D1376739

I Told You I Wasn't Perfect

Denny McLain

with Eli Zaret

TRIUMPH
BOOKS

Library of Congress Cataloging-in-Publication Data

McLain, Denny.
    I told you I wasn't perfect / Denny McLain with Eli Zaret.
        p. cm.
    ISBN-13: 978-1-57243-957-3
    ISBN-10: 1-57243-957-2
    1. McLain, Denny. 2. Baseball players—United States—Biography. 3. Ex-convicts—United States—Biography. I. Zaret, Eli, 1950– II. Title.
GV865.M3965A3 2007
796.357092—dc22
[B]

2006030523

This book is available in quantity at special discounts for your group or organization. For further information, contact:

Triumph Books
542 South Dearborn Street
Suite 750
Chicago, Illinois 60605
(312) 939-3330
Fax (312) 663-3557

Printed in U.S.A.
ISBN: 978-1-57243-957-3

Design by Chris Mulligan, Chicago
All photos courtesy of AP/Wide World Photos unless indicated otherwise.

For Kristi,
The wind beneath our wings.
You are always in our hearts.

And to Denny, Tim, and Michelle,
Thank you for your continuing
understanding, patience,
and love.

Mom and Dad

Contents

Acknowledgments

Thanks are in order for Sharon McLain, who pored through 60 years of pictures to help illustrate this book. She also talked to me for hour upon hour to fill in the blanks and give perspective on key events in her life with Denny.

Sonia Pone, PhD, helped me connect the dots on Denny's behavior, providing valuable insights that helped me make psychological sense of the events in Denny's life.

Steve Brotsky and Alan Sussman brainstormed for titles and took the time to read and comment on early versions of the manuscript.

Two Detroit media legends, Dave Diles and Sonny Eliot, shared stories and gave me historical perspective on the days they knew and covered Denny as a player.

Diles also wrote Denny's 1975 book titled *Nobody's Perfect*, which provided the logical prelude to *I Told You I Wasn't Perfect* some three decades later.

My brother, Phil Zaret, was a consultant and coach on writing many of the non-sports elements in the book.

Pete Chelovich, like a good closer out of the bullpen, helped clean up and clarify some passages in the late stages of submitting the manuscript.

Nick Dolin, producer at HBO Sports, provided a copy of Denny's appearance with Bryant Gumbel.

I used *The Detroit News* microfilm archives extensively for game stories and gleaned from numerous other columns written on Denny both during and after his playing days.

Lawyers Joe Odish and Peter Kupelian helped Denny and me shape some of our legal issues.

Tom Bast of Triumph Books was straightforward in his desire to champion this story, and he took charge of making it happen.

Along those lines, Jeff Witjas and Steve Fisher of the Association of Professional Artists in Los Angeles worked efficiently and effectively with Tom, Denny, and me to bring everything together.

Introduction *by Eli Zaret*

I was getting ready to go to a holiday party in the late afternoon of December 20, 1996, when the phone calls started. Denny McLain and Roger Smigiel had just been convicted on five counts of money laundering, mail fraud, and theft from the Peet Packing pension fund.

The news outlets in Detroit wanted me to explain the unexplainable about Denny McLain, my former radio and TV partner. I knew what the gist of the questioning would be: how could a man who had crafted a successful media career out of the ashes of a prison stay create another mess ugly enough to send him back to jail?

The first to come and see me was a TV reporter from the local NBC affiliate.

"You tell me," I quickly answered Doug Evans of Channel 4, "why a guy with a highly rated morning radio show, a hit TV show, and who was invited all over the country to sign autographs at memorabilia shows would willfully throw all of that away. Why would anybody doing so well want to buy a collapsing meat-packing company in the middle of nowhere? Would you do it, Doug? Would I do it? No way. So why would he? Your guess is as good as mine!"

Denny had been out of jail for a few years when we created the *Eli and Denny* television show in 1990. We were still working together two years later when a family tragedy knocked him far off center. I then watched in puzzlement as Denny systematically dismantled his burgeoning media career in exchange for a shadowy gamble. It was as if he decided to take his life savings to the racetrack to throw it on a 200-1 shot. It seemed like a death wish designed to further plunge his life into despair.

I told the reporters that day how sorry I felt for his wonderful wife, Sharon, who had stuck by him for more than 30 years. I told them how badly I felt for his sons, Denny Jr. and Tim, both really good kids, and his beautiful daughter Michelle, whose three young children wouldn't be seeing their grandpa for a while.

I knew how much Denny loved his family and how he had begged their forgiveness after his first time in jail. Now, here he was again, bitterly disappointing and abandoning them because of his bizarre obsession with engaging in dangerous behavior. I began to wonder if there really was an answer—if there was a way to connect the dots on Denny's lifetime of living on the edge and systematically destroying all of his successes.

I'd never worked with a better entertainer. Nobody could match his lightning-quick wit. But where did all this self-destructive stuff come from? And how could this delightful rogue who loved approval and loved the spotlight have hurt so many people?

Like his family, friends, and the workers at Peet Packing, I too felt betrayed and abandoned by Denny McLain.

The explanation—if there was one—seemed hidden in the speed at which he led his life. Denny was always running, always looking for something bigger and better, even when he seemed to already have everything. Nothing was ever enough. As I tried to look at his life and career, it seemed like his drug was the drug of "more."

It wasn't enough to like Pepsi—he had to have a case a day.

It wasn't enough to win a baseball game—he had to win it in less than two hours.

It wasn't exciting enough to win 20 games at age 22. He had to become a bookie also.

Introduction

It wasn't enough to win 31 games in 1968. He had to add excitement by flying his own plane to games the next season.

And it wasn't enough to leave prison and become a star again in a new field. He had to take the ultimate long shot—buy a doomed hot dog company, deeply in debt and already in foreclosure—and make it a success.

Why was he such a mad adventure-seeker? What was he always running from? Why couldn't he ever just relax, reflect, and enjoy?

Now, in 2006, Denny has traveled a long, extremely painful way in finding answers. And he is, not surprisingly, in the midst of orchestrating yet another comeback while repairing many of the fissures in his personal life.

Denny McLain is one of the most fascinating sports characters of all time. I also believe that there is a little Denny McLain in many of us—a little of the self-centered narcissist, absorbed in our own dreams and fantasies.

The difference may be that Denny is just a more extreme case—extreme enough to lead a life that has been a combination of ecstasy and hell, with little in between.

This is his story, in his own words.

Chapter 1

Kristin

Kristin Dawn McLain, the oldest of my four children, had been to dinner with some friends and was driving home in the early morning hours of March 20, 1992. She was 26 and single, and having recently moved to Michigan from Tampa, she was staying with us until she found a place of her own.

I had gone to sleep early, as usual, because I had to be up at 4:00 AM to host *The Denny McLain Show* on WXYT-AM in Detroit. At about 2:15 my wife Sharon woke me with a nudge. I glanced at the clock to see if I had overslept. When I saw that I still had a few hours of sleep remaining, I turned my head to see Sharon sitting up in bed.

"Kristin isn't home," she said in a voice tinged with worry.

I rolled back over and mumbled, "Relax, she probably slept at somebody's house." I understood Sharon's concern because Kristin always kept us abreast of where she was and what she was doing. But I wasn't in the mood for conversation when I needed to get back to sleep.

When the alarm went off at 4:00 AM, I saw that Sharon was still awake, and her look told me Kristin still hadn't arrived. I was about to get out of bed to shower when we heard a car drive up.

I looked at her and said in a semi "I told you so" tone, "Ya see? She's home." We heard a car door close and then, about 10 seconds later, the doorbell rang.

My first thought was, "Kristin has a key. Why would she ring the bell?" We lived in a very rural area, and it made no sense that anyone else would come to see us in what, for most people, is still the dead of the night. I opened the door and saw a policeman. "Oh! I was looking for a Mr. McLain," he said, "but I didn't know it was you."

I quickly asked him if there was a problem, and he said, "Denny, your daughter is at the hospital—she's been involved in an accident, and you need to get there right away."

Several times I pressed him, "Is she okay? Is she hurt badly?"

All he would give me was, "You need to get to the hospital as soon as you can."

We were babysitting for Markey, the 15-month-old son of our other daughter, Michelle. Michelle was in Gulfport, Mississippi, with her husband, Mark, who was in the navy. I ran upstairs and relayed to Sharon what I'd just heard from the officer and told her we needed to wake up Markey and get going.

We sped to the hospital, and aside from the radio and Markey asking little-boy questions, we rode in silence. As we turned off M-59 in White Lake Township, we saw police cleaning up what looked like an accident scene on the five-lane highway. It was still before sunup, but we could make out a demolished vehicle. I remarked to Sharon, "Man, that musta been a bad accident." The car was so mangled and burned out you couldn't tell the make or the color.

We parked in the first spot next to the emergency room. I grabbed Markey and got out of the car so quickly that I left my keys in it. We told the girl at the ER desk that we were the parents of Kristin McLain and would like to see her. She shot me a nervous glance and said, "Let me get the nurses."

"I would rather see Kristin," I said sharply.

Kristin

Sharon and I both looked at each other knowing that something was awfully wrong. The silence the next few seconds was deafening.

Two nurses emerged from a nearby door and approached with slightly bowed heads. One of them asked, "Are you Kristin's parents?"

When I said, "Yeah," the other nurse recoiled slightly and murmured, "Oh."

Her body language penetrated to my core. Before she could utter another word, I said, "What does, 'oh' mean—and can you please take us to see her?"

"The doctors will be here in a moment to talk to you," the first nurse said, and motioned us to a nearby waiting room. As we walked toward the room I again asked to see Kristin and thought even more strongly, *This is wrong.* Had Kristin been able to talk to us, we'd be going to see her, not headed to a waiting room. Between the antiseptic smell of the hospital and a pair of nurses avoiding conversation, a sense of monstrous agony began overwhelming me and Sharon.

Within 30 seconds, two doctors entered the room. Wasting no time, one of them immediately said, "We've got some bad news."

"What bad news?"

"Your daughter was in a horrible car accident with a truck and another car, and she was unable to make it. She died about two hours ago."

Sharon had held it together until that moment. We had Markey to deal with, and he had probably helped us maintain our composure. But now the dam burst, and she began sobbing and wailing. I might have gone into shock at that point. I showed no expression or emotion. I just remember thinking and saying over and over again, "This can't be happening."

One of the doctors explained that the paramedics and the fire department had been heroic in their efforts. One paramedic even suffered third-degree burns on his arms trying to pull Kristin out of her blazing vehicle.

But there was nothing any of them could do for her. By the time she reached the hospital, the doctors explained, she was already gone.

We had failed to put together that the scene on M-59 was the aftermath of Kristin's accident and the wreckage of her Chevy Blazer.

Through her sobs, Sharon managed to ask the doctors, "Can we please see her? Maybe there's been a mistake?" Before they could answer, she angrily begged, "I have to see her. Please let me see her!"

One of the doctors looked at us. "There was a fire," he said quietly. "I think it's a better idea if we do that a little later. Let the staff first clean things up and then later you can see her, okay? That would be much better for you right now."

I was still too shocked to physically react. I kept repeating to myself, "This can't be true. Nothing like this can happen to my family." Life had been going so well. Who can believe their daughter has been involved in a horrific accident? Nothing prepares you for a moment like this.

I recall almost nothing of the trip back to the house or what we did when we got there. In fact, when we passed the accident site again, it still hadn't registered with either of us that that's where Krissie met her fate. I do know that at some point I called the radio station to let them know I wouldn't be at work that morning. Word travels fast. The station already knew about the accident and had a substitute coming in.

When we got back to the house, we called our other three children to share the awful news before it reached them on radio or television. I remember nothing of those conversations. By midmorning a few friends had heard what happened and came over to console us and handle funeral arrangements.

Friends in the restaurant business sent over tons of food and asked what else they could do to help. There's no answer. No one makes plans for losing a child. You just thank them for asking.

Cheryl Chodun, a reporter from the local ABC television affiliate, called around 9:00 AM from the accident scene and said, "You better get an attorney. This should have never happened." Cheryl described where the accident took place, and it was only then that I put two and two together and realized that Kristin's accident and the accident that we had seen were one and the same.

As I was asking Chodun some questions, Sandy McClure, a reporter from the *Oakland Press* called on the other line and said, "There's more to this than just an accident."

Until we talked to the reporters, we knew none of the details, but suddenly it was turning into a criminal investigation. The reporters told me that a truck had blocked three lanes of the highway and Kristin had been unable to avoid it.

McClure had learned from the state police that the driver, Leonard Martin, had been in the process of backing an 18-wheeler into a tight driveway, and his truck had stretched across three of the five lanes of poorly lit M-59. His taillights created glare off a window and made it difficult to see the entrance to the driveway.

It was then, at 2:00 AM on a poorly lit highway, that Martin had the bright idea to turn off his lights to eliminate the glare while he backed his 40,000-pound truck into the driveway.

Kristin was driving west on M-59 and neared the crest of the hill doing the 50-mile-an-hour speed limit. The truck was sitting at the lowest portion of the highway's dip, blocking the westbound lanes. Not only were the lights off, but the truck's reflectors were also obscured by grime.

Kristin apparently saw him the last 40 to 50 feet, but her move to go around was too late. Had Martin backed into the driveway on his first or second attempt, she would have gotten home—but it was all about bad timing. She skidded 25 feet before ramming into his back wheels, pinning the Blazer under the truck. As the front end of her car compressed, the steering wheel fractured all of her ribs and pinned her into the seat. But she was alive.

With the truck blocking the two westbound lanes and the Blazer jammed under it, Martin tried turning the truck into the middle lane so it would face straight ahead, rather than remain straddled across the highway. It had to have been an attempt to eliminate the evidence of blocking the highway with his lights off. But as he turned, the Blazer came loose and wound up facing back in the direction from which it had come.

Martin's first reactions should have been to turn his lights and flashers on, exit the truck, light flares, place glowing caution triangles on the road, and call 9-1-1. But he didn't do any of that.

While trying to reposition his truck, he left Kristin alone and vulnerable. Less than a minute from the initial impact, a drunken 19-year-old in a pickup truck came speeding over the hill and smashed into the Blazer head on. The pickup caromed off the Blazer and wound up in a restaurant parking lot. Amazingly, neither the driver nor his other two passengers were seriously injured.

An emergency technician who worked on an ambulance and had just gotten off his shift happened to be one of the next cars to drive by. He acted quickly, reaching into the driver's window to try to extract Kristin. But he couldn't pry her free from the steering wheel pinned to her chest.

It was then that the Blazer caught on fire under the hood.

The technician shouted to others arriving on the scene to call 9-1-1 for help, and he ordered Martin to run to his rig for a fire extinguisher. But Martin's extinguisher emptied quickly and was no match for the now-raging flames. Meanwhile, the tech kept yelling at Krissie, "Stay with me. Hang on. We're going to get you out of here."

He ran around to the passenger side to see if he could pry her out that way when there was an explosion, forcing flames through the floor and some 50 feet in the air. The technician escaped the car and wound up with third-degree burns for his efforts.

Kristin

The scene continued to play out as horrified motorists stopped and tried to help. About 15 minutes into the drama, the White Lake volunteer fire department arrived and put out the blaze by throwing sand and dumping a ton of water on it. As the volunteers screamed at Kristin to wake up, they used the Jaws of Life, hoping to free her by the time a helicopter from the University of Michigan Hospital and burn unit arrived.

Finally, some 45 hellish minutes after the initial impact, they succeeded in prying her from the wreckage. She was still alive as they strapped her to a gurney and rolled it toward the helicopter that was waiting to take her away.

But Kristin went into cardiac arrest. The gurney stopped. After two collisions and a fire, a tech announced that it was over.

The chopper headed back to Ann Arbor, and the ambulance took Kristin to White Lake Hospital, where she was officially pronounced dead.

We never did get to see her. The accident had broken almost every bone in her body and the fire had disfigured her.

By midafternoon, after hearing the stories about the accident from any number of reporters, I couldn't take it anymore. I broke away from the gut-wrenching scene at the house to go to the crash site. I was prepared to find Martin and beat the hell out of the demon who killed my daughter. The newspeople were still there, and Chodun, the TV reporter, pointed out Martin, who was now unloading his truck. I walked in his direction and was intercepted by one of the cops, who asked me what I was doing. I yelled, "Are you kidding? This asshole just killed my daughter, and you're asking me why I'm here?"

With the cop standing between us, I yelled at Martin, "What happened? What did you do?" When he stood there mute, I said, "Give me an answer, you gutless bastard, so I can tell her mother. Her mother wants to know why. Is that so hard, to tell us what happened?"

By then, a couple of Martin's associates surrounded him to make sure I kept my distance. Another cop who'd come over said, "Denny, go home. Please go home. This has been a horrible day, but to start trouble will just make it worse." I called Martin every name in the book for not giving me any kind of explanation and walked back to my car.

Later that night I learned that he had been "lawyered up" within an hour after the accident and told to keep his mouth shut. Had he driven his truck as effectively as he shut up, Kristin would be with us today.

All Martin needed to do was follow basic trucking safety procedures, which dictate what to do after an accident takes place. But not only had he tragically erred in causing a young girl to crash into his rig—then he failed to help her.

Further punctuating the grief and horror of Kristin's death was the system's inability to give her justice. The drunken kid got probation, and Martin walked away. They said it wasn't criminal intent and dismissed the charges. We'll never understand that. He was backing into the driveway, blocking three lanes of a highway in the dark without his lights on. Not one bit of safety equipment was out on the highway for other drivers to see—nothing! He didn't follow any of the post-accident procedures that are prescribed to truckers for events like this. How is that not negligence at the very least? And isn't there such a thing as manslaughter? Obviously, he didn't set out to kill anybody, but that's exactly what he did.

The autopsy revealed that Kristin was sober and had her wits about her, like she always did. Timing and the worst possible judgment by a professional trucker just when it counted the most had killed my daughter. I've never stopped asking myself, *Why not put out the flares and the cones? Why not call 9-1-1? Why not call the cops to come and stop traffic? Why not use the fire extinguisher right away? Why, why, and why?*

Kristin

If Martin had a conscience, he never displayed it to us in any form. It was as if he'd just delivered another load—nothing more and nothing less.

Kristin Dawn McLain had come over that hill and never had a chance.

◆　　　◆　　　◆

She was born September 28, 1965, the first child and a gift from God to a 21-year-old pitcher enjoying his first full season in the major leagues. I thought she was the most beautiful child I had ever seen.

In the 1966 season, Sharon would wait for me to come home from the ballpark so I could give Krissie her nighttime feeding. I would goo-goo her and burp her. I can close my eyes now and feel her falling asleep on my chest as we lay on the couch.

From the very beginning, I thought of Krissie as my perfect reflection—a fighter, a kidder, and a quipster who came up with more Yogi Berra sayings than Yogi himself. She was as close to the perfect child as any parent would want, and she grew into a wonderful big sister for our sons Tim and Dennis Jr., and Michelle, our fourth and youngest.

Her first boyfriend and longest-running love was a kid from school named Brian. He picked her up for their first date in his dad's car and endured an interrogation at our front door that almost had him peeing in his pants. When it got to the point where he was visibly shaking, I finally backed off. Brian got her home on time and never once in high school did Krissie miss her curfew.

We loved Monopoly, and I always played banker. A devious banker can always cheat his way to victory. Krissie was every bit as competitive as her dad, hating to lose any game at any level. Our last Monopoly game was Christmas, 1991.

I cheated as always, but her brothers, sister, and mom kept landing on her hotels. There were only two of us left. In the final move that ended my 20-year winning streak, I landed on her hotels and went bankrupt.

After whooping with delight, she said, "Dad, it takes one to know one. Denny (Jr.) kept feeding me money under the table. You lived by the sword and now you've died by it!"

We all had a terrific laugh, and it seems now like the laughing never stopped until that fateful night three months later.

I had been released from prison in August 1987, and by 1990 I had established a successful second career as a radio talk show host in Detroit. The other three kids were all nearby—Michelle was just married and soon to start a family; Denny, our second oldest, was in the military and was on his way to the Persian Gulf; and Tim was in college.

Kristin was running a day care center in Tampa. She loved kids, so the job suited her. She had a social life and was content with her situation. But I wanted her with us. I had put the horror of prison behind me and desperately wanted to play daddy again for all my kids. I had such guilt for causing them so much pain and humiliation, and I wanted to somehow make it up to them.

I had conveniently rationalized that her neighborhood in Tampa, that had already begun to experience some violence, would soon be infested with drugs and gangs. She wanted to stay there, but what she wanted wasn't my priority. I convinced myself that the gangs might grab her or a stray bullet might hit her.

She was an adult and deserved to make her own choices, but I was a free man now and demanded that the family be together again. Like my dad, I ruled my roost with an iron fist. I told her I wouldn't pay her rent anymore because I wanted her to become the producer of my radio show.

I ordered her to move and learn the radio business. She was good with people, and I wanted her with me at the radio station, even if I had to pay her myself. Like always, it was my way or no way, and after a number of arguments she caved in.

Kristin

I sent a truck to move her to Michigan and started her with a job at a plumbing supply company owned by a friend. Sharon, with mixed feelings, had stayed on the sidelines through all of this. But when Krissie finally yielded to my pressure, Sharon was also thrilled to have her first child and best friend close at hand.

After all, Kristin was home and we were all together again.

Chapter 2

Dad

My father, Tom McLain, grew up in Chicago and was such a fine high school shortstop that the Cubs offered him a minor league contract. But soon thereafter, Tom's father, Tom Sr., died a grisly death—impaled by a tree branch while trying to rescue the family cat. Tom Sr. was only 36 at the time, leaving my father with the responsibility of taking care of his three younger siblings.

There was also another deterrent to Tom's dream of a baseball career: his girlfriend Betty told him that if he ran off to play baseball there'd be no marriage. Tom married Betty in 1941 at the age of 18. Uncle Sam drafted him two years later, and he was already in combat in Germany when I was born in March 1944 on the south side of Chicago, just one block from Midway Airport.

When Tom returned from the war, he took jobs as a truck driver and insurance adjuster. Soon, my brother Tim was born, and with two jobs and a demanding wife, Tom worked like a dog. To relieve the stress, he smoked three to four packs of unfiltered cigarettes a day and guzzled a ton of beer.

My dad usually had a cold one between his legs when he drove the family car, and when he got home from work he would either head right to the icebox or order Tim or me to get him a beer.

Tim and I would always brace for the worst when Tom McLain opened the front door. Would he be a sober dad we could love, or would he already be drunk after popping a few with the boys on the way home?

When Tom was drunk we would tread lightly. He could be physically and verbally abusive, whipping us for real or perceived offenses, or treating us like slaves with a "get me this, get me that" attitude. Tim and I served as Dad's remote-control channel flipper before there ever was such a thing, leaping up to change the station or get him a refill.

Tom's rules were that when he got home I better have my homework done and have practiced the piano for an hour. During the baseball season I also had to work on my pitching. When I didn't produce as expected, he'd take out the leather belt and beat me.

His anger was as terrifying as the belt was painful. And the more he had to drink, the worse the beating would be. Tom ruled by that strap, with the omnipresent message: "Mess up and you've got one coming."

When I was guilty of something that didn't necessarily merit the leather, he'd smack me on the back of my head with his open hand, and it would sting like hell. He was 6'3", 250 pounds, and had huge, powerful hands. After he smacked me a few times at the dinner table, I never sat near him again.

As wrong as whipping a child is, what made it even worse was that my mother rarely stepped in. She not only allowed him to deal with us when he was drunk, but she also set us up. She'd tell him, "Dennis hasn't done his homework," or, "Dennis only practiced piano for half an hour." She was a miserable person, incapable of consoling me or even giving me a hug on a bad day. We were never close.

We never once talked about alcoholism in my house. Instead, Betty would rationalize Tom's drinking by saying, "He's just one of the guys, relieving the pressure. Your dad works two jobs and pays for your clothes, tuition, shoes, baseball gloves, and everything else."

Dad

My mother was angry almost all the time, and it seemed like she got to release some of her pent-up venom through the end of Tom's belt.

Tom's smoking was just as scary as the drinking. He always had a cigarette in his mouth or hand, and he'd fall asleep and destroy a sheet or a couch cover with a burning ash. Fortunately, my biggest fear never came to pass—that he'd set the house on fire and burn us all to death.

My curfew was sunset, and one spring night when I was 12 and we were living in the Chicago suburb of Markham, I played ball until 9:00 PM and didn't make it back home until after the sun went down. A 14-year-old girl had moved into the neighborhood and was willing to give hand jobs to just about any boy who showed up. She would even do it to two guys at the same time. I had been with her that night—it was my first experience with sex. I was late; I knew what was awaiting me at home; and I didn't have the nerve to face it that night. So I hid in the back yard of a vacant house about 200 yards down the street, terrified about the consequences of breaking one of Dad's rules.

A few weeks earlier, three young boys, two of them named Schuessler and another named Peterson, had been raped and killed. It was the first highly publicized children's crime ever in Chicago. My parents feared the worst and called the police to report me missing.

I figured I'd say that since I knew I was going to be late, I'd decided to run away rather than suffer a beating.

At about 10:00 I peeked down the street and saw what looked like every cop car in Markham in front of my house. I knew then that the gig was up and it was time to try to sell my story. When I got to the front lawn, I saw a look of relief on my mother's face and remember her saying, "Thank God, you're all right." Then she grabbed me by the arm and said, "Your dad will be right back, and you can give your story to him." Tom had been driving all over Markham, talking to neighbors, checking stores, the baseball park, and anywhere he thought I might have been.

15

When he got home, I tried the story about nobody loving me and running away. He didn't buy it. After the police left, he picked up the strap, glared at me, and said, "Pull down your pants." He whipped me until I screamed bloody murder.

It was the first and only time my mother ordered him to stop. It must have affected him also because it was the last beating he ever gave me. I had bruises and broken skin and couldn't even take a bath for a few days. In the 1950s pre–Dr. Spock, spare-the-rod society, the belt was an accepted form of discipline.

Despite the smoking, drinking, and intimidation, I still believed my dad loved me. Even as he would flail away at me with the strap, he'd yell, "You're going to grow up to be somebody. You're not going to waste your life!" He had so much pent-up anger and frustration from working so hard and sacrificing his dreams at my mother's demand, and he wanted us to have what had escaped him.

Without Tom McLain, I never would have been a baseball player. He wanted me to be the player he wasn't able to be and decided that I was ready to play competitively at seven years old. Unfortunately, Little League ball had yet to arrive in Markham, and the Little League's minimum age was eight.

The nearest league was in Midlothian, Illinois, about 10 miles south of Markham. Tom called one of the coaches and told him we had just moved into the area. He also told them I was eight.

It was my first exposure to organized play, and I dominated in every aspect of the game. I hit harder and fielded better than the older kids, and Tom was thrilled. He'd suspected I was a player, and now he knew it. I played shortstop in the first game and got a hit every time up.

Not surprisingly, the opposing coach did his research and discovered we'd given a phony address. The McLains were washed up in the Midlothian Little League almost as soon as we'd started.

Dad

Undaunted and unembarrassed, Tom McLain single-handedly brought Little League–style ball to Markham the next year, putting together a couple of teams and establishing the Markham Boys League. He talked the school board into building a baseball field and found sponsors to put in fences, dugouts, and a concession stand. In time for the next season, the Markham Boys League was incorporated into the Little League organization, and it is still in place today.

Tom coached our team and didn't use me as a pitcher until our second season, when I was nine. In our first game, I pitched and struck out 15 batters and probably walked as many in a six-inning game. It was that day that my dad's focus changed from making me the next great Cubs shortstop to becoming the next great Cubs 20-game winner.

I loved baseball and felt safe around my dad when we practiced and played. Baseball was my refuge, where I could avoid the fear and crushing discipline that was enforced at home. It was only on the ball field that my dad and I could truly enjoy each other's company. We embraced the competition and loved winning. Playing baseball—and to a somewhat lesser degree, playing piano—were the only ways I got approval and a sense of importance.

Dad wasn't a cheerleader. He'd never jump up and down or shower me with superlatives. I never remember getting a hug, a kiss, or even a handshake. But for him to just come up to me after the game and say, "Nice goin', good game," meant the world. I lived for that and was always striving to play better.

When I was 10, in the third year of the Markham Boys League, I was pitching for our team, American Legion, against our archrivals, the VFW. Late in a close game, the mother of a player on the other team directed a derogatory comment my way that could clearly be heard by everyone.

After we won, Tom ran to the other side of the field and got in her face about it. I remember putting myself in her shoes. Tom was pissed, and that meant that somebody was going to get hurt.

The lady's husband came to her rescue, and while yelling at Tom, may have accidentally spat in his face. In an instant, Tom delivered a crushing right hand to his jaw, knocking the guy unconscious before he even hit the ground. I'll never forget the thudding sound of his fist and watching the guy crumple to the ground. He lay there, out cold, with his jaw bent at a grotesque angle.

People were shouting and screaming, and a Markham cop ran over from a nearby field. When he sized up the scene—an unconscious man with his jaw twisted under his ear, he arrested Tom. The guy sued, and Tom pleaded guilty to a lesser charge. As I recall, our homeowner's insurance covered the settlement of some $10,000, a ton of dough in the '50s.

My father was easily provoked and wasn't prone to back down from a fight. When I was 11, in December 1955, my mom and dad went to a party at the VFW hall in Markham on a Friday night to watch Sugar Ray Robinson challenge middleweight champion Carl "Bobo" Olson.

Robinson was on a comeback after a two-year retirement and had struggled against some mediocre foes before his title shot at Olson. Olson had won 23 straight fights. Ironically, his last middleweight loss had been a 15-round decision to Robinson in late 1952, when Robinson was champ. Robinson then vacated the title in 1953, and Olson beat Randy Turpin to become the new champion.

Now it was two years later and Olson still held the belt. He was a 3-1 favorite over Robinson, who at 34 was almost seven years his senior and believed to be past his prime. There was added excitement because of the racial angle—Olson was white, Robinson was black—and Olson was avenging his earlier title loss to Robinson.

At the all-white VFW hall that night, my father took a huge gamble. He liked Robinson to win the fight and risked $100 we didn't have to try to win $300 from a number of people anxious to back Olson.

In the second round, Robinson unleashed a terrific barrage and knocked out Olson to regain the title and stun everyone at the VFW hall.

One of the guys who lost money to him made the mistake of calling Tom a "nigger-loving bastard" as he paid his debt. Tom beat the living shit out of the guy, right in front of everybody in the VFW hall.

Tom only made a few thousand dollars a year, and on that night he not only brought in some much-needed dough, but he also got to vent his pent-up anger on somebody other than me.

◆   ◆   ◆

When I was too old to play in the Markham Boys League, Tom drove me 15 miles to Harvey to play in the Babe Ruth League, where I continued to mow down the opposition. My aunt lived there, and we used her address to pass the residency rules.

My development as a baseball player was the family's top priority, and my father arranged his work schedule to accommodate my practices and games. Tom had been a shortstop and didn't know a hell of a lot about pitching, but he was smart enough to sense how dangerous throwing curveballs could be to a young arm. He'd say, "You've got to wait 'til we find the right guy to teach you to throw the curveball. If you do it before you're 18 or 19, you'll lose 10 percent off your fastball."

He added, "If I ever catch you throwing a curveball, you won't have to worry about losing your fastball—you'll lose your whole arm. I'll make sure of that."

I was in eighth grade, about 13 years old, when I tried experimenting with the curveball in the backyard while Tom was at work. Sure enough, it made me sore to the point where I had to miss a start. When I told him I couldn't pitch, he slapped me on the back of the head and said, "Why's your elbow bothering ya?" Before I could lie, he yelled, "You've been screwing with the curveball, haven't ya?" He was furious, but by that time, he'd stopped whipping me.

Near the end of that season our team played a playoff game on the south side of Chicago. In attendance was Father Austin Coupe, baseball coach at Mount Carmel High School. I pitched a shutout and went 4-for-4 with a huge home run. After the game, Father Austin sought out Tom, and the two all but settled it right there. Tom wanted me to continue my Catholic education, and Father Coupe offered me a full scholarship to pitch for him.

I made the starting rotation at Mount Carmel as a 14-year-old freshman, and as a sophomore, I was scheduled to pitch on May 4, 1959. At game time, Tom wasn't in his usual spot in the stands, and I knew right away something was wrong. He always arranged his work schedule to see my games.

I even waited around for him after the game before taking the bus home.

When I got to our street, his car was parked in front of the house and a lot of people were standing in the front yard. I approached my mother and was about to ask what the heck was going on when, with an expressionless look on her face, she said, "Your father is dead." Just like that. No, "I'm sorry," or anything to soften the blow. Just, "Your father is dead."

Tom McLain had suffered a heart attack while driving to my game. He was a block away from Comiskey Park when he pulled over to the curb and died, slumped on his steering wheel. Like his father, Tom Sr., he was only 36 years old.

Over and over again I walked around the block in a daze that night. How would I play baseball without my dad? How would our family survive? And would I have to quit school at 16 to support us?

I never forgave my mother for her coldness and lack of compassion that day. But strangely, some years later when we were having a rare heart-to-heart talk, she casually said, "Did you know that you never cried after your dad died?"

Dad

She was right. I hadn't cried. Maybe I was relieved that he was gone. It had been a while since he'd beaten me, but only his death could remove the threat of further beatings. My home had been a sort of prison, run by two people whose intimidation and punishment had been a constant presence.

It's so sad that my dad never experienced the joy of true physical and emotional closeness with his kids. I guess he just didn't know how to do it. He wasted too much energy drinking, intimidating us, and trying to please Betty, who was never happy anyway.

My dad died in May 1959 and by July Betty started dating a chef, a terrific guy also named Tom. She married him less than a year later, but she had invited him to move in with us several months before the wedding. It crushed me that she would entertain another man in my father's bed so soon after he was gone.

My stepfather was generous, hardworking, and treated me very well, but I was never comfortable with the situation and resented him. Betty told me many years later that we would have lost our house had my stepfather not come into our lives.

Without Tom McLain to fear, I stopped worrying about consequences. My stepdad never interfered with my freedom and, without my dad around to carry out her mission, my mother had no reason to rat me out anymore. I didn't steal, get into fights, or become a juvenile delinquent, but suddenly I had no rules to follow and nobody to control me.

And it was from that point forward that I just started doing whatever the hell I pleased.

Chapter 3

The Bushes

In four years at Mount Carmel, I pitched, played shortstop, and finished my high school career with a 38–7 win-loss record. We won the city championship three times, and in my junior year I led the city in wins, batting average, and home runs.

I also played some football as a freshman. On the very first play of the very first game, I ran 80 yards right up the middle. The next time we got the ball, I threw a 50-yard touchdown pass. The coach was Tom Carey, a former Notre Dame star who thought he'd fallen upon the next Paul Hornung—a guy who could run and also throw the ball as far as anyone he had seen.

I was at Mount Carmel on a baseball scholarship, and after news of my debut football performance reached him, Father Austin came up to me at practice the very next day, grabbed me by my face mask, and said, "Take those pads off now. I'll kick you from here to Alabama if I see you in a football uniform again. You came to Mount Carmel to be a baseball player, and that's what you'll be." I never even went to a Carmel football game after that for fear I'd lose my scholarship.

In May 1962, about a month before I graduated, Father Austin came to me with the exciting news that Notre Dame was prepared to offer me their first-ever baseball scholarship. I would've been the first in our family to ever go to college, and no school was more attractive to a kid from

23

Mount Carmel than Notre Dame. But once the Major League scouts started waving money, even the Golden Dome had to be ruled out.

I got offers from the Yankees, Phillies, and White Sox. Mickey Mantle was my idol, but the Yankees scout had a huge hole in the bottom of his shoes. Obviously, my mother's compulsive neatness kicked in, and I turned the Yankees down.

The hometown White Sox, at $17,000, offered the most. It was $10,000 up front and the other $7,000 if I made it to the majors. That was huge dough, and I was a Chicago boy. My dad would have been proud—he'd never made anything close to $10,000 in an entire year.

I snatched the Sox check, and less than three hours after my graduation in June 1962, I said my good-byes and hopped a plane for the Harlan (Kentucky) Smokies in the Appalachian Rookie League.

It was the first plane ride of my life, and when the plane started to taxi down the runway, I was so petrified, I thought about screaming to have 'em let me off. I kept two vomit bags on my lap the entire trip.

I was a jumble of excitement and sadness because I was leaving everything I knew. Except for a trip to nearby Matoon, Illinois, for the State Babe Ruth League Championship Series, I'd never been south of Markham. Now I was headed for the heart of Dixie.

The plane flew into Knoxville, Tennessee, and I picked up a Greyhound bus to Harlan. Harlan was a depressed, coal-mining town near the three borders of Tennessee, Virginia, and Kentucky. It took me less than five minutes in Harlan to become depressed myself. I'd heard about minor league cities, but this was culture shock. I got in around midnight, asked a guy at the bus station where the hotel was, and heard a version of English I wasn't familiar with. I wondered if I'd have to learn sign language to survive this town.

He pointed to a building down the street.

The Bushes

"That's it?" I asked in disbelief. I thought, *If they send the bonus babies to a rat trap like this, then what happens to the other guys?*

My room was on the fifth floor, and there was no elevator. The lobby had fans that made loud grinding noises, and there was an old coot in a rocking chair spitting tobacco juice into a spittoon with a hound lying next to him.

Welcome to Harlan.

It felt like it was 100 degrees in the hotel that first night, and it never felt a single degree cooler after that. There weren't even fans in the rooms. It was also one bathroom for the whole floor. Guys lined up in the morning, waiting for their turn. I remember thinking that if I'd gone into the army I'd have been taken better care of than this.

The citizenry of Harlan looked like the back row at a Willie Nelson concert, speaking in a barely intelligible southern drawl through their remaining teeth. They all seemed reasonably kind and gentle, but obviously, the dentist had left Dodge some time ago.

Harlan was a coal-mining town, and a sulphur-like stench permeated the air. It smelled like black lung disease waiting to happen. Unless it was really windy, it was with you all day. But that's what these people did for a living. There were only about a thousand or so in the whole town, and most of them worked in the mines.

The night after I arrived, there was a huge fight between a few of our players and the local boys. One of the Harlan gals had gone off with one of our players, and our guy got the shit kicked out of him behind the dance hall. It was a clear message to the rest of us that these boys owned their women. It was way too early in my career to tempt death for a little hillbilly action.

The minors are everything *Bull Durham* was about and less. Clubhouses are small, filthy, and nauseatingly odorous. Yesterday's sweatshirts and underwear hang on clubhouse clotheslines, and the rock-strewn infields look like the streets of Baghdad.

I Told You I Wasn't Perfect

I made my rookie league debut against Salem on June 28, 1962, in the hottest, most humid conditions I'd ever pitched in. I was excited and felt really loose on the mound, and I was sensational. I'd never even pitched nine innings before, but I did that night, striking out 16 and throwing a no-hitter. I threw all fastballs because I still hadn't learned to throw a curve. The irony was that it was the first and last no-hitter of my career.

All I could think of when the game was over was to get to a phone and call my girl and my mom. Back then, you had to dial the operator and then have her patch you to another operator and then another until you finally got through to Chicago. It felt like it took an hour to finally get through to my redhead girl back home, Karen Herrington. Her dad answered the phone, said she was sleeping, and hung up on me. One down, one to go.

Then I managed to reach my mother, who said, "Nice going. By the way, your brother is sick." That was it—nothing more or less about my pitching performance. My mother could just cut my heart out.

It had only taken a few innings that night for me to realize I was in the wrong league. I'd also been away from home for three days and was already lonely. I had a no-hitter under my belt and figured I was entitled to do what I wanted. So I decided to visit Karen. I asked someone with the ballclub, "How far to Chicago by car?" He told me, "About eight hours."

Our third baseman was Ronnie Boyer, younger brother of major league third basemen Ken and Cletis. We had an off day the day after I pitched, and I borrowed Ronnie's car to make the "eight hour" trip to Chicago, which turned out to be about 15 hours. It was all back roads because the interstate hadn't been built.

I convinced a teammate who was also from Chicago to come with me, and we took off. I hadn't yet convinced Karen to sleep with me; in fact, I'd never convinced any girl to sleep with me, but I reasoned: who wouldn't want to make it with a bonus baby coming off a no-hitter who also drove all night to see you?

The Bushes

When I missed practice the next day, Glen Miller, the Sox minor league director, started tracking me down. He didn't know if I was dead, kidnapped, or left to rot in a Kentucky coal mine. He got Karen's number through my mom and called her to deliver a message: "If and when he gets to your house, he'd better call me ASAP."

When I hit her door, instead of a smile or a hug, I got a look that told me I was in trouble. I quickly called Miller, who told me to get back to Harlan by game time tomorrow night or not bother showing up at all. "I'll make sure you never pitch another f*cking pro game in your life," was his blunt warning.

I visited Karen for a few minutes as her hovering father supervised. I called my teammate, and we headed off for a grueling nighttime drive through the twisting mountain roads. We made it back to Harlan by game time the next day, and Miller told me that another incident like this would destroy my career. Actually, I got the threat. The other guy got released.

The episode taught me a universal sports lesson: as long as you win, you can do almost anything you want short of murder. I'd gone AWOL because I could, and I'd continue to push in order to find out where my limits were.

I gave up two unearned runs in my second outing, and we lost. But I fanned another 16, giving me 32 strikeouts and a 0.00 ERA in two games. Miller called me into his office the next day and said, "You don't need to be here any longer. You're going to Clinton, Iowa." Then he smiled and added, "By the way, your girl will only be three hours away, and that's gotta help."

Clinton was in the Class-D Midwest League. I may've contributed to ending one guy's career, but Denny was movin' on up.

I'd bought myself a Pontiac LeMans convertible and a LeMans hard-top for my mom with my $10,000 bonus and still had about $2,000 left.

I picked up my car in Markham and drove to Clinton, which was right on the Mississippi River and just three hours away from Chicago, as Miller had promised. The difference between Harlan and Clinton was night and day. Thank God I was back in the Midwest, where they at least spoke a version of English I could understand.

The Clinton players were older than the ones in Harlan. One of our guys was 30 and had been knocking around for 12 years trying to catch on, even as a coach. I saw more than a few guys like this in Clinton, and I thought there had to be a better life than playing minor league ball for that long.

But if you didn't graduate from high school, what else was there to do except hang on as long as you could? The minor leagues are all about long shots, and some guys never stop clinging to hope, despite the awful odds.

As for me, the hitters in Class D had seen a lotta guys who threw the ball hard, and many of 'em could handle my fastball. When I really had it going, it didn't matter who was hitting. But if I didn't have my "A" game, it could get ugly.

I still threw all fastballs, and my new manager, Ira Hutchinson, decided it was time to teach me the curve. It was hopeless—either they hit it or watched it, knowing I'd never have the guts to throw two in a row. I rode the roller coaster in Clinton, taking some of the worst beatings in my life, but in some games looking like a budding Cy Young.

My biggest problem came with a 3-2 count. Since my only effective pitch was a fastball, they'd sit on the fastball knowing they'd get a strike. I threw hard but wasn't able to throw strikes in the places I learned to throw them a few years later.

Besides the trials and tribulations of baseball, young minor leaguers also struggle to live on their own and deal with new people. You can't run around much because you don't have money, and back then you spent what you had on the phone. Almost my entire paycheck went to phone calls to call Karen and Mom. It was really expensive back then, and I'd stand in the booth shoveling quarter after quarter into the damn phone. God, I hated Ma Bell.

Most of us didn't even know how to use a washer and dryer. I'd take my clothes to the cleaners and, for $3 a load, they'd do it all. That had to be the most disgusting job in town. We'd wear the same underwear a few days in a row to avoid extra loads of laundry.

There was a truck stop near the ballpark that had its own little restaurant. The ballclub had a meal deal there for us, and day after day it was meatloaf, chicken, mashed potatoes, corn, and a bulletproof dinner roll. But the big thing was grits. Grits for breakfast, grits for lunch, grits for dinner.

You could stuff your face for $2 a meal, and we all ate there. The waitress was older than most of us and would leave her shirt slightly open—kind of a cleavage-for-better-tips deal. The bus would pick us up there and we'd travel to minor league garden spots like Cedar Rapids, Burlington, Davenport, and Decatur.

We only got $2-a-day meal money on the road. Nutrition wasn't an issue back then, but survival on $500 a month was. We lived in apartments, and guys would share the rent of maybe $100 to $150 a month. The living conditions were better and the clubhouse was more spacious than Harlan, but it was still 22 guys crammed in a locker room built for 12.

As in Harlan, every time you'd sit down to put your pants or shoes on, somebody's ass was in your face. And the towels stunk, as if they didn't want to waste any detergent on 'em. You were always tempted to look under things to see where the rotting body was stashed. We'd be sitting around and somebody would say, "Smells like something died, doesn't it?"

Ira had heard about my wanderlust from the guys in Harlan, and he warned me early on about driving home. "Don't you dare leave this city or area, y'understand?"

Besides my salary of $500 a month, I still had a little bonus money in the bank, and a few nights after I got to Clinton, I decided that another escape escapade was in order.

My body was screaming for sex, and Karen back home was still my best shot at finally getting it. I thought I could put the slip on Hutchinson by leaving a few hours after the game when he'd gone to bed.

I paid the toll bridge fee and raced back to Markham in the Le Mans convertible, top down, music blaring, and nothing but losing my virginity on my mind.

I got to Karen's house about 3:00 AM. When she heard the Le Mans drive up, she snuck out the back door dressed only in short shorts, a T-shirt, and no bra. I'll never forget the image of her approaching my car, the porch light revealing her bouncing breasts.

We grabbed and groped like the sex-starved teenagers we were, and as she started to straddle me with my zipper undone, a flashlight froze us. It was her dad, and he fumed, "Get the f*ck outta here—and after you get the f*ck outta here, never come back."

Karen had told her father she was in love with me, and he wouldn't allow her to be involved with a ballplayer. He wanted her to go to college, and he knew it wouldn't happen if she ran off with me.

I headed for my mother's house—my virginity intact—to get some sleep before heading back to Clinton. I made it back to Iowa by 5:00 the next afternoon and strolled into the clubhouse in time for batting practice.

Ira called me into the office and quietly said, "That'll be a hundred."

"What for?" I asked, feigning ignorance.

"You took off last night and I told you to stay in f*ckin' Clinton. Don't do it again."

I was stunned. "How the hell did you know?"

"None of your f*cking business. I'm the manager and I know what's going on with my team."

Two weeks later I tried it again—over the bridge, pay the toll, and take the Le Mans to Chicago. When I got back the next day, Ira called me in again.

"This time it's $200. When are you going to figure out that I'm not kiddin'?"

"How the hell did you know?"

He stared at me. "The next time it's $500. I'll ask you the same f*ckin' question again—do you understand?"

$500 was a month's salary.

A few weeks later I went again.

Thinking that something was going on at the bridge tollbooth, I drove 20 miles north to the next bridge and crossed. When I got back the next day, Ira fined me $500, a full month's salary. I found out later that Ira's spy at the bridge had gotten transferred to the other bridge that very week.

I paid the $500 and stayed put in Clinton.

I liked Hutchinson and appreciated how he tried to teach me the curve. I went 4–7 in 16 games and struck out 93 batters in 91 innings. He told me that one-pitch pitchers never last, but he believed in my potential.

That winter of 1962–1963, the Sox sent me to play in an instructional league in Sarasota, Florida. While I was there, I got a letter from Sharon Boudreau. I was a lifelong Cubs fan, and her father was Cubs legend and Hall of Famer Lou Boudreau. I'd met Sharon when I was 14 at a Babe Ruth game in Harvey. She was a year older than me, knock-out gorgeous, and so totally out of my league that I'd never had the guts to pursue her. But when news of the Sox offering me a big league contract reached the local newspaper, Sharon sent me a congratulatory letter.

This started some hot and heavy mail and telephone correspondence, and when I came home around Christmas, we started to date. By the way, did I already tell you I was impulsive? On New Year's Eve, 1962, I took her to see the movie *West Side Story* and asked her to marry me that night. She said yes, and two teenagers, instantly in love, were on their way.

The White Sox invited me to spring training in 1963 because they had to. Baseball rules dictated that if you gave a player a bonus of more than $4,000, you had to put him on your big league roster after a year. If you didn't do it, he'd be put on waivers and you could lose him altogether.

The Sox were in a bind. They had two available roster spots but had three pitchers in that category: Dave DeBusschere, Bruce Howard, and me. DeBusschere had gotten a much larger bonus, so it came down to Howard and me. If they kept both of us, they'd have to sacrifice a roster spot for an established major leaguer.

I'd met Bruce in Clinton, and we'd shared an apartment with a few other guys. We were both having good springs. As spring training drew to a close, Sox manager Al Lopez devised the brilliant plan that whoever won a pitch-off in an intrasquad game would stay and the other guy would be thrown into the minor league draft.

The news was all over the minor league clubhouse that morning—Howard and McLain were gladiators in a winner-take-all death match. It was the Coliseum all over again.

I pitched well: struck out eight or 10 and lost 2–1 to Howard. Immediately after the game, they called me in and told me I was being put on waivers. Howard was about to turn 20 and had a breaking ball. I was about to turn 19 and Lopez hadn't been able to teach me the curve, although he hadn't really tried all that much.

I was stunned. How could they let me go? C'mon. I'm a Chicago kid. It had never entered my mind that I'd be the one let go.

Lopez had a hell of a staff in the early '60s with guys like Gary Peters, Ray Herbert, and Juan Pizarro. He wasn't into starting from ground zero young kids. His thing was, "When they get to me, they better be able to pitch," and he'd decided that Howard would develop sooner.

The Bushes

I was totally dejected and wanted to quit. I feared I'd never learn how to throw a curveball because Lopez had essentially told me that. I was thinking I'd just go back home and work at the steel factory near my house for the rest of my life.

I called Sharon. I told her I was miserable and ready to quit.

Sharon had been around baseball a whole lot longer than I had—she'd been there when her dad was traded, released, and later fired as Cubs manager—and he was a Hall of Famer. She knew what I was going through and told me, "This is what you've wanted all your life, and this is what your father wanted. It's what the game is all about and this is just a blow." She also let it be known that she didn't want to marry a quitter, and if I didn't stick it out she didn't think we had much of a future.

As fate would have it, when I'd pitched with Clinton the summer before, there was a guy in the stands one night named Ed Katalinas. Ed was the Detroit Tigers chief scout, and he'd been pounding the pavement in the Midwest. He had come to a fork in the road in Iowa and had to decide whether he'd go one way to Burlington, where the Pirates had a club, or take the other road to Clinton. The distances were about the same, and he was going to both places eventually.

Katalinas did what any sane man would do—he flipped a coin. Heads was Burlington, tails was Clinton.

Katalinas had no idea who I was, but I happened to be pitching in Clinton that night, and when he got back to Detroit he told the Tigers that if my name ever came up on the waiver wire, they needed to grab me.

It hadn't even been a year since I'd graduated from high school, and I fought my swirling emotions that early April day in Sarasota, deciding if I really wanted to remain a part of all this. I cried to Sharon that I couldn't even go to Notre Dame because I'd played pro ball and had blown my chance for a scholarship. I'd also blown most of my bonus money.

Late that afternoon, a White Sox official came by to tell me that the Tigers had just paid the $8,000 waiver fee and that someone was coming to get me to take me to a place called "Tiger Town." It sounded like a zoo or a theme park.

A few hours later, Katalinas rolled into the complex to drive me and my baseball future the two-plus hours to Lakeland, Florida. By the time we got to Tiger Town, Katalinas had me again thinking I really was the next Bob Feller.

Tiger Town had been a military airport during World War I, with the barracks redone to house the players. Here I was again—no air-conditioning, bathrooms down the hall, cockroaches, and a million guys running around in shorts, playing cards, and talking about the girls in Lakeland.

Lakeland represented a new start for me. I was excited to be there, and most importantly, the Detroit Tigers wanted me.

It had been an amazing day, from total rejection when Lopez said, "We don't think you're ever going to be able to throw the curve," to Katalinas making me feel valuable again. And Katalinas told me I'd get a chance in Double-A right away, a huge step from Class-D ball at Clinton.

I learned at Tiger Town that everybody in the minors is just trying to improve and get to the next level. Rejection is part of the game, and now that I'd finally experienced it, I was already feeling tougher and more experienced.

I don't think many of us remember how fragile we are as 18-year-olds. We're a moment away from either side of the spectrum—from being totally positive and believing we can succeed, to throwing in the towel and spending the rest of our lives in a steel plant.

My dad taught me that the most responsible thing for somebody to do is to work, and he worked himself to death by 36. My dad also had to make the decision: "Do I get married or do I go play baseball?" He chose Betty. With Sharon's help, I chose to go keep my dad's dream alive and not go home to get a job.

The Tigers sent me to Duluth, Minnesota, in the Northern League. My new manager, Bobby Mavis, immediately tried teaching me the curve. Like the others before him, Bobby eventually gave up. I still couldn't get it to bend, but luckily, my fastball was even better than it had been the year before. I was gaining strength and experience and raced out to a 13–2 record.

The minor league pitching coach blew through town every now and then to try to teach me the curve, but I still wasn't getting it. I'd throw 115 pitches per game, and 110 were fastballs. But I kept the ball in the park, threw strikes, didn't walk anybody, and they scored runs for me.

I played with future major leaguers Pat Jarvis and Jim Rooker in Duluth. Rooker was a few years older than me and had been married since high school. He had two kids at the time, and it blew me away how young guys would start families and then bounce around from city to city and league to league.

Surprisingly, many of the young wives seemed to love it, even though there was no substance to the lifestyle outside of the baseball park. You're totally wrapped up in trying to get to the majors and nothing else seems important. It's your pitching, your rest, your big league fantasies, and your girlfriend. That's it. It's the reason so many ballplayers are shallow. Even in the majors they don't know who the vice president is half the time.

I was on a roll all summer. Sharon came to Duluth around the All-Star break. We still hadn't slept together, and the time had come. I'd asked her to marry me on New Year's Eve right after we'd started dating, and I was paying about $60 a month for the ring.

She came in on a Friday and wouldn't let me spend the night at her hotel. She was really making me work. We'd make out and dry hump like rabbits in heat. I don't think she had intended to give it up, but it probably didn't matter. I was so incredibly hot for her that I must've finished in my shorts four or five times. If the goal of her visit was to keep me hungry, then her trip was a smashing success.

◆   ◆   ◆

Late in the 1963 season, the Tigers bumped me up a notch to Knoxville in the Double-A South Atlantic League, otherwise known as the Sally League. It was my fourth team and fourth new state in a little over a full season of pro ball.

I was making about $125 a week now, and I was put in a hotel that was also a popular hangout for hookers. As I'd leave to go to the ballpark, I'd get looks and comments I'd never gotten before. "Hey, cutie," and, "Hey, good lookin'," were some of the things they would throw out at me. Man, Double-A ball was okay.

Before I moved into an apartment with three other players, we had a night off and I was sitting in the lobby reading the sports section. One of the gals sat right down next to me and asked me to take her to dinner. "Sure," I said and took her to the hotel restaurant.

After a few minutes, I innocently asked, "What do you do for a livin'?"

"What would you like me to do?" she coyly replied.

"Excuse me?" I said, still not getting it.

"How's $10 for a blow job and $20 for around the world sound?"

I panicked. I had been so desperate to get laid, but I couldn't handle it. I had never even been undressed in front of a woman. I excused myself, saying I was going to the men's room and went outside to get some air. I didn't go back to the hotel until 3:00 in the morning to avoid any chance of seeing her. I wonder how the rest of her dinner went.

The Bushes

I struck out five of the first six hitters in my first appearance before getting my brains beat out. This was a better league, and although I was still striking guys out, I started giving up more hard shots. Baseball was getting tougher, and near the end of the season I was missing Sharon badly and spending most of my salary on long-distance calls. Thoughts of quitting began running through my mind again.

I loved playing baseball, but it was such a struggle. You're not only competing against players who want the same things you want, but you're also competing with everybody on your own team. It wasn't like you weren't pulling for each other—I don't think I ever sat on a bench and pulled against somebody I was playing with—but you also didn't want the other guy to get called up before you. It was every man for himself, and that's an especially tough thing to deal with when you're young and so damn lonely.

When I was in Duluth and winning all these ballgames, Bobby Mavis said, "Keep it up and you'll be in Detroit before the year is over." The Tigers weren't doing well in '63. There was a big transition going on, and we all got greedy. We knew something was happening with the big club, but we didn't know who'd be the one to get an opportunity.

You'd be in Duluth, Winnipeg, Bismarck, or wherever the hell else, and you'd hope a Tiger starter like Frank Lary got his brains beat or Hank Aguirre broke his leg.

I went 5–4 for Knoxville, which gave me an 18–6 record for the year. I wasn't too thrilled with my performance late in the year, and that's why I was stunned when they told me in mid-September that the Tigers were impressed and I was going to the Show.

I tried to put up a front that it was really no big deal. But going to the big leagues also meant that the remaining $7,000 of my White Sox bonus would kick in.

The first thing I did was call Sharon, and she was as excited as I was. She kept saying, "I told you so, I told you so. Go get 'em Denny, go show 'em."

37

I was told to meet the Tigers in Washington, where they were playing the Senators.

I checked into the Shoreham Hotel, found my room, and was stunned. It had all of the amenities one could imagine, even air-conditioning. It was too late to catch the team bus, so I took a cab to RFK Stadium and tried to enter through the player's entrance. A security guard called the clubhouse, got clearance for me, and sent me on my way. The first time I passed an entrance to the seating area, I walked up the ramp to eyeball the field. The Senators were taking batting practice, and my heart was racing. I thought, "Here I am. Denny McLain, just 19 years old from the south side of Chicago, and I'm going to step on that field to play baseball."

I knew the Tigers were just giving me a cursory look. Winning 18 games in the minors with only a fastball wasn't any big deal. I spent that first game in the bullpen drinking it all in, even though there were all of 1,976 paid in attendance for a Senators team that would soon finish the year 56–106.

I didn't expect the welcome wagon when I got to the majors, but Rocky Colavito was nice enough to offer me his warm-up jacket to wear in the bullpen, and Al Kaline made it a point to come over and say hello. Gus Triandos was also friendly to me that night, and manager Charlie Dressen came by to tell me we'd have time to chat the next day.

Hank Aguirre was called in to face the Senators in the tenth inning of a 5–5 game. With two out, Dressen came to the mound to tell Aguirre to keep the ball away from the lefty-hitting Jim King. Aguirre didn't listen well, and King hit it out of the goddamn park. I had never seen a baseball hit that hard or that far in my life. The sound alone was exhilarating, and I told myself to savor the moment.

Dressen and I hit it off immediately. I threw over the top, and he loved guys like that. Sandy Koufax threw over the top, and Koufax had been Charlie's protégé when he coached the Dodgers in 1958–1959. Almost immediately, he taught me how to spin the ball and convinced me that with some work I could learn a curve and become a pitcher, not just a thrower.

He preached one of the most important and simplest lessons ever: "With your stuff, all you have to do is throw strikes, and you'll get a lot more guys out than will ever hit you. Strikes, strikes, and more strikes. Get it?"

The second day I was there, Charlie told me I'd make my major league debut two days later at Tiger Stadium. Ironically, I'd face the same Chicago White Sox who had given up on me back in April.

I didn't sleep or eat much for the two days. I kept on repeating to myself that this was get-even time with Al Lopez. I was determined to show Lopez what a horrible mistake he had made in the spring.

My debut was September 21, 1963, against a Sox pitcher named Fritz Ackley, who was also making his big league debut.

The first hitter I faced was Mike Hershberger, and I walked him on four pitches. Hershberger took a big lead, and I whipped the ball to Norm Cash and picked him off. It was the first batter I'd ever picked off in any league ever. I looked into the dugout and heard Dressen screaming, "For crissakes, all you old sumbitches can't pick anybody off, and this kid gets the first guy who ever got on against him. Pay attention. Goddamnit!"

Charlie had a wonderfully subtle way of getting his message across.

In the third, I walked Don Buford on a 3–2 count, and I picked him off, too. Now Charlie thought he had Koufax, Feller, and Dizzy Dean all rolled into one.

I walked in my first official at-bat, and we trailed 1–0 in the fifth inning when Ackley fed me a high fastball that I blasted into the left-field seats to tie the game. It was my first official major league at-bat, and it was also the last homer I ever hit in the majors.

My throwing error in the top of the eighth allowed a run that made it 3–3. But Norm Cash put us ahead 4–3 with a solo shot off Jim Brosnan in the bottom of the eighth.

I was really nervous in the ninth and kept looking in the dugout to see if I was going to get yanked. Charlie never budged. I struck out Pete Ward and ex-Tiger Charlie Maxwell to end it with my seventh and eighth strikeouts of the game.

I got hit hard by the Senators and lost my next game but beat Baltimore 7–3 in the last game of the season. It was the major league debut of Wally Bunker, who went on to become a pretty good pitcher.

I gave up 10 hits and seven walks but went the distance. I hadn't pitched that well, but the next day in the paper Dressen was asked what had pleased him most about the season. He said, "The kid who pitched the last game and the kid who played right field."

The kid in right was Willie Horton, who'd hit .326 in 43 at-bats after he got called up. I finished 2–1 with a 4.29 ERA and 22 strikeouts in 21 innings.

◆   ◆   ◆

Since Sharon wasn't Catholic, my mother wouldn't approve our marriage. I was disappointed, but I'd long ago learned to block out my mother's rejection. A few weeks later, Lou Boudreau gave Sharon and me $1,000 and told us to go get married. We hired a justice of the peace and that was that.

Our first night was spent in a hotel on the lake in Chicago, and I'll never forget being so thankful we'd waited on sex until then. We still have the bottle of champagne that her mother bought us to drink that night.

As we lay there in each other's arms—two kids not yet 20 years old, I thought about how she had boosted my spirits back in April, just five months before. Would I have actually given up after Bruce Howard beat me in spring training and spent the rest of my life working in a shop?

The Bushes

There are moments that change lives, and Sharon's insisting that I stay with baseball was one of those.

It all added up to a damn good year.

Chapter 4

Rookie

The Tigers assigned me to Triple-A Syracuse to start the '64 season, and I was thrilled when the Tigers called me back to the majors in mid-May.

I pitched a few times and developed a lesion under my right shoulder blade that hurt like hell. Our trainer, Jack Homel, used to rub the damn thing until I cried. But by August I was throwing well again.

I got in 16 starts in '64, and my final outing was October 1, in New York, in the season's final week. I was 3–4 with an ERA of about four runs a game and was feeling really good about myself. It was a crisp fall day in New York, and I was ready to take the mound in Yankee Stadium.

The aura in Yankee Stadium was just amazing. I'd walked out to center field the day before and looked at all the monuments. I could've sworn Ruth and Gehrig were still there—somewhere. You can just feel the history and nostalgia in the stadium.

The Tigers were over .500 but not involved in the pennant race that had the Yankees leading Baltimore and Chicago. As luck would have it, I was pitching well, and we had a 4–1 lead on the Yankees in the bottom of the seventh.

Mickey Mantle was at the plate with a 3–1 count, and our veteran catcher, Gus Triandos, signaled for a changeup. It's the pitcher's job to either throw the pitch or shake him off, and Charlie Dressen had taught me the changeup in spring training. Charlie was my mentor and was considered a professor of pitching.

Charlie liked me, but what wasn't to like? I threw the ball in the high 90s and wasn't scared of anybody. Charlie had helped me develop the curve in my September call-up the year before, and now he was telling me that I had as good a changeup as Sandy Koufax.

When he played in the '20s and '30s, Dressen was listed at 5'5", 146 pounds, but he looked even smaller that that. And they never made any more colorful characters than Charlie. When we were at home, he used to make what he called "African chili," and you ate it or you wouldn't play. It was hot peppers, beans, rice, and raw onion, and it was so hot it would burn your dick off.

Dressen's first big league managerial job was with the 1951 Brooklyn Dodgers, and he was in the dugout that fall when Ralph Branca gave up the "shot heard 'round the world" to Bobby Thomson. Dressen would tell the story that as soon as he saw Branca throw the fateful pitch, he put his head down and said, "Oh, f*ck no." He knew it was coming over the plate cock high, and he had told his team that if you didn't pitch Thomson totally down, you were in a lot of trouble.

I thought about what Charlie had said before the game. He was smart, organized, and efficient, and he was the only manager I ever had who would bring the whole team together before every game to talk over the tendencies of opposing hitters. Charlie would give strict instructions, and as the starter that day, he stressed that I was to never throw Mantle a changeup. Dressen specifically said, "As good as your changeup is, you better not throw it because Mantle will hit that f*cker to Pawtucket by the time they chase it down."

So we were in the seventh inning, and I was peering in at Triandos, who was calling for the changeup. I didn't shake him off because I wanted to throw the pitch. Triandos was sitting safely outside by six or eight inches.

Rookie

Was I gonna throw him a changeup with the score tied 2–2? Hell no. The meeting was only two hours earlier, so I couldn't make the excuse that I forgot. So I said to myself, *Shit, I got a three-run lead.*

It was a great pitch—right where Gus called for it—six to eight inches outside and below the knees. Mantle reached out and pulled it deep into the stands in the right-field corner. Years later, I saw Mantle hit the ball right-handed into the upper deck right-center bleachers in Detroit, and that's an awesome poke. But I was still a rookie, and I couldn't believe anyone could hit a ball like that.

I got out of the inning with a 4–2 lead and was thinking, *How in the hell do I avoid the dugout?* Normally I'd come back and sit right in front, nearest to home plate. So I headed for the end of the bench, avoiding eye contact. No sooner had I sat down, than Charlie started screaming loud enough for the hot dog vendors to hear.

"What the f*ck did I tell you in that f*ckin' clubhouse meeting? Why do we have a clubhouse meeting if you're gonna go out there and do your own f*ckin' thing? What in the f*ck is wrong with you? You think Sandy Koufax would throw a f*ckin' changeup to Mickey Mantle? Nobody can throw a changeup to Mickey Mantle. If you ever throw another pitch I tell you not to, you'll never pitch in this organization again!"

I said, "Yes, sir. You're right, Charlie. I like it up here, and it won't happen again," but I was also thinking, *Jesus Christ, it's not like I killed somebody.*

We won the game 5–2, and the Yankees held on to win the pennant by a single game over the White Sox.

Chapter 5

I Arrive

I was determined to shoot out of the pack of promising pitchers and become the real thing in 1965, and the process began in Mayaguez, Puerto Rico.

The Tigers sent most of their young players to play winter ball under Tiger coach Bob Swift, and we had a truly remarkable team. Swifty took his orders from Charlie Dressen, and with Mickey Stanley, Willie Horton, Jim Northrup, Joe Sparma, Bill Freehan, Ray Oyler, and me, we had a young nucleus that was capable of developing into championship caliber.

The league was outstanding and featured every Puerto Rican who played in the majors, including Roberto Clemente and Orlando Cepeda. I struck out Cepeda four straight times one night in San Juan. Cuban-born Luis Tiant, who, like me, was a major league rookie in 1964, also played in the league.

It was a great time. We all lived in an apartment complex that was still under construction. It had a restaurant on the bottom floor, and our deal was along the lines of the old the gas station in Clinton, Iowa. You could buy all your meals for $4 to $5 a day, and you never knew if the so-called "chopped steak" might have been chopped cat or dog. I don't know how many Rin Tin Tins we ate that winter, but nobody had the guts to ask or, God forbid, look in the kitchen to see what was really going on. One night Oyler claimed he found a dog's toenail in his meatloaf.

Gambling was legal in Puerto Rico, and most of us gambled. But the casinos presented problems for Americans. The taxis stopped running at midnight, and one night Sparma and I were on a roll, up $400 or so, and we played well past midnight. We had been warned not to walk back to town late at night because of roving gangs. We weren't attacked, but we did get the shit scared out of us by a seemingly endless number of growling dogs.

Swifty caught wind of our escapade and fined us $100 each. We only made $1,000 a month, and he said if he found out that we'd gone again, we'd regret the day we ever even heard the word "casino." Swift was a good guy and one of the more learned coaches in game, but he always felt he had to demonstrate his toughness to prove he was in charge.

The way around his edict was simple. Pitcher Jack Hamilton and I ran a casino in the apartment complex four or five nights a week.

I'd won a total of six games in the major leagues in '63 and '64, but I really began finding my way in Puerto Rico. My breaking ball was becoming very effective, and I was getting everybody out. I finished 12–4 with a 1.92 ERA and pitched the championship winner in Santurce.

Winning was the easy part. Leaving Santurce that evening with the title was another story. Angry fans threw rocks at our bus as we began to drive away. I'm not big on stereotypes, but it sure seemed that the Latinos got very emotional over baseball. The whole town was waiting for us back in Mayaguez. When I got off the bus, the crowd lifted me on its shoulders and marched me around the town circle.

What a moment that was. When they put me down and I got my bearings, I realized they'd picked my pocket of about $200. I reported it; they took up a collection and I wound up with almost a grand.

Winter ball morphed into spring training, and we knew we'd be better than we were in '64. In '61, the year Roger Maris and Mickey Mantle hit 115 homers between them, the Tigers won 101 games and finished eight games back from the Yankees. The Tigers became a .500-type team in '62 and '63, and by '64 our attendance had dropped to a 20-year low of 816,000. Management was counting on the young bucks to usher in a new era.

Northrup, Oyler, Horton, and I had all put in time at Syracuse in '64 and were primed to make a splash in the majors. Of our pitching staff, *The Detroit News* wrote, "Dave Wickersham, Mickey Lolich, and Hank Aguirre are the three top starters, and young Denny McLain seems capable of joining them with some solid performances."

Back then, you had your starters, and everybody else just filled out the staff. A relief pitcher was essentially just the next guy going to minor leagues. You may have had a number-one relief pitcher, and going into '65, ours was probably Terry Fox. Fred Gladding and Larry Sherry were okay also, but the game back then was all about the starters trying to pitch nine innings.

By mid-May I had five starts and no wins. Dressen was experimenting with me, Sparma, and Phil Regan to determine who would emerge as the fourth guy in the rotation, and none of us had been really convincing. On May 19, before a modest crowd of barely 5,000 at Tiger Stadium, I shut out the Senators 4–0. Washington manager Gil Hodges praised me for "getting my fastball over," and our catcher, Bill Freehan, concurred by saying, "When Denny spots his fastball, he can be tough."

I started and lost to the Yankees on May 31 and lasted only four innings against the Angels on June 7. On June 12 I gave up a three-run homer to the Twins' Jimmie Hall, but I beat Camilo Pascual 8–5. I was 2–3 and still just one of those "guys filling out the staff."

On June 15 at Tiger Stadium Wickersham started against the Red Sox and got hit hard. The Sox had two runs in with one out in the first inning when Dressen ordered me to warm up. After Tony Conigliaro singled in the third Sox run, Charlie brought me in with two men on and one out.

The wind was blowing right in my face, and I zipped three fastballs past Ed Bressoud. Bob Tillman was next, and I got him on four fastballs to end the inning. It seemed like the wind was actually causing my fastball to rise.

In the second inning, I struck out pitcher Earl Wilson and then blew away leadoff man Lenny Green for four strikeouts in a row. I felt invincible by this time, and three more fastballs got Dalton Jones to end the inning and make it five straight strikeouts. There were 9,000 fans on hand, and we got a nice roar as we headed back to the dugout.

Carl Yastrzemski led off the Sox third, and I fanned him on four fastballs for six strikeouts in a row. Although I wasn't aware of it, six tied a major league record for relief pitchers held by the Phillies' Jack Meyer in 1958 and Pete Richert of the '62 Dodgers.

Felix Mantilla was next, and I put him away with five fastballs for number seven and the record.

The last batter in the third inning was first baseman Lee Thomas. I had Thomas 0–2 and decided the time had come to throw my first breaking ball. Freehan gave me a target on the outside corner, and I hit it perfectly. Thomas was completely fooled. Unfortunately, so was home plate umpire Johnny Stevens. For me to throw a curve for a strike was unheard of. Stevens hesitated a split second and called it a ball.

I was pissed. I had no idea that seven straight strikeouts was a record, but I still wanted Thomas. Eight straight would have been a major league record for starters or relievers. Thomas tapped the next pitch to second baseman Jerry Lumpe, who easily threw to Norm Cash to end the inning.

The Red Sox got two off me in the sixth, and after trailing 5–2, Charlie had Fred Gladding pitch the last two innings. We won it 6–5 on Horton's three-run homer in the eighth.

I finished with 14 strikeouts in 6 ⅔ innings, and along with Gladding's four, we matched Bob Feller's single-game record of 18, set back in 1938. Freehan also set a major league record with 19 putouts. All in all, it was a wild night—starting with the Red Sox knocking out Wickersham, my strikeout streak, Horton's dramatic home run, and the equaling of Feller's record.

The game got everybody's attention and turned into a career-changing experience for me. Even though I didn't figure in the decision, I went from being one of the guys in the bullpen to a guy they were going to rely on for a while.

I became entrenched in the rotation at that point and won six in a row to push my record to 7–3.

We hosted Cleveland in a twi-night doubleheader on July 21 with 33,000 fans on hand. I pitched the second game after Lolich beat Sam McDowell in the opener. I'd been throwing well for more than a month, but this night was different. Early in the game I got the sense that I was doing things I'd never done before. My control had always been good but never like this. I'd get a guy 2–2, 3–2, and I then hit the corner with whatever catcher Johnny Sullivan called.

Charlie had told me before the game that Chuck Hinton was a dead fastball hitter around the knees or lower. You could throw it on the ground and the son of a bitch would hit a homer. I was a high fastball pitcher, and with two out in the second, I faced Hinton. I got him to 1–2 and threw a fastball down and away. It wasn't more than six inches off the ground, but it was also over the plate, ankle high, and Hinton hit it nine miles. It impressed the shit out of me. It also convinced me again that Charlie knew what he was talking about.

I gave up two hits the rest of the way, and we won 2–1 on Don Demeter's two-run homer off loser Sonny Siebert. I fanned 12, walked none, and had never felt in such complete control. Dressen said to the reporters, "I told you so that the kid was gonna be a big-league pitcher."

The *Detroit News* game story began, "Young Denny McLain bared a killer instinct last night in winning his seventh straight game...." I'd become a full-time starter before that night, but that was when I became the ghost ace. I was the best pitcher on the ballclub, although you couldn't say it categorically. But I knew it, and everybody else knew it.

We played another twi-nighter at home against Chicago four days later before 38,000. I was extremely excited because I was on a roll and going against Bruce Howard. Two years ago, at age 19, the White Sox had made me think of quitting when they kept Howard instead of me. Howard came into the game with a 4–5 record, and I was ready to stick it to Al Lopez again.

We scored seven runs in the second inning to chase Howard, and I was breezing along. Sometime around mid-game, the temperature dropped 10 or 15 degrees as it went from very hot to semi-cool.

I got the first two men out in the sixth on just a few pitches, and then, on the first pitch to cleanup hitter Pete Ward, I felt something pop in my shoulder. I pitched a five-hitter for my eighth consecutive win in a 13–2 blowout, but I could barely lift my arm the next morning. It was the first time it had hurt to any significant degree since the failed curveball experiment in my backyard as a kid.

I went to trainer Jack Homel the next day to see if he could rub the soreness out, but he couldn't put a dent in it. He suggested I go to the team doctor, who set me up at Henry Ford Hospital with Dr. David Mitchell. Mitchell told me that a shot of cortisone would likely do the trick.

It was that day, that conversation, and that moment that cortisone came into my life.

I thought I'd get a shot in the ass like they do with penicillin. Instead, they took me into sterile room and I started thinking, "Are they gonnna cut my arm off?" Mitchell had me lie on a table and wiped iodine all over my shoulder. He told me to turn my head and I'd just feel just a pinch. He was right. But that was just the Xylocaine to deaden my shoulder for the big needle.

I Arrive

I thought he was done, so I turned back to my right and saw a six-inch needle about to go into my shoulder and I almost passed out. Mitchell told me to relax because the first needle was just the setup. This one had the cortisone in it, and he started probing around. When he hit the troubled spot, it still hurt like hell, Xylocaine or not.

I might have won 20 in 1965 if I hadn't come down with a kidney infection in late August. I was sitting on the bench in Los Angeles before a doubleheader in late August and felt really sick. I told Homel I thought I might pass out. He told me it was probably the smog alert they were having, and since we were going to Minnesota after the game, that'd probably cure it.

By the time the second game rolled around, I was violently ill. And on the plane to Minneapolis, the pilot called ahead to have an ambulance ready. They thought the pain I was experiencing might have come from my appendix. I was checked into a Swedish Catholic hospital, and they told me there were kidney stones between my bladder and penis. The next night my nurse came in to see if I was feeling any better. I told her that the medication was taking care of some of the pain, but I wasn't too thrilled with the news that they were going to put a tube up my penis.

She said, "I can't imagine anyone wanting a tube in their thing. I do have a better way, but you need some nerve. The doctors tell me that if it doesn't pass this way, the pain might be even worse."

"I'll take a chance," I said. "What is it?"

She told me to lay back and turned the light off. She put her hand under the blanket and jerked me off. Everything rushed out, including blood and the stone, and the pain passed. My fever also went down and I felt like I could jump out of bed and dance. Unfortunately, a few more pieces were still in there, and it took another uncomfortable week to pass them.

On September 21, I defeated the White Sox again at Tiger Stadium, fanning 12. Beat writer Watson Spoelstra wrote in *The Detroit News*,

53

"Claimed from the White Sox two years ago for the $8,000 waiver price, Denny delights in beating Chicago and is 3–1 against them. He has become one of the AL's most formidable right-handed pitchers."

My first daughter, Kristin, was born on September 30, and on October 2 I finished the season by beating the Senators 9–1. I missed a shutout on my own throwing error in the ninth. It had been the most satisfying season of my life. I was still only 21 years old and had won 16 of my last 20 decisions after going winless until May 19. I finished 16–6 and was chosen Tiger of the Year by the writers. I was honored at a dinner and gave my first and worst speech. I told a decent Charlie Dressen joke and then thanked the writers who voted for me. I tried to be funny by adding, "As for the writers who didn't vote for me, go f*ck yourselves." Our owner, John Fetzer, was there, and the hushed reaction told me I'd missed the boat. Fetzer sought me out, told me he sensed my discomfort, and accepted my apology.

It was great to already be considered a good player, and I was determined to make 1966 an even better season. I wanted to become one of the best, like the Giants' Juan Marichal or the Dodgers' Sandy Koufax.

Both of them made big news in 1965. Marichal won 22 games with a 2.13 ERA, and on August 22 Marichal had infamously bludgeoned the Dodgers' Johnny Roseboro with his bat. The Giants finished just two games back in a great West Coast pennant race.

Koufax pitched a perfect game against the Cubs in September and finished the year 26–8, with a 2.04 ERA. He broke Bob Feller's strikeout record of 348 with 382. He missed Game 1 of the World Series against the Twins for Yom Kippur but won Game 7 to clinch the championship for the Dodgers.

Chapter 6

Farewell Charlie

We'd won 89 games in 1965 and looked like a young club on its way. Willie Horton hit 29 homers with 104 RBIs, and Charlie Dressen was enthused that his top three starters—Mickey Lolich, Joe Sparma, and me—were all under 25 years old. Mickey Stanley, our best all-around athlete, was only 23 and ready to help now. We picked up Bill Monbouquette from the Red Sox in the off-season to be the fourth starter.

With Al Kaline, Bill Freehan, Norm Cash, and All-Star shortstop Dick McAuliffe, we showed a lot of promise, and the writers predicted we'd contend in '66.

It was a fascinating period in baseball. Sandy Koufax and Don Drysdale held out in spring training, looking for a three-year, $1 million deal that they would split at $166,000 a season for each. They finally settled with Koufax getting $120,000 and Drysdale $105,000.

Over the winter, Reds GM Bill DeWitt traded an "old" Frank Robinson, so he thought, to the Orioles for Milt Pappas and Jack Baldschun. Robinson liked to crowd the plate, so in his Orioles debut, Red Sox pitcher Earl Wilson welcomed Frank into the AL by hitting him in the back his first time up.

The Mets won the chance to sign Tom Seaver for $50,000 when Commissioner William Eckert picked their name from three he had in a hat. He had voided the Braves' signing of Seaver because they had done it during Seaver's college season.

And Emmett Ashford became baseball's first black umpire.

Emmett immediately became the most demonstrative umpire in history. He would yell, "Steeerike!" and while other umpires would play it cool and pause a moment before calling a pitch, Emmett wouldn't screw around. Ashford understood the full nature of his job, which included being entertaining without showing up the players.

About a year or so after he entered the league, we were playing the White Sox and John Wyatt was pitching in relief for us. John was a mediocre pitcher near the end of his career and had begun relying heavily on his spitball. He didn't throw it as well as Gaylord Perry, but he was as good as Perry in disguising its source.

Wyatt was unusually effective this night, with his pitches darting in and out of the strike zone, often diving straight down as they neared the plate. Not only couldn't the White Sox hitters get near it, but Bill Freehan looked like a boxer, stabbing and jabbing to get it to hit his glove. White Sox manager Eddie Stanky was incensed, and his hitters continually asked Emmett to check the ball.

We had a one-run lead, and Wyatt expected the manager to pinch-hit for him. As a middle reliever, he almost never got an at-bat. But the manager caught him off guard and sent John up to hit for himself.

As he settled into the box, Sox catcher Duane Josephson said, "Emmett, do you smell that?"

"Time out," Emmett roared, "what the hell is that smell?" Like a dog in heat, Emmett was furiously sniffing Wyatt up and down.

"What is that awful smell coming from you? It better not be an illegal substance, Mr. Wyatt!"

"Emmett, it's not an illegal substance."

"Then what the hell is it?"

"Emmett, it's Preparation H, and I am suffering from hemorrhoids. Is that illegal?"

Trying to hold back his laughter, Emmett says, "No, it isn't illegal. But are you using it on the goddamn baseball or not?"

"I am disappointed in you, Emmett, that you would accuse a brother of doing anything illegal."

By now, Wyatt, Ashford, and Josephson were fighting back the laughter with Emmett wiping away the tears.

Finally, Ashford said, "When I came into the league they told me you were a real asshole, and now you've proven it. Play ball!"

There was nothing illegal about Preparation H unless they could figure out how John was getting it on the baseball. Had someone lit a match to his shirt, Wyatt might have burned down the ballpark. It was the first and last time that Wyatt used Preparation H for his spitter, but man, he had the best one any of us had ever seen.

The Indians won their first 10 games in '66 to set an AL record, and Sam McDowell was on fire. On May 1, he threw his second consecutive one-hitter, just the fourth pitcher to ever do that.

I got off to a great start, too. On May 6, a really cold night in Chicago, I had a nasty changeup and one-hit the White Sox in a 1–0 victory, getting 22 of the last 23 hitters. J.C. Martin's lead-off single in the second inning was the Sox's only hit.

The win put me at 4–1 with a 1.98 ERA, and it was my first career win in Chicago. I told the Chicago writers, "I like to rub salt in the wound, and there's nobody I like beating more than Chicago, especially right here."

One of the writers had written that the Sox had cut me in '63 because I was "flaky." I got in his face, telling him it was bullshit—that I was 18 and used my bonus money to go home a few times. Of course, the writers then ran to Sox GM Ed Short and fanned the flames with my quotes.

Short called me a "pop-off" and shot back, "If McLain had looked good in spring training, we would have kept him."

Short was right. I was a pop-off. I loved the attention, and I'd say whatever I could to keep the writers around. I'd played piano at a number of clubs in '65, and I bragged, "I want 16 concert appearances this summer, and I can fit 'em in on my off days and sneak in two or three at the All-Star break."

We were 16–10 on May 16 when Charlie Dressen entered the hospital with his second heart attack in two years. Bob Swift took over. I pitched that night and beat the Yankees 7–2 on a two-hitter. I was 6–1 with a 2.05 ERA after getting the last 16 Yanks in order.

At that point, we traded Don Demeter to Boston for Earl Wilson to help our pitching because it was obvious that Monbouquette wasn't working out.

On May 25 the Indians came to town, and I was slated to face Sam McDowell, who had led the league with 325 strikeouts and a 2.18 ERA in '65. I told the writers, "I'd like to see who the best young pitcher in the league is. I want to beat McDowell so bad my teeth hurt." I was still a kid, mesmerized by the power of the press and incapable of controlling what streamed out of my mouth.

My teeth actually did hurt because I drank up to a case of Pepsi every day, and they were rotting out. But I was just trying to hype the event and sell tickets. I told the writers that I'd sent McDowell a note last year asking him what made him think he was so hot. I added, "You couldn't print in the paper what he wrote me back."

More than 25,000 showed up, and we hadn't gotten more than 15,000 for a single game since the season opener. It turned into a bust because Sam had a sore shoulder and left in the second inning, and the Indians chased me in the third in a 13–2 rout.

On June 24 we were 42–24 and looking good. But Swift couldn't handle the pitching staff, and it started catching up to us. Then, in mid-July, Swift tragically came down with stomach cancer and Frank Skaff took over.

Amid the chaos, I was having another very good year. I was 13–4 in early July, and I had been a combined 29–8 since May of '65. All-Star manager Sam Mele selected me to start the big game in St. Louis against Sandy Koufax, who was 15–4.

I was 22 years old and felt invincible against what the press was calling the most fearsome lineup in All-Star history. I threw 28 pitches in three innings and retired nine consecutive hitters. I made Willie Mays look bad swinging at a slow curve before he took strike three. I got Roberto Clemente on a fly and got Hank Aaron looking at strike three to end the first. I got Willie McCovey and Ron Santo to hit into outs and then fanned Joe Torre on three pitches to end the second. So much for a murderer's row.

I got the bottom of their order one-two-three in the third and left with a 1–0 lead.

It turned out to be a classic, with Maury Wills's tenth-inning single off Pete Richert scoring Tim McCarver for a 2–1 National League win. The writers seemed impressed by my performance. Mays said to them, "How old is he? Somebody has taught him about pitching real quick—he's fast and mixes his pitches."

I entertained the writers, saying, "I don't like to waste pitches, even when I'm 0–2. My philosophy is, why waste a pitch when you can get them on three?" This was really Charlie Dressen's theory—don't waste pitches if you have good stuff. If you are a shit-baller, you have to pick and pick, but a hard thrower shouldn't. Never give a sucker a break.

I may have only been 22, but I felt like I had the world by the balls.

Unfortunately, our season was falling apart. With Skaff's lousy managing, pitching coach Stubby Overmire's total lack of pitching insight, and some of my own poor performances, things got real ugly after the All-Star break.

On July 20 the Orioles abused me for eight runs in four innings, and I got into an argument with Overmire after the game. I had been ahead of a hitter but gave up a homer on a bad pitch, and Stubby went off on me. At first I thought he was kidding. When I realized he wasn't, I got upset and told him to get lost.

I broke out of a slump with a shutout of the White Sox on August 2. Pete Waldmeir of *The Detroit News* was looking for a column, and I gave him one.

"With all the managerial problems we've had," I told Waldmeir, "you don't know who to listen to, and the coaching of our pitchers has been less than great." Then I dropped the bomb: "This has got to be a country club team. The players run it. If we want to do something, we do it. Actually, it's a little ridiculous. I've been here three years and played for three managers, and I wouldn't be surprised if we had a new one after this week."

The shit hit the fan the next day with the comment about "a country club team" rattling cages all through the organization.

On August 10 Dressen had a third heart attack and died. It was awful. I'd seen Charlie a few times after his attack in May, and you could tell the end was near. How I loved that man for believing in me as a 19-year-old and then helping me to become the pitcher he believed I could be.

We also knew that Swift's cancer was ravaging him, and there was just an uncomfortable feel about the entire season. Some guys even sank to gallows humor, making jokes like, "Who'd want to manage this club—we kill every manager who comes aboard." By August 29, I'd fallen to 15–11 as we faced the Orioles in Baltimore.

Baltimore had always hit me hard, and in the first inning, Frank Robinson hit a curveball out of the park with Luis Aparicio on base for a 2–0 lead. In my career against Baltimore, I'd given up 31 runs in 26 innings. It was also Robinson's 41st homer en route to winning the Triple Crown in his first AL season.

Farewell Charlie

By evening's end, I walked nine Orioles and struck out 11. We won 6–3, and I found out later that I'd thrown 229 pitches. The genius, Overmire, when asked about my pitch count, said, "We don't keep a complete count anymore. But I know he had 35 in one inning."

Can you even imagine something like that occurring today? Your best pitcher needs cortisone shots at age 22, and you allow him throw 229 pitches? These are the intelligence levels we dealt with back then.

On September 26 we beat California 2–1 for my 20th victory. I finished the season 20–14 with a 3.92 ERA and 192 strikeouts. Four cortisone shots over the course of the season had helped me get through.

We finished in third place with 88 wins. The Yankees, who'd played in five consecutive World Series from 1960 to 1964, finished dead last in the 10-team AL. When they had drawn 413 fans for a late-September game with the White Sox, legendary announcer Red Barber had the cameras pan the empty seats. Not amused, the Yankees quickly fired one of the all-time greats. Hard to believe that a Red Barber, trying to inject some humor into a game with 413 fans, would get canned.

The Orioles swept the Dodgers in the World Series, and on November 18, 30-year-old Sandy Koufax retired. He had a 27–9 record in '66, but his arthritic pitching elbow was history. Koufax said, "Too many shots, too many pills, and I don't want to take the chance of disabling myself. I don't regret the 12 years in baseball, but I could regret one season too many."

On the final day of the season the Tigers reassigned Skaff as a scout and hired Mayo Smith as manager. Then we lost Swift to cancer in the off-season. Two managers had died in one season, and we had fired the third.

The feeling was that 1967 had to be better.

Chapter 7

Shorthorn

Winning 20 games in 1966 at age 22 was a very big step from my breakout year in '65. In a *Sport* magazine article previewing the 1967 season, Joe Falls wrote of how the turmoil and confusion caused by the deaths of Dressen and Swift may have affected our cohesion. Falls wondered, "There are some great individual players, but are they a team?"

Our future Hall of Famer Al Kaline had hit only .281 and .288 the last two years, and the Twins had turned down an offer of Kaline and Dave Wickersham for Jim Kaat and Jimmie Hall. Now, as the '67 season rolled around, Kaline was bitching about being asked to play center field. "I don't know if it's the mental pressure of having to do some of the work of the guys next to me," Al complained, "but it's a hard job, and I don't enjoy it as much as right. If they would just let me play right, guys wouldn't be talking about trading me all the time."

The remark about having to cover for other players almost caused a mutiny in the club. Kaline had more than a few teammates who were sorry the Twins turned down the deal. New manager Mayo Smith was Kaline's 10th manager in his 15 years with the club, and, wanting to establish some stability, Mayo told Kaline he'd play right field all year.

After my "country club" remark in early August, Jim Campbell called me in and ordered me to claim that Pete Waldmeir had misquoted me.

So I said, "The Lord can strike me dead if I said any of those things."

Falls also wrote in his *Sport* article:

> Denny McLain squabbled with teammates, opponents, coaches, the front office, and newspapermen in '66. He said the efforts of pitching coach Stubby Overmire "were something a joke" and even called the Tigers a "country club team."
>
> McLain swore he was misquoted on the "country club" line and said, "the Lord could strike him dead" if he really said any of these things. The writer who "misquoted" him fired back at McLain, "I hope no one will be hurt in the rush to the dugout if the skies cloud up and it starts lightning the next time McLain takes the mound."

I began '67 as the ace of the staff, hopeful of winning at least 20 again. The Orioles had swept the Dodgers in the '66 World Series, but we'd won 89 and 88 games the past two years and felt we were ready to contend with Baltimore or anybody else who stepped out of the pack.

I struggled in spring training with a sore arm and pitched badly in my last exhibition appearance, walking five Red Sox in three innings. Earl Wilson, who went 13–6 with a 2.59 ERA for us after coming over from Boston, told a writer, "Give me one reason why I shouldn't pitch the opener."

Mayo kept the peace again by telling Wilson that after I opened on the road, he could pitch the home opener a few days later. Mayo had also brought over John Sain as pitching coach. Sain had a reputation as the best in the business, but the Yankees and Twins fired him for siding with his pitchers rather than managers Ralph Houk and Sam Mele.

I pitched poorly and lost the opener in L.A., giving up four runs in four innings, including a two-run homer by Don Mincher. My arm was bothering me, and I could tell that the number of cortisone shots I'd need would rise considerably above the four I had in '66.

On the personal side, I'd begun gambling pretty heavily on basketball and football with a guy named Ed Schober. Ed was the Detroit area merchandising director for Pepsi and had learned through numerous newspaper and TV interviews that I was consuming his product to the tune of a case or so a day. Naturally, Ed called and signed me to a promotional contract, and every week a blue-and-white Pepsi van would deliver 10 cases of my favorite beverage.

For $15,000 a year, big money in those days, and a refrigerator and garage fully stocked with Pepsi, all I had to do was mention my love for Pepsi when the opportunity arose, try to drink one during interviews, and make a few personal appearances. Ed Schober immediately turned into Mary's little lamb, sure to follow me everywhere I went. Ed was a jock sniffer right out of central casting, beside himself with excitement to hang around the Tiger clubhouse.

Sharon and I liked the Pepsi deal so much, we got a little English sheepdog puppy and named the damn thing Pepsi. Ed's family and ours were inseparable, and we'd get together at least a few times a week.

In '66 I was teaching and playing the Hammond organ all around the Midwest, including a little club in Flint called the Shorthorn. It was a nice place that held about 125 people and had the best prime rib. I wasn't the world's best piano player, but I could entertain the crowd with music and banter, and there sure as hell wasn't another 20-game winner in the world who could play the Hammond as good as me.

Like the Pepsi folks, Hammond had also caught wind of the fact that there was a wacko pitcher on the Tigers who played their product. They signed me to a $30,000 promotional contract to play and talk up the newest organ they had at the time, a sleek X-77 that had enough bells and whistles to look like the cockpit of a jet. The promotional deals with Pepsi and Hammond easily exceeded my baseball salary. I could hardly believe how much money I was making.

Ed and I started placing our bets through the Shorthorn's owner, a guy named Clyde Roberts, who looked a lot like the Pillsbury Doughboy. One day Roberts came over and said, "Check it out. You're losing $200 to $300 a week on college and pro basketball. Since I know a lotta other guys who place a ton of action, why don't we start taking the action instead of giving all the money to the bookies?"

I talked about it with Schober, and we came to the stunning conclusion that it made perfect sense—let us be the bookies. So there you had it—a 22-year-old 20-game winner and the director of merchandising for Pepsi of Michigan bankrolling a bookie operation.

We'd make a fortune. We agreed to keep all bets to $100 or less, and Clyde would make certain that any bigger bets were cleared through Schober or me. Clyde also assured me that there would be no need to have mob ties because he had a guy who'd "protect" the operation.

Ed and I figured that all we needed was a few customers who were as bad at handicapping as we were and we'd be set.

Clyde's pal at the Shorthorn, the guy who was going to protect the operation, was a short, dark-skinned lowlife named Jiggs Gazell. Gazell was a caricature of a gangster like you'd see on *The Untouchables*. He wore those old gangster hats and was always impeccably dressed. He was to handle the bets in Flint while I played baseball all over America. We rented an apartment and bought a table and chairs and installed a phone so that they had a place to take the bets. Jiggs and Clyde would phone in the bets to Ed each night before the action would be authorized. It seemed foolproof.

Jiggs and Clyde had me see one of their regulars, Larry, an officer at the Citizen's Bank across the street from the restaurant, who lent me $7,500. I gave Clyde and Jiggs $4,000 in cash to bankroll the business.

Shorthorn

To get the deal done, I had to give Larry a $500 kickback, and he became one of our first customers. Every night I played at the Shorthorn, Larry the Banker was in there getting stone-cold drunk.

Lo and behold, shock of shocks, we bolted out of the gate on a four- or five-week losing streak, and before I left for spring training in February 1967, I had to borrow another $3,000 from Larry, with the customary $500 kickback.

Like a 20-game winner who felt he had the world by the balls, I was arrogant enough to call in some of my spring training bets from the pressroom in Lakeland. Our general manager, Jim Campbell, was tipped off by a sportswriter and called me into his office to ask if I was doing any betting. Campbell had me by the balls, and the best I could do was distort the truth and tell him I was just betting a little basketball but nothing of any significance.

Would Campbell suspend a 20-game winner? Hell no. When you win 20 ball games, you can get away with just about anything. Campbell called me into his office and said, "If you're going to gamble, Jesus Christ, don't do it in front of the writers." I never placed a bet in the pressroom or locker room again, although I still studied the spreads, the scoring averages, freethrow percentages, and everything else down to their shoe sizes. God, I just loved everything about gambling, from picking teams to placing bets to watching the action.

But the bookmaking dream team wasn't producing results. Gazell and Roberts were lax in informing Ed of the day's bets, and after eight or nine weeks of steady losing, I finally said to Schober, "What's wrong with this picture? When we were betting, we paid Roberts every week. And now that we're his partners, we're still paying Roberts every week."

By midsummer I was down over $15,000 and knew that Roberts and Gazell were ripping us off. So I wrote it off as something stupid that I wouldn't do again. What else could I do—run to the cops and tell them I was being scammed?

I figured Ed and I were never a part of their bookmaking operation. Roberts and Gazell were keeping their winning bets and sticking me and Ed with the losers. It was early August when I told them to stick it up their ass.

Aside from the Shorthorn and the pennant race, there was some seriously scary stuff going on in Detroit. The city had developed a number of four-man cop squads called STRESS units that busted illegal drinking joints and streetwalkers. Blacks reviled these police teams that came to their neighborhoods harassing and humiliating people. Detroit wasn't alone. Blacks all over the country were rebelling. The weeklong riot in Newark began on July 12.

In newspaper polls, Detroit blacks had for years cited police brutality as their number-one problem. Housing had become a mounting source of white–black tension in Detroit in the '60s. Blacks were integrating the suburbs and were forced to pay higher rents than whites for equal accommodations in the city.

The auto plants had begun outsourcing and cutting back on assembly line workers, and young black workers were being put out on the street. In 1967, while white America appeared to be enjoying great prosperity, blacks were frustrated and alienated by the pace of racial change they felt was too slow.

Ironically, the hippies in California were calling 1967 the Summer of Love, but reality told a much darker story. In early July, H. Rap Brown had come to Detroit for a Black Power rally and, thrusting his fist in the air, bellowed, "If Motown doesn't come around, we are going to burn you down!"

It was just a matter of time.

We played the Yankees at Tiger Stadium on Saturday afternoon, July 22, 1967. In the early morning hours of July 23, a STRESS unit raided a so-called "blind pig," an after-hours drinking and gambling joint on 12th Street and Clairmont in northwest Detroit. The cops had expected to round up a handful of people but instead found a crowd of 82 holding a welcome-home party for a few returning Vietnam veterans. Instead of busting the place and dispersing the crowd, the cops called for support and hauled in all 82. After the last paddy wagon left, a few who had watched it all take place broke the windows on a nearby white-owned clothing store.

That touched it off. Gunfire, looting, and arson escalated through northwest Detroit and spread to the east side. Within two days, the National Guard came, then the 82nd airborne, and it seemed like the more the police and military tried to stop it, the worse it got.

We came back to play a doubleheader against the Yankees on Sunday afternoon, and the smoke rising over the left-field wall got everybody's attention. There wasn't blanket media coverage back then, and by Sunday morning many people weren't fully aware of the extent of the death and devastation that was going on.

At the end of that first ballgame, Jim Campbell came down to the clubhouse to bring everybody up to date on how bad things were and to warn us to be extra careful. He told us to get home right away after the second game to protect our families.

Our radio announcers, including Hall of Famer Ernie Harwell, never said a word about the riots. The edict from Campbell was that baseball must be in a world of its own. There was a war taking place on the other side of our left-field wall, but Campbell wouldn't even allow a public service announcement for the fans' safety.

The Orioles were due in town the next day, and the two clubs decided to move the series to Baltimore. Campbell arranged to have the games televised in hopes that watching Tigers baseball would distract the looters and arsonists.

It didn't.

When five days of rioting were over, 43 were dead, 1,200 were injured, and more than 7,000 people had been arrested.

Attendance plummeted for us the rest of the summer because people were reluctant to venture downtown.

On August 3 I shut out the Orioles 5–0 and was 13–12 on the year. We were 10 over .500, three games behind the White Sox, and right in the midst of the pennant chase.

On August 4, a few weeks after telling my former "partners" at the Shorthorn that we'd quit the gambling operation, Ed Schober called me in a panic. He told me that a guy named Ed Voshen had put down $8,000 on a horse named Willamston Kid, and it had won the eighth race at the Detroit Racecourse. The horse had paid $21 to win, and Clyde and Jiggs we telling Schober that we owed Voshen $46,000.

I said, "That's bullshit. I already told those guys we were out. And even if we hadn't backed away, any bet of consequence had to be approved by us."

I went to the Shorthorn on an off day to plead our case with Clyde and Jiggs. Jiggs argued that Ed had never turned down a bet in the past, and he couldn't find Ed that afternoon.

As I was getting up a full head of steam, Jiggs picked up a fork and slammed it into the table dangerously close to my pitching hand. He looked at me and said, "It won't miss your fingers the next time if you don't pay up. Can you pitch with a fork in your f*cking hand? They're gonna f*ck up one of us real bad, and it ain't gonna be me. I'm telling 'em that the money is yours and you owe it. And these motherf*ckers will put a fork right through your hearts for $46,000."

Whoa.

Schober begged me to meet with Voshen and explain why the debt wasn't ours to pay. Twice I sat in the parking lot of a restaurant for meetings set up by an intermediary named McCann, and both times Voshen was a no-show. I thought it was very strange that a guy I allegedly owed

Shorthorn

$46,000 would miss a meeting, and I suspected that Voshen was just another front for the Shorthorn guys to scam us. Finally, McCann, who claimed that Voshen also owed him money from gin games, agreed to a 20¢-on-the-dollar payoff.

I cashed two checks for $8,000, and since I was busy with a little thing called a pennant race, I sent Schober to pay off McCann and hoped it would put the Jiggs and Clyde tandem out of our lives for good. I still don't know what the hell really happened. If I had a baseball star on the hook for a lot of money, would I discount the debt? Hell no. I think if you're smart, you say something like, "If you don't pay me all of the money, I'll drop a little note to the commissioner of baseball."

And I sure as hell didn't want the commissioner to ever hear about any of this.

Chapter 8

The Race Is On

I pitched well in August, winning five and losing two, despite the pressure from the Shorthorn boys and my ever-aching arm.

On September 2, I was 17–14 and pitching in the fifth inning of a scoreless tie in Minnesota. I tried picking Tony Oliva off first and threw wildly into right field, setting up the game's first run on a sacrifice fly. The Twins went on to win 5–0.

The loss dropped us into fourth place, but only two and a half games out of first in an amazing race with the Red Sox, Twins, and White Sox.

I gave up four runs in five innings in Kansas City on September 6, but Fred Gladding took over in the sixth and we won 8–5. I was awful again on September 10 in Chicago. I gave up two runs in the first, one of them on a wild pitch, and then wrenched my back with the first pitch of the second inning. I never wanted to come out of a game, but I had no choice and we wound up losing 4–0.

These were critical games for us, and I wasn't helping by trying to pitch with a bad shoulder and back. My concentration was nowhere at this point because Schober and I were spooked by the ghost of Ed Voshen and worried about being exposed. I kept expecting someone to tap me on the shoulder and say, "Hey, where's my money?" or that my car was going to blow up.

The sore back caused me to miss my turn on September 15, but I was able to start against the Red Sox on the night of September 18, 1967. All four contenders were now within a game of each other, with the Tigers in first place by a mere half game. It was a wonderful testament to the people of Detroit that night, as 43,000 came to the city to see us after 43 Detroiters had been killed in the riots less than two months previous. I remember looking into the stands that night, wondering how many of them might have been packing pieces.

I started the game by walking Jose Tartabull. A ground-out sent him to second, and then Carl Yastrzemski knocked in Tartabull with a double to center. Reggie Smith got on on an infield hit, George Scott hit a sacrifice fly, and Dalton Jones singled in a third run. Back in May, Jones had beaten me 1–0 with a homer, and now the son of a bitch got me again.

We still trailed 3–0 in the third inning when I walked Mike Andrews and gave up a single to Yastrzemski. It was my fourth straight poor outing, and Mayo yanked me.

I was furious at myself, and my arm was screaming in pain. The frustration of letting down my teammates was weighing heavily on me, and as I stormed up the tunnel to the locker room, I used my glove to knock out every lightbulb along the route.

I got into the locker room and when I went to kick my locker, my ankle caught one of the steel separators between the lockers. It wasn't a really big whack, but hard enough to get my attention. What hurt more at the time was the way we went on to lose that night. Yastrzemski hit his 40th homer off Fred Lasher to tie it at 5-all in the ninth, and in the tenth, Jones got his fourth hit of the night—a homer off Mike Marshall to win it in dramatic fashion. The loss threw us into a three-way tie for first with the Red Sox and Twins at 85–66.

I got home and couldn't go to sleep because I was still agitated about letting everyone down. Typically after pitching, I'd get home and eat, turn the TV on, have my Twinkies and Pepsi, and fall asleep on the couch.

The Race Is On

It was about 2:00 AM when I was startled out of my sleep by a big noise in the garage. It had to be a critter, my dog chasing a critter, or some fan destroying my garage because of my horse-shit pitching performance that night. The TV was all fuzz because the stations had signed off. When I jumped off the couch to see what the ruckus was, I didn't realize that my left leg had fallen asleep under the weight of my body. As I got up to run to the garage, my left ankle bent underneath me and down I went. I never made it to the garage, and I never heard anything else. But I'd sprained my ankle. Isn't there a statistic about 90 percent of all accidents occurring at home? I was one of the 90 percent.

The injury happened on a Monday. I got treatment every day and hoped I'd be able to pitch in Washington that weekend. Our other three starters, Mickey Lolich, Earl Wilson, and Joe Sparma were keeping us in the race, and I wanted to do my part. By the end of the week I told Mayo I could pitch in Washington on Sunday, but he said, "F*ck it, I got my rotation already set." I was furious.

We lost 5–4 on Sunday when our bullpen tandem of Fred Lasher and John Hiller squandered a 4–2 lead for Sparma. We were back in fourth place, a game and a half out, heading into the final six games.

We split two games in New York with Wilson losing 2–0 and Lolich beating Mel Stottlemyre 1–0 with a terrific complete game shutout. But we were still a game and a half out with four to play, all against the Angels at Tiger Stadium.

California was over .500 and in fifth place in the 10-team American League. They had a decent team and a good manager in Bill Rigney. I got treatment after treatment and even took a cortisone injection in the ankle. Cortisone is a steroid and was the wonder drug of the day. Although this type of cortisone is for anti-swelling and pain relief, not strength enhancements, I had more steroids running through my muscles, tendons, and veins than Jason Giambi and Barry Bonds combined.

I Told You I Wasn't Perfect

We got rained out on Thursday and Friday and watched the drama unfold with the other contenders. The White Sox totally choked under manager Eddie Stanky, losing their last five to fall out of the race. On the final weekend, Minnesota was in Boston, and because of the rainouts, we faced back-to-back doubleheaders with the Angels.

If we could beat California three out of four, we'd be guaranteed at least a tie for the pennant. In Game 1 Saturday afternoon, Lolich threw his third straight shutout and beat the Angels 5–0.

We led 6–2 after seven innings of Game 1. Wilson, who led us with 22 wins in '67, pitched the first five innings but walked the leadoff hitter in the sixth, and Mayo handed it over to the bullpen.

When Earl was with the Red Sox, if he had a lead after five innings, the number a starter has to pitch to get a win, he always wanted the great reliever, Dick "the Monster" Radatz, to save it for him. Earl would even fake an injury if he had to. Mayo hated him for that and called him "pussy boy" behind his back.

In the eighth we still led 6–4, but the Angels had men on first and third against Fred Lasher with nobody out. Mayo brought in Hank Aguirre, the crafty veteran, to face pinch-hitter Bubba Morton.

Morton tapped back to the mound as the runner at third, Don Mincher, headed home. Catcher Bill Freehan was yelling for Aguirre to throw him the ball, but Aguirre threw it to first instead, allowing Mincher to score and reducing our lead to 6–5.

Aguirre panicked and never even peeked at Mincher running down the line. What made it even more pathetic was that before the play, Freehan had yelled to Aguirre, "Throw it here if it's hit to you." It was an inexcusable blunder on a play we practiced in spring training 'til we were blue in the face.

The Angels scored three more to beat us 8–6. Mayo had me up and down four different times in the bullpen during the doubleheader but never brought me in.

The Race Is On

My ankle hurt like hell, but I was still pissed off, thinking that if Mayo had pitched me in the seventh, we would have won. But I'd been useless for a month and Mayo was fuming about my injuries. I'd already won 17 games, for God's sake, but his attitude seemed to be that we'd win it without my help.

Now we had to sweep the Sunday doubleheader to be guaranteed a tie for the pennant.

As I left the clubhouse after the Saturday doubleheader, Mayo grabbed me and said, "If Sparma wins the first game tomorrow, we'll see how far you can go in Game 2. I know your ankle's hurting, but go as long as you can. I'll make sure the trainers get you what you need."

I said, "Sure, Mayo, whatever it takes."

We came back for the do-or-die doubleheader and were surprised that Tiger Stadium wasn't sold out. Thirty-nine thousand people showed up to witness the fateful finish.

Sparma pitched extremely well and won the first game 6–4. We had our bags packed because if we won the second game we were to fly to either Minnesota or Boston for a three-game playoff, depending on who won their final day showdown in Boston.

I took the hill for Game 2 and gave up a second-inning homer to Rick Reichardt. But we fought back in the bottom half against a rookie pitcher named Rickey Clark. Ed Mathews doubled, and Northrup homered to give us a 2–1 lead. Don Wert walked, and I sacrificed him to second and looked like a cripple as I tried to run down the first-base line. McAuliffe tripled off Clark, and we took a 3–1 lead.

I went out to pitch in the third inning and just couldn't land on the foot. Either I was going to break my ankle or take a line drive in the ass. I gave up singles to Bobby Knoop and Jay Johnstone. I got a break when Roger Repoz lined to Mathews at first for a double play. But Jim Fregosi doubled to center to score Knoop and reduce our lead to 3–2. Mayo came out and pulled me.

I was horribly disappointed. Our whole season was on the line—somebody had to step up and do the job—and it wasn't gonna be me. I wasn't mad at Mayo as much as I was pissed off at myself. I had been more than willing to take another shot to kill the pain, but trainer Bill Behm had warned me that it could've seriously affected my career.

Behm told me that if I couldn't feel the pain I had a chance of breaking my ankle. I'd taken a few greenies, a form of amphetamine; Contac, a sinus medication that gave you an amphetamine-like boost; and some aspirin. But the pain was still too much.

Mayo replaced me with John Hiller, and Don Mincher immediately slugged a two-run homer to put the Angels ahead 4–3. The Angels got three more in the fourth off Hiller, Mike Marshall, and Dave Wickersham to lead us 7–3.

Over in Boston, the Red Sox and Twins knew that if we lost, the winner of their game would win the pennant outright. The Sox came from behind to beat the Twins 5–3, with Yastrzemski getting four straight hits and knocking in two runs with a bases-loaded single in the sixth off Dean Chance. Yaz's great finishing performance also locked up the Triple Crown for him with a .326 average, 121 RBI, and 44 homers that tied him with the Twin' Harmon Killebrew.

The Red Sox then sat around their clubhouse to listen to our game with the Angels. Our fans knew all too well that if we didn't come back to win the game, we were done, and that's when it started to get really ugly.

Trailing 8–3 in the fifth, Eddie Mathews caught a foul pop down the first-base line a few feet from where a cameraman was positioned and then turned and threw the ball at the guy. What a classless act. The cameraman was allowed to be there, but Mathews thought he'd be a tough guy.

The Race Is On

In the seventh inning drunken fans ran onto the field and interrupted play while trying to dodge the cops. At this stage of events, the antics of the fans made better entertainment than we were producing.

Mayo was in the midst of using eight pitchers, and the game was taking forever. We did manage to narrow it to 8–5 on Dick McAuliffe's two-run single in the seventh. Then in the ninth, we got a few men on, and McAuliffe came up representing the tying run. He'd already gotten two hits and knocked in three runs, but he grounded into a 4–6–3 double play and we lost 8–5. It was only the second double play he grounded into all year.

The game had taken 3:12, interminable in that day and age, with the double play concluding our afternoon of slow torture. We had won 17 of 29 games after September 1 but couldn't pull off the pennant.

The moment the game ended, the pleasure seekers ran out on the field en masse, tearing up home plate and throwing chairs at police and ushers. Stadium management turned on the sprinklers to chase them away. As we gave the postmortem to reporters in the clubhouse, you could hear chairs hitting the walls and bottles thrown from the upper deck breaking on the concourse. It was ugly in our clubhouse also, with a few of our hitters blaming the pitching staff for its performance over the weekend.

Hitters tend to forget when they get shut out, and it was an ugly scene as guys guzzled beer to relieve their anguish while calling each other gutless and heartless.

In the trainer's room, Mathews and Wilson had a shouting match, with Mathews directing his wrath at Earl for coming out of the game the day before. We agreed with Mathews that Earl didn't have the fortitude to finish close games. I always wondered how many wins we sacrificed because Earl refused to finish what he started.

Both the Tigers and Twins finished one game back of Boston. The Red Sox had come in ninth the two previous years and had gone into the season as a 100-1 shot. The people of New England were now calling their unlikely pennant success the "Impossible Dream."

I'd gone winless for the month, and some of the writers implied that I should have been tougher and found a way to kill the pain. When I walked out of the clubhouse, the best I could muster for Mayo was, "See ya next year."

"We'll see, partner, we'll see," was his less-than-encouraging reply. As I hobbled to my car, I thought there was a pretty good chance he'd trade me sometime before the 1968 season began.

Chapter 9

A Pretty Good Year

The Tigers tried to trade me all winter after the 1967 season but couldn't find the right deal. My cockiness and inability to control my comments to the press had grated on Tigers management and thrown up red flags all over the league.

I'd also pitched poorly down the stretch and had the "mysterious" September ankle injury. Clearly, my star had fallen since the 20-win season in '66, and the fans who heartily booed me in spring training in '68 were voicing disappointment that I was still around.

My arm had bothered me a lot in '67, and I'd probably taken 10 to 12 cortisone shots over the course of the season. But I strengthened my entire right side by bowling all winter, and I knew I'd show people how wrong they'd been. I also got contact lenses over the winter and wouldn't be bothered with my glasses fogging up anymore.

Earl Wilson had emerged as the ace of the staff with 22 wins in 1967, and even though I had 37 wins the last two seasons, I fell to fourth in the rotation behind Earl, Mickey Lolich, and Joe Sparma.

The thing I wasn't sure about was how good our team was. We didn't run well, our hitting was pretty average, and our bullpen had taken the heat for losing the '67 pennant. On the plus side, we matured as a team in that year. We started hitting cutoff men and played the game smarter despite the lack of involvement from our manager, Mayo Smith. Mayo drank so much that it usually took him three or four innings to sober up and get his head into the game.

You've gotta throw a signal out there from time to time, but whenever Mayo moved a body part in the early innings we just worried that he was falling over. As a result, the players had learned to manage themselves in '67.

Baseball strategy is pretty situational, and there are few geniuses on dugout benches. The great managers know how to utilize players and motivate them, but we learned to coach and motivate ourselves and became pretty good at it by the time '68 rolled around.

Wally Moses was Mayo's top assistant and knew the game well. Moses coached us on how to signal to each other when Mayo was asleep at the wheel. When a guy like Jim Northrup wanted to run, he'd flash the hitter a sign.

We also had baseball's best pitching coach in Johnny Sain. Sain's whole life was pitching, and he didn't even want to know the other players. If you were a pitcher, you loved him. If you were a manager, you always thought he was undermining your authority. He wouldn't allow the manager to have anything to do with his pitchers, and he spoiled the hell out of us—especially the ones with talent.

As spring training ended, the nation was shocked by the assassination of Martin Luther King Jr. The opener was delayed a day because there was a national day of mourning, and Mayo used the extra off day to call a workout. We had three black players—Willie Horton, Gates Brown, and Wilson—and Wilson was furious that he wouldn't be able to stay home to watch the funeral on TV.

Earl's problem was that he was always furious. He was angry that the white players got all the endorsements and income-producing opportunities. He was right about that, but if you really want a piece of the pie, you have to at least smile and make nice every now and then. Earl was the best-dressed player of his era, but he was also one of the gruffest.

Earl lost the opener 7–3 to the Red Sox, and I started the next day. Jon Warden relieved me in a tied game, but in the ninth, Gates Brown hit a pinch-homer off our ex-teammate John Wyatt to win it. Gates had been hurt much of '67 with a dislocated wrist and had only hit .187. The Tigers also tried to trade him in the off-season, but nobody wanted him. Needless to say, sometimes the deals you don't make are the best ones. They were stuck with both Gates and me for '68.

Starting with Gates' pinch-homer, we reeled off nine straight wins, including three in extra innings. In my second start, I battled Cleveland's Sam McDowell for seven innings. Willie Horton hit a two-run homer with two out in the ninth off Indians reliever Jack Fisher to win it 4–3. I didn't get the victory in either of my first two starts, but the way we won them both in comeback fashion began to define our season.

Bowling thousands of games in the winter was really paying off, and I was genuinely surprised at how easy pitching had become. The other guys had off-season jobs, while I was bowling up to 100 lines a day and gambling all the way. I craved the action and found no shortage of takers who wanted to beat the pitcher. My advantage came when the crowd gathered for the last few frames and the other guy would succumb to the pressure. I loved the 10th frame like I loved the ninth inning. The athlete always has the edge at crunch time.

I'd throw a ball and run down two or three alleys, sliding on my knees, knowing it was going to be buried into the 1–3 pocket for a strike. I played the showman. Give me a little crowd and I'm in my element. I averaged over 200 in the leagues and probably higher than that in money games.

On May 5 I went the distance and moved to 4–0 as we broke a little three-game losing streak with a 5–2 win over the Angels. The three losses, including a pair of one-run heartbreakers, had dropped us to 13–8. The fans booed us during the losing streak and it really bothered me.

Detroit was in the midst of a newspaper strike, so the reporters were either wire service guys or out-of-town reporters. Our guys loved not having the Joe Falls and Pete Waldmeir types to deal with. They were tough, agitating writers, and there were always half a dozen of us feuding with at least one of them. Now, with no local writers around writing garbage, it was a great time to play in Detroit.

But I could still create my own stinking piles of garbage with even the tamest of writers. After the Angels victory, the conversation got around to the fans who had booed during the losing streak. I asked the writers, "Why would fans rip on the home team, especially a team that had nearly won the previous last year and had started out 13–5?"

Here's how the Associated Press reported the story:

> McLain said, "Tiger fans are the biggest front-running fans in the world. Norm Cash and I were going bad last year and they got on us real bad. How do they think a guy's wife feels after he goes 0-for-8, 0-for-16 and the fans cut loose while she's in the stands? If they think we're stupid for playing this game, how stupid are they for watching us?"
>
> Asked if fan's attitudes had an effect on losing the pennant by a game last year, McLain replied, "I think it did. There were certain guys on this club who didn't want to go out and play last year because of fan abuse. Now the fans are on Kaline." (Kaline is hitting .241, with 2 RBI in 22 games.) "He's produced for 15 years and he'll produce again this year. They don't realize how good a ballplayer he is. I don't care if I get booed here the rest of my life.

A Pretty Good Year

"Detroit is a great town. I like it. I've bought a home and have roots. But the fans in this town are the worst in the league."

When the crowd of reporters scurried out to file their story, Tom Loomis of the *Toledo Blade* was still in the room. I said to him, "I only meant 1 percent of the fans." But it was too late.

I was 24 and so in love with holding court and dropping verbal bombs that I ignored the consequences. I was pitching well and felt bulletproof, like I could do or say whatever I wanted and get away with it.

If we removed the booze from the parks it'd all be different, but I was upset at how the fans treated Kaline and Cash in the middle of the pennant race in '67 and continued to do so in '68. I believed that fans had the right to boo and get loud, but getting personal and profane is dead wrong.

I thought somebody had to say that there's a contingent that drinks too much. Everybody's busting his ass to win, and boos from the home fans really piss you off. The mature thing is to realize that you play for yourself and your team. But I was naïve enough to think, "Do I really want to win for these people?"

We all loved Cash because he'd play hurt and hungover and always found humor in things. Norm's remembered for bringing the table leg to the plate during Nolan Ryan's no-hitter, but no matter how well he played, the fans never forgave him for being unable to repeat his incredible 1961 season when he hit .361 with 132 RBIs.

I was right about the two-faced nature of fans. But you never win when you rip your fans. I'd say what I thought, embellish it to make good copy, and then absorb whatever pain came with it. I lacked the maturity to think out of the moment and handle all the angles.

Another thing that troubled us early in the '68 season was bad attendance. Aside from the opener, our largest home attendance in April had been 10,147. With the newspapers on strike and smoldering racial tensions still in the air, people were either disinterested or simply reluctant to come downtown.

My May 5 comments about the "worst" fans would be thrown back in my face all season. I tried to apologize every way I could, but it was too late to get my foot out of my mouth. Shortly after I made that comment, the team went on a road trip, and Sharon took the kids to visit her parents in Chicago. When she stopped for gas the attendant said, "Do you know you've got a bomb under your car?"

She said, "I've got a what?"

It was a smoke bomb. He went underneath to get it and told her, "Whoever hooked it up didn't do it right." It could have been put on at the ballpark or in the neighborhood. We never found out.

We came back from the road trip to host the Orioles. I was 5–0, we were in first place with a 19–10 record, and it was my first home appearance since ripping the fans. From the moment I stepped on the field, our first crowd of over 20,000 treated me like I was an ax murderer. Boog Powell hit a three-run homer off me in the first, and I was gone in two innings to the loudest chorus of boos and taunts I'd ever heard. It felt as bad as being beaten by my father. I was guilty and this was the punishment I had coming.

I was also right about the booze. Detroit fans were allowed to bring beer into the ballpark as well as buy it there, and drunkenness fueled two wild incidents in June alone. We had a two and a half–game lead when we hosted second-place Cleveland on June 7. More than 31,000 fans saw us battle back from 3–0 down to tie it in the eighth on Cash's homer off Indian reliever Mike Paul.

In the Indian's ninth, Paul drew a leadoff walk from Fred Lasher and was bunted to second. Tony Horton singled to right, and Paul rounded third, heading home. Northrup's throw got to Bill Freehan the same time

A Pretty Good Year

Paul did, and Bill applied the tag. Home plate ump Jim Honochick called Paul out but then changed it to safe, indicating that Freehan had juggled the ball.

Freehan wheeled and pushed Honochick, staggering him backward. Mayo ran from the dugout and grabbed Freehan to keep him off Honochick, then berated Honochick himself. By the time third-base ump Bill Valentine arrived to grab Mayo and join the tug of war, booze and beer bottles and other assorted garbage hit the field and smashed onto the dugout roof. It was extremely dangerous, and as inconceivable as it seems today, they actually allowed fans to hold bottles in their hands back then!

Mayo got ejected while Freehan was allowed to stay in the game. The Indians' run put them ahead 4–3.

We had two on with two out in the ninth when Stanley blooped one over second that center fielder Jose Cardenal couldn't reach. Cardenal then threw wildly to home, Freehan and McAuliffe scored, and the place went stark raving nuts over the 5–4 win. That's what we were all about in '68. It had been quite a night. It began with a silent tribute to Bobby Kennedy, who'd been slain two nights earlier, before the garbage and beer bottles preceded a thrilling victory.

On June 19, we had 32,000 at Tiger Stadium to see us host the Red Sox on a steamy and ideal beer-drinking afternoon. Joe Sparma had a 4–2 lead in the seventh. With two out and one on, Joe Foy bounced one back to Sparma, who muffed it, allowing Foy to reach first safely. Ken Harrelson stepped up and blasted a three-run homer to put the Sox up 5–4.

In the top of the eighth, reliever Daryl Patterson walked a few guys and then, on a sacrifice bunt, threw high to first when he had an easy play at third. We were playing like shit, and as the Red Sox scored three more runs, the beer cans, fruit, and other garbage started raining down again.

Harrelson was playing first base, and when the Red Sox took the field for the bottom of the ninth, an idiot hit him in the back with a cherry bomb that fell to the ground and exploded, scaring the shit out of him. Harrelson shook his leg, acting like he was trying to shake the crap out of his pants. But when another cherry bomb exploded near him, Harrelson started running to the dugout. The umps talked him into staying on the field so the crowd wouldn't be further incited. Harrelson compromised by standing in shallow right, as far from the stands as he could get, and the game ended moments later.

These were Tiger fans and this was 1968. Unrest was all over the country, so why not at the ballpark? With extra police on hand, we beat the Red Sox 5–1 before 31,000 the next night to put us eight games ahead of Cleveland. I pitched a three-hit complete game, struck out 10, and had a 12–2 record.

We went to Cleveland after the Red Sox series, and on June 24 Mayo thought about benching slumping Jim Northrup who had one hit in his last 20 at-bats. Kaline had been out since late May after angrily jamming his bat into the bat rack and breaking his hand. The story fed to the media was that Oakland's Lew Krausse had broken it with a pitch. But what really happened was that after striking out, Kaline had a temper tantrum. Thinking that he was tougher than the bat rack, Kaline jammed his bat in the rack and began wincing in pain. In the middle of a pennant race he actually injured himself.

With no alternative than to put poor-fielding Gates out there, Mayo changed his mind and kept Northrup in the lineup. Northrup fanned his first two times up, but in the fifth, with the bases loaded, hit a grand slam off Eddie Fisher.

We loaded the bases again in the sixth, and the Indians brought in lefty Bill Rohr to pitch to Northrup. Northrup hit his second grand slam in consecutive innings, tying Jim Gentile's record. God I loved that Northrup—when I pitched, he hit.

A Pretty Good Year

We won it 13–2, and I went the distance, the second of seven straight complete games I'd pitch in that stretch. On Sunday, July 7, the day before the All-Star break, I gave up homers to the A's Sal Bando and Reggie Jackson, and we were tied 4–4 in the ninth. But Horton homered off Ed Sprague to win it 5–4.

I was 16–2.

Kaline returned that week. In the 45 games he was injured, we played at a 31–14 clip and went into the break with a nine and a half–game lead. The talk around the clubhouse was, "Who needs Al?"

It was also around then that my roommate, Ray Oyler, asked me, "You gonna win 30?"

I said, "F*cking right—30's a chip shot now."

With 16 wins and almost all the attention even I could want, I decided to show off by renting a private jet to help us party over the break. It cost $9,000, but who cared about money? Freehan was also an All-Star, and Sharon and I invited Bill and his wife to spend the day in Las Vegas before flying to the game in Houston.

When we were at 41,000 feet and could see Vegas from 175 miles away, it felt like the most peaceful moment of my life. I decided then and there that I would lease a plane after the season, no matter what it cost.

The Vegas break was glorious and I was in my element. We were wined and dined 24 hours a day at the Riviera Hotel—given chips and lavished with booze. All I was asked to do was be visible, talk to people, and give autographs. It was my first trip to Las Vegas, and I was intoxicated by the action and attention. The Riviera talked about signing me to play the organ after the season, and I couldn't wait to get back to this fantasyland.

I got no sleep in Vegas but threw down a few Pepsis and flew to Houston Tuesday afternoon. I stumbled over to the Astrodome for the first ever indoor, artificial turf All-Star Game.

Willie Mays singled to left off Luis Tiant to start the game. Tiant tried to pick him off and threw wildly. Tiant then wild-pitched him to third, and Mays scored when Willie McCovey grounded into a double play. It turned out to be the only run of the game in a 1–0 NL win.

I pitched the fifth and sixth innings, allowing just a single to Hank Aaron.

The Freehans went back to Detroit Wednesday morning, while Sharon and I took the jet back to Vegas for more gambling and hijinks.

I flew Sharon home and then took the jet to Minnesota to join the team. Suddenly, at about 18,000 feet, it sounded like a small bomb exploded. The door had popped open, and if it had been at a much higher altitude, you wouldn't be reading this. The pilot and I thought we were going to crash and quickly grabbed the oxygen masks. We told the air-traffic center we had an emergency and quickly descended so we could remove the masks. We flew the rest of the way to Minnesota at 10,000 feet with no further damage.

The adrenalin rush was incredible. When we landed I thought, "How could anything possibly go wrong for me in 1968?"

Chapter 10

30

By Friday night, I'd recovered from the All-Star break fun and excitement and beat my pal Jim Kaat and the Twins 5–1 on three hits. On July 16 I shut out the A's 4–0 in Oakland on eight hits, eight strikeouts, and no walks for my seventh consecutive complete game, ninth straight win, and an eye-popping record of 18–2.

The media coverage was growing more and more intense, and I appeared on the cover of the July 29, 1968, issue of *Sports Illustrated* with a headline, Detroit's Denny McLain in Antic Pursuit of 30 Wins. The Tigers were on top, and I was the talk of the baseball world. Mark Mulvoy wrote:

> Until this season McLain, 18–2, was better known for his performances outside the white lines than between them. He had quickly gained a reputation as Super Flake—a hot-tempered, eccentric kid with a million-dollar arm, million-dollar tastes, million-dollar dreams, and a 10¢ attitude.
>
> "When you can do it out there between the white lines," McLain says, "you can live any way you want to. I like to travel fast and always go first class.
>
> "I always say what I want—what I think—without any reservations. And I guess you could say it's gotten me into plenty of trouble. But I've only been misquoted once. (The

"country club" quote from '66.) From now on I'm going to try and be a bit more diplomatic."

McLain has also amended his "worst fans" comments to "some of the worst fans." He contends, "We've got a lot of bad fans in the ballpark. The other team takes its life into its hands if they've got us beat in the late innings. The fans throw bottles and firecrackers, and one night when Boston was in here they hit Ken Harrelson in the back with a firecracker. They could have blinded him."

We had an incredible knack for winning games in our last at-bat in '68. One of the wildest took place on Friday, July 19, in our first home game since the All-Star break. And 53,000, more than the listed capacity of Tiger Stadium, came to see us host the rival Orioles. Baltimore and Cleveland were both in striking range at seven and a half games back.

The Orioles had fired Hank Bauer the previous week and replaced him with a 37-year-old unknown named Earl Weaver. The Orioles chased Mickey Lolich with four runs in the first six innings and led 4–2 going into the bottom of the ninth. We'd only gotten two hits all night, including Dick McAuliffe's two-run homer off Wally Bunker. But Jim Northrup singled, Al Kaline walked, and Norm Cash bounced into a fielder's choice.

Weaver brought in ace reliever Moe Drabowsky, who got Freehan to bounce into the second out, scoring Northrup, leaving us with two out and one on. Mayo decided to let 25-year-old rookie shortstop Tom Matchick stay in the game to hit against Drabowsky.

We may have had the worst-hitting trio at shortstop in baseball history. Dick Tracewski, Ray Oyler, and Matchick split 650 at-bats in '68, with Oyler hitting a microscopic .135, Tracewski a pathetic .156, and Matchick just .203. There was no way any of them should have been allowed to hit with the game on the line.

Matchick got the count to 3–2, and Drabowsky appeared to get him to fly out to end the game. Frank Robinson stood at the fence, waiting for the ball to plop in his glove, but there was a slight breeze, and the ball carried a little farther than expected. As it descended, it caught a piece of the second deck overhang and momentarily shocked everybody. It was a game-winning, two-run homer, and the crowd, having thought the game was over, suddenly went berserk. In the clubhouse, McAuliffe said to Matchick, "If you weren't so ugly, I'd kiss you."

I pitched the next afternoon, and the Orioles knocked me out of the box in the fifth inning when Frank Robinson and pitcher Dave McNally both homered off me. The O's also swept us in a Sunday doubleheader before 49,000 fans and pulled to within five and a half games.

I got a lot of help a few days later in winning number 19 in Washington when we scored two in the eighth to pull it out 6–4.

On July 27 we went to Baltimore to face the second-place Orioles, who now trailed us by six and a half games. Almost 46,000 fans were there to also see the O's prevent me from winning number 20. No such luck. We hit five homers, and I pitched a complete game three-hitter with seven strikeouts in a 9–0 whitewash.

I was 20–3, and a writer told me afterward that it was the earliest anyone had won 20 since Rube Marquard in 1912.

I thought, "Rube who? Nineteen twelve what?"

The Detroit newspapers were still on strike, but George Vecsey covered the game for *The New York Times.* He wrote:

> Denny McLain has survived a smoke bomb, a heavy diet of cola, and an airplane with a door that wouldn't close. The American League isn't troubling him much, either. McLain has pursued his version of the good life since joining the Tigers in 1964. He has maintained a winter career as a

concert organist, has drunk 100 bottles of his favorite cola a week (he is now having extensive dental work), and chartered a small plane for a holiday jaunt to Las Vegas. It was during that trip—before and after his appearance in the recent All-Star Game—when the door of the plane wouldn't close properly, and McLain and his pilot made a landing he now describes as "scary." McLain also described Detroit fans as the "worst in baseball" earlier in the year and found a smoke bomb planted in his car.

Critics have said he was not serious enough—usually when he wasn't winning. He won 20 in 1966, but a broken toe, suffered when he tried to walk while his foot was asleep, made him miss several starts late last season, hardly endearing him to disappointed Tiger fans.

But McLain has ability, as he demonstrated tonight and on at least 19 previous dates this season....

I had my 20 wins, but we still were fighting to maintain our lead. On August 11 we led the Orioles by five and a half and the third-place Red Sox by 10. That day we hosted Boston before nearly 50,000 in a Sunday doubleheader.

The first game lasted nearly four and a half hours. We used six pitchers, including a struggling Mickey Lolich, who Mayo had recently relegated to the bullpen. Lolich had pitched and won in relief the day before and had now held the Sox scoreless from the tenth until the fourteenth inning.

With two out in the bottom of fourteen, Gates Brown pinch hit for Lolich and homered into the lower deck in right off Lee Stange for a dramatic 5–4 victory.

Mayo started John Hiller against Gary Bell in Game 2 and tried to hide poor-fielding Gates in left field to rest Horton, who went 0–6 in

Game 1. It was tied at 2–2 in the ninth when the Red Sox rallied for three runs off Warden and John Wyatt to take a 5–2 lead. It had been an awfully long day, and we figured we'd at least managed a split. The crowd started quietly filing out after seven hours of baseball.

Lo and behold, with a walk and four singles we scratched out three runs off Bell and two Sox relievers to tie it 5–5. With men on first and third, Sox manager Dick Williams brought in left-handed Sparky Lyle to pitch to Gates, who promptly singled past first baseman George Scott to drive in the winning run.

We ran out of the dugout and mobbed Gates as the crowd went wild.

Gates had been a wayward kid who Jim Campbell signed out of the Ohio State Penitentiary in the early '60s. He had put it all behind him and became a model citizen and an inspiration to a lot of kids in the city. He was also one of the most delightful characters I ever got to know in the game. I don't think there was a day on the road we didn't play cards for serious money. Gates took thousands of dollars from me playing poker and taught me how to gamble at cards the hard way.

As a career pinch-hitter, Gates peaked in '68, hitting an amazing .462 on 18–39. He was a master at relaxing and staying mentally prepared while sitting for hours awaiting a possible chance to hit. One day in '68 Mayo called on him to pinch hit for Lolich a few innings earlier than he'd expected. Gates drove a ball into the right-field corner and, after he slid into second base, the umpire called timeout because he saw blood on the front of Gates's uniform.

Our trainer, Bill Behm, was ready to run out and help, but Gates waved him off, saying he was okay. When the inning ended, Gates ran right down the tunnel to avoid getting near Mayo. Mayo had told Gates time and again not to eat in the dugout, and when called on to pinch hit, Gates had stuffed a hot dog in his shirt. The ketchup bled through after he slid in on the hot dog. He was busted.

I Told You I Wasn't Perfect

We stayed safely ahead of the pack, and I kept winning ballgames. When we rolled into Boston on August 16, I was 24–3, with six consecutive wins. We were seven ahead of Baltimore and up by 11 on the Red Sox. I'd pitched five straight complete games and, although Mayo wanted me to get to 30, he told me he wanted me to back off the cortisone shots and start having the bullpen help me from time to time.

We led 2–0 in the sixth on Kaline's two-run homer when their pitcher, Jim Lonborg, reached first on a bunt down the third-base line. Mike Andrews singled to right, Freehan allowed a passed-ball on the first pitch to Dalton Jones, and the runners moved over to second and third. I could forgive Freehan. Lonborg had already plunked him his first two times up, and the two would tie a major league record that night when Lonborg later hit him with a pitch for a third time.

With men on second and third, Freehan came to the mound to settle me down and decide how we'd deal with the meat of their order: Jones, Carl Yastrzemski, and Hawk Harrelson.

Freehan said, "We're gonna go up the ladder with fastballs and get all of 'em."

"Fine with me. What else is new?" I always felt that meetings were more for the catcher rather than me. Hell, I knew what I was going to do.

We threw three strikes to Jones. The first at chest level, then shoulders, and the third one was eye level, and he swung and missed. Same thing with Yaz—letters, shoulders, eyes—six pitches, two outs.

Harrelson stepped in and I couldn't believe it, but Mayo started walking to the mound. He gets there and I say, "What do you want?"

"Walk Harrelson."

"F*ck him. No way." I had no desire to load the bases.

Mayo had Fred Lasher warming up in the bullpen and said, "If you're not gonna walk him, then gimme the ball. You've pitched a lot of innings this year. Let us save one for you."

I said, "Yeah, I've pitched a lot of innings, and I'm gonna finish this one."

Mayo stuck out his hand again and said, "Gimme the ball."

I said, "I'm not giving you the ball," and I walked to the back of the mound.

He followed me and almost pleadingly said, "There's a lotta people here, and you better give me the f*cking ball."

I said, "Jesus Christ, I've won 24 f*cking games for you, and Harrelson is an automatic out. I could tell him what I'm throwing and he'd still have no chance."

By this time, Cash had come over and was laughing his ass off. When Mayo asked Freehan how I was throwing, Cash whispered to me, "All Mayo's gotta do is ask the ump for another ball."

Freehan told Mayo, "There's no need to take him out. Harrelson got [umpire Ed] Runge so pissed off when he struck out in the fourth, I don't think we even have to throw him a strike."

You can't get the crowd against Runge or he'll make you pay for the rest of your days in the majors.

Mayo gave up, and Freehan said, "We'll go with all sliders off the plate."

The first slider was an inch or two off the plate, and Runge called it a strike. The next slider was about six inches off, and Runge called strike two. Harrelson gave him that quick look that said, "You gotta be kiddin' me."

If that wasn't bad enough, Runge now caught my eye. As I was looking in for the sign, he used his left leg to push Freehan even farther outside the plate. I threw it a foot outside and Runge called strike three.

When we got back to the dugout, Freehan told me that Harrelson turned and said to Runge, "Are we even?" Runge said, "Yeah, if you've learned your lesson."

It was one of the best innings I ever pitched, and we won 4–0. I was 25–3, including 16–0 on the road, and had gone the distance in 22 of my

31 starts. I was also up over 250 innings, and the price I paid for that was a constantly aching shoulder.

On August 20, in Chicago, Pete Ward hit a grand slam off me in the sixth to end my portion of a forgettable 10–2 loss. My shoulder was termed "tired" by team physician Russell Wright, who explained to the media that the tired feeling was caused by "minor irritation of the trapezoid muscle." The trapezium is between the shoulder and neck. Wright said, "Denny is just built abnormally. His right side so overpowers his left. So after he pitches a game, the muscle on the right shoulder gets dragged too far over into the bones on his neck. I wouldn't say there's any danger of his missing a pitching turn."

I really was over-built on my right side, but it was more from bowling all winter than pitching. These medical people had no clue. The next day they called it "an inflammation of the tendon in the front of his right shoulder." In other words, it was time for more cortisone, and I flew back to Detroit to get shot up before my next start and to continue the push to 30.

A *Life* magazine reporter named David Wolf had been traveling with me for an article that appeared in an early September issue. He wrote: "McLain was swaggering when the Tigers reached New York. On the way to Yankee Stadium he leaned from a car window and called over at a lady driver: could she make love to a four-game loser? The woman gasped and sped away as Denny laughed."

That wasn't the real quote. I asked her if she'd ever f*cked a four-game loser. That's me—just showing off to a guy holding a pen and paper.

I lost 2–1 in New York two nights later when the Yankees' Roy White hit a two-run homer off me in the first inning and Mel Stottlemyre pitched a four-hitter. *Life* quoted an unnamed teammate after the Yankee loss, saying, "It's good he lost. He was starting to act like he already won 30."

Now what kind of asshole would say that? I found out it was the overwhelmingly jealous Mickey Lolich. I was the last guy he wanted to see win 30 games, and Lolich's toughest time was '68.

On August 28 in Anaheim, Northrup and Freehan homered, and we beat the Angels 6–1 on six hits. I struck out 11 and became the first AL pitcher to win 26 since Bob Feller and Hal Newhouser back in 1946.

Back home on Sunday, September 1, 42,000 packed Tiger Stadium. The game was delayed 45 minutes because of rain and it threw me off. Don Buford led off with a line single to center, and Curt Blefary followed with a two-run homer into the right-field stands. We were down 2–0, and the game had barely begun.

Mayo ran out to the mound and asked, "How ya feeling?"

"Okay."

"You sure?"

I told him, "I feel pretty good. I'm loose but I've gotta settle down. Maybe I'm just overthrowing."

That should've been enough, but Mayo was always worrying about my shoulder and was thinking that the rain delay had caused my shoulder to tighten up. He asked, "Do you want out?"

"F*ck no, Mayo, it's the first goddamn inning—there's 42,000 people here—it'll get better."

Freehan was there and Mayo looked at him. "How's he throwing, Billy?"

Bill looked Mayo right in the eyes, smiled, and said, "How would I know—I haven't caught anything yet."

It broke the tension, and the three or four of us on the mound had a good laugh.

We got out of the inning and Northrup hit a two-run shot off 17-game winner Jim Hardin to tie it in the bottom of the first.

The rain returned, and we waited another 50 minutes before we could continue. I went back to the shower to have the hot water loosen me up.

We got two more in the second and took a 4–2 lead into the third. But I walked Buford, and Blefary singled to right. Frank Robinson singled in Buford to cut our lead to 4–3 and put men on first and second.

Boog Powell was the next hitter, and I could never get that son of a bitch out. I hated hitters who hung out over the plate, and Powell was one of those. I'd already tried everything with him. I used to yell to him, "Fastball's coming—I might as well tell you so we can speed up the game." And I'd throw him a fastball. Other times, I'd lie and see if that would help, but it never did.

This time, I tried to go up and in, but the ball was cock high, right over the plate, and Powell hit a screamer right at my crotch. I got my glove in the way in the nick of time, threw to Oyler at second base, who doubled up Blefary and then tripled up Robinson at first for the old 1-6-3 triple play. We won 7–3 and I pushed my record to 27–5.

We hosted the Twins on September 6, and Horton's three-run homer helped us get four runs off Jim Kaat before he retired anybody. I went the distance with a dozen strikeouts and was 28–5. The 28 wins were the most since Robin Roberts in 1952, and it put me ahead of the pace of the last two 30-game winners, Lefty Grove and Dizzy Dean.

I was running a marathon, trying to get to 30 before my arm fell off. The pain after the games was overwhelming. I'd ice it, swallow aspirin, and have a few drinks the next day to alleviate the pain.

The media coverage was getting crazy. We flew to Anaheim, and reporters were everywhere. Not only that, but in that same week feature articles and cover stories on me appeared in the *Saturday Evening Post* and *Time.*

Joseph Kane traveled with us for three weeks and wrote the cover story in the September 13, 1968, edition of *Time.* Kane noted that the toughest thing about it for him was keeping up with me as I tore through hotel lobbies and television studios.

As great a fantasy as winning all those games was the incessant attention. In 1961 Roger Maris found it to be a nightmare and ran from it whenever he could. For me, it was a drug. Not only was I swarmed by writers wherever I went, but I also had magazine writers traveling with us and in my face for three straight weeks.

It was heaven.

Kane wrote about my phone constantly ringing with appearance and endorsement offers as well as my plans to play the Hammond organ in Vegas in the off-season. He wrote: "'Music has always been the number one thing in my life,' McLain typically exaggerates. 'Baseball is a means to an end. I want ultimately to be a professional musician.'"

It wasn't enough to be winning 28 games. I had to also make it sound like it wasn't even what I did best. Here's more from Kane and *Time*:

> Last month, after victory number 25 in Boston, he spent two solid days hopping around New York and Detroit, appearing on the *Today Show*, huddling with his agent, attending promotional meetings for his Quintet records. In 48 hours he managed only five hours of sleep, and when he went out to pitch the second half of a doubleheader against the White Sox, Denny was dreadful. He was sent to the showers in the sixth inning and the White Sox won 10–2. Denny had no excuses. But he had no apologies for his energy-sapping extracurricular activities. "If I have to sit still, I lose my mind. If I'm coming or going I'm okay, but once I stop, I get nervous." Despite these occasional lapses, Denny boasts: "On the days I pitch, I'm the best there is."

It's embarrassing to read the braggadocio four decades later. On the other hand, I'm not so opposed to the way *Time* described my pitching style:

Not since blue-bearded Sal Maglie, who used to point his glove like a pistol at a batter's heart during his follow-through, has there been an angrier, more arrogant, or more confident man on the mound. A chunky 5'11", 190-pounder, McLain stands there stiff-backed, briefly fingering the rosin bag before throwing it violently to the ground. [I never touched a rosin bag in my entire career, so I don't know where the hell he got that.] Like a high school wise guy, he tilts his cap so far down over his eyes that he has to cock his head back to see the catcher's signs. Then, with the barest hint of a nod, Denny is ready to pitch. He squirts a stream of spittle out of his mouth, the left corner of his upper lip curls back in a sneer; his hands come slowly together at his chest. Suddenly he wheels to the right, rears back, and throws. If it is a strike, McLain licks his teeth with obvious satisfaction. Back comes the ball from the catcher and, as if bored with the very sight of the batter, McLain turns away from the plate.

More often than not, Denny's second pitch is identical to the first. So is the third. He delights in tweaking danger by the nose just for the sheer, perverse fun of it. An opponent who hits a home run off McLain's fastball will probably get another hummer the next time he comes to bat. Denny is always anxious to prove that any hit was a fluke.

We flew to Los Angeles, where I'd shoot for number 29 on Tuesday, September 10. There was so much going in L.A. that I had to have my agent, Frank Scott, out there with me to run interference. We got into L.A. on Sunday night after the Twins series, and Frank had me all over town on Monday.

The highlight was visiting with Tom and Dick Smothers by the pool at Tom's house as we went over the script for an hour-long fall special in which they wanted me to star. Glen Campbell, one of the hottest guys in show business, was there also. Campbell had a harem of gorgeous, bikini-clad starlets hanging on everything he said. I thought, "Show biz—is this unbelievable or what?"

We went by the studio of the *Steve Allen Show* and taped a segment on the set where he had me play a song on a Hammond they'd set up. Allen and I then went out on the street and played catch with his sidekick, Pat Harrington.

About 20 minutes before I went out to warm up that night in Anaheim, Ed Sullivan showed up in the locker room. He'd already booked me for after the season but wanted to meet me first. We put a Tigers hat on him and took him around the clubhouse to meet some of the guys.

We beat the Angels 7–2 for win number 29. I also managed to get three hits, including a triple and a two-run fourth-inning single that put us ahead 5–0. I walked one and fanned 12 but gave up homers to Rick Reichardt and Tom Satriano in the sixth. It didn't matter because it was over by then. I was 29–5 with 304 innings pitched.

We landed in Detroit at 7:30 Friday morning after taking the red-eye from Los Angeles. I'd shoot for number 30 Saturday on national television and hopefully get some sleep. I'd played pinochle all night on the flight and had barely dozed off.

Before the game Friday night, I met with Dizzy Dean and Sandy Koufax outside our dugout. Dean was there to symbolically pass the torch from the last 30-game winner to the next, and Koufax was part of the NBC crew that would broadcast the game.

I had always been in awe of Sandy because he was such a gentleman. The late Charlie Dressen had brought Sandy to the major leagues and had always pumped me up by telling me that I was a right-handed

Koufax and would do great things. In '68, it was looking like Charlie had been right. To be compared to Koufax was the ultimate accolade for me, especially coming from my pitching mentor, the dearly departed Charlie.

As for Dizzy, he was just a good ole boy who wanted to talk about the football season and point spreads. I was surprised that he would be so vocal in talking about gambling and odds in our dugout. He told me he was pulling for me, but I found it hard to believe that he wanted his status as the only living 30-game winner to change. I sure as hell wouldn't pull for him if it were the other way around.

In a *Sports Illustrated* article on my shot at 30, Alfred Wright captured the scene in one long paragraph:

> Brash and Irish, he often acts as if it was his world and the rest of the people were just passing through. He is also pure show biz from the top of his square head to the soles of his itchy feet. So it was fitting that he spent the first half of the week winning his 29th game against the California Angels within sight of Disneyland and making occasional strafing runs on Hollywood itself. Back home in more prosaic Detroit…he managed to create a kind of ersatz Hollywood of his own right in his suburban split-level. From morning to night, the place was choked with booking agents in sideburns and mod suits and their mini-skirted chicks—all of them shouting at each other over the long distance phone while McLain, accompanied by his four-piece combo, was down in the den, shattering neighbors' eardrums with his X-77 Hammond organ as ABC-TV cameras cranked away.…It is the incandescent flame of show biz that burns in Denny's heart. Thirty games? Ho-Hum. *The Ed Sullivan Show*? Yeah, baby!

My brother Tim drove me to the game, and before I could even enter the clubhouse, Joe Falls of the Detroit Free Press hawked me at the door. Falls asked me to go in a back room for a private interview, but I wouldn't. He quickly asked me how many times I'd pissed and what I had for breakfast.

I stepped into the clubhouse and was taken aback by a huge throng of reporters milling around my locker. I thought there might have been a gift or something in there that they were waiting for me to open. But they were just waiting to ask me whatever insignificant questions would help them get whatever story they were looking for.

Pitchers never talk to the media before games. It's looked at like it's voodoo and that you'll lose your focus. I didn't care. I never understood how a writer could have anything to do with my performance. It doesn't take three hours to get ready. It usually took me 20 to 30 minutes—warm up and maybe sit down with the catcher if you didn't know hitters already.

What a special day it was and what an absolutely marvelous time to be alive. I loved it all. I was the circus leader and these were my animals following me around. I told the writers that I'd been on the phone until about midnight. Logically, one of them asked me what I'd dreamt. I said, "I dreamt about losing my contact lenses, and I spend more on contact lenses than most guys make."

The game had no pennant implications because we had a nine and a half game–lead over second-place Baltimore and led the A's by double that. It was a perfect, sunny day, and 44,000 at the ballpark were there to see someone win 30 for the first time since 1934. Chuck Dobson was pitching for the A's. Before the game, A's backup catcher Jim Pagliaroni walked around with a sign that read, "Dobson goes for #12 today."

I breezed through the first three innings.

In the fourth, Danny Cater singled and Reggie Jackson hit a good curveball into the lower deck in right to put us in a 2–0 hole. But like we did all year, our guys came right back. Jim Northrup walked, Willie

Horton singled, and Norm Cash hit a three-run homer off Dobson to give us a 3–2 lead.

The A's tied it in the top of the fifth when Bert Campaneris singled in Dave Duncan, who I'd put on with a leadoff walk. It was still 3–3 in the sixth when I threw a lousy changeup to Jackson, who blasted it into the upper deck in right for his second homer of the game and a 4–3 A's lead.

I got the A's out one-two-three in the ninth, fanning Jackson and Dick Green to end the frame. Now, it was up to my teammates to pull out number 30 against A's reliever Diego Segui.

Kaline pinch hit for me and led of with a walk. Dick McAuliffe popped out, but Mickey Stanley ripped a single to center and Kaline scooted to third. The stadium was wild with excitement. I just sat there, knowing that we'd come back like we had so many times all season.

Northrup topped a bouncer to Cater at first base. Cater, who led all AL first basemen in fielding, charged, caught it on a high hop, and threw it up the third-base line and over catcher Dave Duncan's head. Kaline fell while ducking to avoid getting hit by Cater's throw and crawled back on his hands and knees to touch home with the tying run.

The tension and excitement was incredible now. The A's brought the outfield in to try to cut down Stanley on a possible play at the plate. I was pacing uncontrollably up and down the dugout when Horton drove a 2–2 pitch over Jim Gosger's head in left and Stanley ran in with the winning run, clapping all the way.

When Horton hit it, I jumped up and banged my head on the dugout roof, almost knocking myself out. Kaline caught me and all but carried me out of the dugout to join the celebration on the field. By the way, what a great cover *Sports Illustrated* had—Kaline's holding me up as much as he's hugging me.

My teammates clumsily hoisted me on their shoulders as a scrum of reporters and cameramen chased behind, screaming questions. Koufax and Dean joined the fray, and I remember turning to the stands to see a woman behind the dugout throw her panties at me. The cops kept the fans from streaming onto the field, and my teammates set me down so I could shout answers to the horde of reporters gathered near home plate.

After a few minutes of that, I was ushered to the clubhouse in order to let the pandemonium die down.

I'd been in the locker room for about 10 minutes talking to reporters when PR man Hall Middlesworth fought through the crowd and, in a panicked voice, shouted, "You gotta go out there because they're not going to leave." I ran down the tunnel and heard the fans chanting, "We want Denny. We want Denny…" I waved and blew kisses and said thank you. I thought for a moment about all that had happened since I'd called them the "worst fans anywhere" back in early May.

People sure forgive a winner, don't they?

Chapter 11

Viva Las Vegas

We had a 10½–game lead with 11 games to play, so it was just a matter of putting away the pennant and waiting to face the Cardinals, who were 12 games ahead in the National League.

On September 17, three nights after the craziness of winning number 30, almost 47,000 were on hand to see us try to clinch against the Yankees. I'd been sick as a dog with a cold or flu, and Mayo Smith suggested that I just hang out in the clubhouse if I needed to. He also said that if we clinched that night, he'd hold me back a day from my scheduled start the next day.

Joe Sparma started for us against the Yankees' Stan Bahnsen, and I watched the first few innings from the bench. We were on a seven-game winning streak and were sure this would be the night. In the third inning I took Mayo's advice and retreated to the clubhouse to rest up for the celebration.

The trainers had given me every legal drug imaginable for sinus and cold relief, and when I went to use the bathroom, I saw the cases of champagne sitting in tubs of ice in the shower room. I figured that 30-game winners are entitled to start early, so I popped a cork, turned on the radio, and relaxed on an easy chair in Mayo's office. The champagne eased my headache, and by the seventh inning the bottle was gone and so was I.

As good as I was feeling—high on all the medications and champagne— I might have been able to pitch a little relief that night.

When Don Wert singled in the winning run in the bottom of the ninth for a 2–1 victory, I was out cold on the trainer's table. I didn't even know the game was over until everybody ran in the clubhouse screaming and yelling. I got up, opened another bottle, and sprayed our owner, John Fetzer, and GM Jim Campbell until their suits were soaked.

Fetzer had trusted Campbell to build his team, and he'd done it. Most of us had played together at Triple-A Syracuse and here we were, just a few years later, as American League champions. This was the last year of single-division play where each league had 10 teams. Baseball was preparing to expand in '69 and go to a pair of six-team divisions in each league.

Our team could drink heavily and didn't need a special occasion for an excuse. But clinching the Tigers first pennant in 23 years gave us carte blanche to act like idiots. The next morning was the first and last time in my life that I woke up and had no idea what had happened for the last six or seven hours.

My first dose of reality after a wild clubhouse bash was to come to my senses in the back of a limo in Dearborn. The party was still raging on around me, and I had no recollection of how I got there. My roommate, Ray Oyler, and Norm Cash were also there, and across from me in the back seat of the limo was the ugliest woman I'd seen in my life—no lie, she was a female version of Saddam Hussein. Of all the sickening sights to wake up to.

If not for alcohol, how would you ever experience adventures like these?

Fortunately for all of us, Wednesday's game was rained out, and by the time we faced the Yankees again on Thursday afternoon I'd recovered from both my cold and the cheap champagne. Mayo said he only wanted me to go five or six innings. We had a 4–1 lead after six. When I got back to the dugout for the bottom of the sixth, he said, "Look, you've pitched enough, let's get you some rest for the World Series." I told him, "No way.

I'm not giving up the lead, and three innings isn't gonna make it any better or worse. You've gotta leave me in to finish."

As was typical, Mayo didn't pursue the argument any further. By the top of the eighth, we had a 6–1 lead. My 31st win was a lock. Jake Gibbs grounded out to start the inning and Mickey Mantle was up next. Mantle was my idol. As a kid I wanted to wear number seven, hit from both sides of the plate, and play center field—just like the Mick.

Mantle was tied with Jimmie Foxx for third on the all-time list, with 534 homers, trailing just Willie Mays and Babe Ruth. But he had only 16 homers on the year and hadn't hit one since mid-August. After an injury- and booze-filled career, our beloved Mick was an ancient 36 years old and set to retire after the season.

When he emerged from the dugout for his last ever at-bat in Detroit, everyone in the ballpark and all the Tigers in the dugout stood and cheered him. With the pennant clinched and the game decided, I signaled our catcher, Jim Price, to come to the mound. I told Price, "I want Mantle to hit one."

Price, not the quickest of minds, gave me a dumb look and said, "Whaddya mean?"

I said, "Let's just let him hit one."

It was obvious that it still hadn't registered, and it made me a bit irritated. I said, "Look. I'm going to throw a pitch, and I want him to hit a home run. He needs one more to move up on the all-time home-run list."

Price's eyes opened a little wider, and he said, "You're kidding, right? *Jesus Christ, Price, he can't hit a six-run homer!*"

"Okay. How am I supposed to tell him?"

"All you gotta do is say, 'Be ready, Mick.'"

Price trots back in, and I see him say something to either home plate ump Nestor Chylak or Mantle. I figured it must have been Chylak because I threw the first ball on an arc, maybe 50 miles per hour, and

Mantle takes it for strike one. I can't believe he didn't swing. Mantle turns around to Price and says, "What the hell was that?"

Finally, Jimmie says, "Just be ready."

Price puts the glove in the middle of the plate, I throw it the same speed, and Mantle takes it for strike two. Now he's 0–2, and I'm thinking, "Is he that stupid? Does he really think I'm trying to set him up and trick him? Maybe I should just strike him out."

Mantle turns back to Price and says, "Is he gonna do it again?" Price says, "I'm not sure, let me ask him."

So Price comes trotting out, and I put my hands on my hip and say, "What the f*ck? What are we missing here?"

Price says, "Mick wants to know if you're going to do it again."

I almost fell off the mound laughing. "Of course I'm going to do it again. Tell him to be ready this time."

Price gets back to the plate and says to Mickey, "Yeah, he's gonna do it again." Everybody's smiling by now and everybody's pulling for him to hit a homer. I throw the next one the same way and it slides a little outside and Mantle barely fouls it off.

Now that it's obvious what's going on, I yell into him, "Mickey, where do you want the f*ckin' ball?" And he puts his hand out about balls high on the inside part of the plate. I nod my head and throw it there—and Mantle hits a line drive into the upper deck just inside the foul pole.

Hitting a ball out of the ballpark, even in batting practice, is tough to do, so he still had to hit the ball. It shows you what kind of a player he was, and at that moment, in my mind, he deserved it. It was surreal, as if in slow motion—so dramatic, well-defined, and so right—the ball soaring out and Mantle trotting around the bases drinking in the moment.

When he got to second he took his hat off and acknowledged the crowd. When he got to the plate, he looked at me, waved the cap again, and shouted, "Thank you."

Viva Las Vegas

As a final touch of class, someone in Tigers management had retrieved the ball from the upper deck and had brought it to the dugout. As Mantle stood there and acknowledged the cheers, Al Kaline rolled the ball across the diamond to Mantle.

Joe Pepitone was the next batter and, as soon as he stepped in the box, he smiled and put his hand belt high over the middle of the plate. I threw one at his chin, and all I could see were Pepitone's arms, legs, and ass flying in all directions before hitting the ground.

The crowd and the press loved the entire Mantle–Pepitone drama, and most versions of it over the years have been pretty accurate. It was a Hall of Famer being honored in the best fashion of all, having him perform what he was most famous for. I cherish it as one of my warmest baseball memories.

We won 6–2, and I was 31–5. Mantle told the reporters afterward, "I'm a big fan of Denny McLain."

I just told them, "Mantle hit a good pitch."

About a week later, soon-to-be-fired Commissioner William Eckert sent me a letter saying that an investigation may be held for "compromising the integrity of the game." Jim Campbell called him and nothing came of it.

I pitched again four days later and lost 2–1 at Baltimore to drop to 31–6. A rookie named Roger Nelson five-hit us with relief help from Pete Richert. I had one start left to get to 32 wins, which would have been the most by any pitcher since the lively ball era began in 1920.

We hosted the Senators on September 28, the next to last day of the season, and I threw a two-hitter into the bottom of the seventh of a scoreless game. With Freehan on second and one out, Mayo sent Gates Brown up to pinch hit for me. I thought, "All of sudden Mayo decides he's actually going to manage? I have a two-hit shutout and he's taking me out? Bullshit!"

Gates was intentionally walked and then Mickey Stanley singled in Freehan off of Camilo Pascual. We led 1–0 after seven, I was the pitcher of record, and it was up to Don McMahon to save it for me.

The Senators got two runs off McMahon and Jon Warden in the ninth and number 32 went down the drain with the 2–1 loss.

◆   ◆   ◆

My arm was awful by the end of the year. I'd had put so much strain on it by starting 41 games and completing 28. I threw 336 innings, struck out 280 batters, and pitched on two days' rest three times. I was always at my best on three days' rest, the four-day rhythm of the era. But this was before we had our union in place and we had been in a pennant race. We were expected to sacrifice our futures and perform this way.

Cortisone, xylocaine, Contac, and greenies had fueled me, along with my obsession to go nine innings. I'd get my normal three days' rest before facing Bob Gibson in Game 1 of the World Series in St Louis.

Gibson had as great a year as I did but had fewer wins, 22, and innings, 304. But his 1.12 ERA, 13 shutouts, and 268 strikeouts gave him one of the best seasons in history.

Gibson and I, along with the overall dominance of pitching that year, changed the course of the game. By season's end, there was talk that they would lower the mound and tighten the strike zone. American League batting had dropped 17 points in the last five years, with scoring down by a thousand runs per league. Carl Yastrzemski's league-leading .301 batting average in 1968 was the lowest in history.

Mayo Smith never managed much because he was scared he'd screw something up. He was often criticized and laughed at for his inaction and lack of daring. But his decision to move Mickey Stanley from center field to shortstop for the World Series was unprecedented in baseball history. Really though, when you have three shortstops in Ray Oyler, Dick

Tracewski, and Tom Matchick, all incapable of hitting .200, just how gutsy was it?

Stanley was our best athlete and had done a respectable job when Mayo put him at shortstop for the last six games of the season. Mickey was our version of Jim Thorpe—the best multisport athlete I've ever seen. He could run like a deer and had the quickest feet when a shot was hit his way. They talked about Brooks Robinson and his first step at third base, but Stanley's first three steps in the outfield were the quickest I'd ever seen.

The other reason it was a worthwhile gamble was that Mayo had to put Kaline in somewhere. Some of the guys didn't think that Kaline should start the Series, including Mayo, but he was under pressure and had the shortstop situation to solve. Al had played only 102 games and scrambled for playing time at first base and the outfield after missing a month and a half with a broken hand. Norm Cash was our first baseman; Jim Northrup had 21 homers to Kaline's 10 and had 90 RBIs to Kaline's 53; Willie Horton hit 36 homers and had a great year; and Stanley was a Gold Glover in center who batted second.

As respectfully as I can say it about a Hall of Fame player, Kaline wasn't the most loved SOB in the clubhouse, and we did win the pennant without him.

Our guys resented Kaline for turning down a $100,000 salary when Jim Campbell offered to put him on par with the top players in the game. While the media played him up as a hero for being so modest, we all knew that it cost us serious dough. If one player reached a certain financial threshold, that door was then opened to other players, or it at least raised the bottom of the base. This was pre–free agency, and the players needed to stick together and help each other in matters like these.

I'm certainly not saying that I was Mr. Popularity. No doubt, I got on everyone's nerves with my self-promotion and running my mouth on any subject at all. And with the defending champion Cardinals heavily favored to beat us, I didn't make any more friends when I said on the eve of the opener, "I'm sick of hearing what a great team the Cardinals are. I don't want to just beat them, I want to demolish them."

I got so sick of all the hype and garbage about how great the Cardinals were and all the "year of the pitcher" crap that I told one writer I'd be "more on edge for my Riviera opening in Las Vegas at the end of the month." What an idiot I was to say dumb things like that.

The Cardinals were baseball's first minority-dominated team, with Gibson, Curt Flood, Lou Brock, and great Latin players like Orlando Cepeda and Julian Javier. Brock had stolen 62 bases in '68 while our entire team had stolen only 26.

We stayed at the Chase Hotel in St. Louis, and a bunch of us were in the bar whooping it up the night before the first game. I played piano and we sang for hours. After Lolich and some of the others went to bed, Northrup, Cash, Wert, Sparma, and our wives stayed there until the joint closed. This was the World Series, not a wake, and we didn't know if we would ever have the opportunity to do this again.

I only had a drink or two, but I was tired from entertaining the entire joint right up until closing. We had a great time the night before the biggest game of our lives, dumb bastards that we were.

Before the game, our doctor injected me with cortisone. I popped a few greenies for energy and off I went. It wasn't until 2006, when the steroid crisis was rocking baseball, that the commissioner got around to even discussing banning greenies.

But by the third inning, my shoulder was killing me. I struggled with my fastball and control and kept on falling behind in the count. I only gave up three hits in my five innings pitched, but I walked Roger Maris and Tim McCarver in the fourth and then gave up singles to Mike Shannon and Julian Javier to fall behind 3–0.

Viva Las Vegas

It wouldn't have mattered if we'd been in bed by eight the night before because Gibson was unhittable. Kaline and Cash struck out three times and all of us looked like we were in shock.

Mayo pinch hit for me in the sixth and Brock homered off Pat Dobson in the seventh to make it the 4–0 final. In the ninth, Gibson fanned Kaline, Cash, and Horton, making them look awful chasing his slider. His 17 strikeouts broke Sandy Koufax's World Series record of 15.

Lolich won Game 2, 8–1, beating Nelson Briles and 23-year-old Steve Carlton, who relieved him. Lolich even homered off Briles, the only one he hit in his entire career.

Game 3 was in Detroit, and Kaline's two-run homer in the third off Ray Washburn gave Earl Wilson a 2–0 lead. But when Wilson gave up a walk, single, and double in the fifth, Mayo brought in Dobson, and McCarver's three-run homer put St Louis ahead 4–2. Cepeda hit a three-run shot off Don McMahon in the seventh, and we were cooked 7–3.

We now trailed two games to one, and it was my turn to pitch Game 4 on Sunday. The game was delayed 37 minutes by rain, and it totally screwed up my preparation. I stood in the shower to have the hot water loosen up my shoulder, but by the time the first pitch came, I'd already cooled down.

I'm not a mudder, and Game 4 was as bad as it gets. When I walked out for the first inning, it was drizzling, and when I threw the first pitch, it was coming down in buckets. Actually, the first pitch went okay. It was the second pitch that Brock hit into the center-field stands 430 feet away.

I got Flood to ground out, but I covered first on a Roger Maris bouncer and lost my balance going over the bag. Maris was safe and McCarver singled him to third. Stanley couldn't come up with Shannon's grounder in the hole and we were down 2–0.

I was helpless in the third: Flood singled, and with two out, McCarver tripled him in. Then Shannon doubled McCarver home. I walked Javier and by then they had to stop it because the rain was ridiculous.

I Told You I Wasn't Perfect

I came in and told Mayo I'd had it—my shoulder was killing me. I was short-arming the ball and told him to put somebody else in before I gave up 10 more runs.

After an hour and 14 minute delay, Sparma, Hiller, and Dobson helped get the Cardinals to a 10–1 victory. Gibson had beaten me again with a complete game five-hitter and even homered off Sparma to lead off the fourth. I sucked, and Gibson pitched in the same weather I did.

It had been an awful day for the 53,000 at Tiger Stadium. Not only had the home team gotten clobbered and their 31-game winner fallen to 0–2 in the Series, but we had stalled as much as we could in the fourth and fifth innings to try to get a rainout and have it replayed—and even that didn't work.

I waited around for the reporters as I was required to do, and I told them I was done for the Series. I didn't think I could pitch again and said so. The depression of getting my brains blown out and putting us behind 3–1 with Gibson able to pitch again was the worst feeling in the world.

I believe I had a partially torn rotator cuff for several years. Dr. Mitchell and the people at Ford Hospital knew what the problem was, but there was no surgery available for it. Besides the cortisone every few weeks, it was rubdowns, pills for pain, greenies, and Contac. By '68, there was never a time I pitched without some pain.

Once I got loose I was normally okay after a few innings as long as I didn't have to sit too long. Every pitcher dreams of getting a six-run inning, but I hated the thought because then I had to get loose again.

Game 5 was the next afternoon, and Drs. Mitchell and Livingood told me I should take another cortisone shot to try to pitch Game 6, assuming Lolich managed to win Game 5. I said, "Fine—let's go."

Our announcer, Hall of Famer Ernie Harwell, invited blind guitarist and singer Jose Feliciano to sing the national anthem before Game 5. It was a long version of the song and at that point in time, singers weren't supposed to give their own interpretations. This was the height of the Vietnam War and the protest movement. The National Guard was all over the field in a patriotic display, and here's this blind Latino supposedly "butchering" the anthem. It was viewed as almost sacrilegious rather than an impressive artistic interpretation.

Four hitters into the game, Cepeda hit a two-run homer and Lolich trailed 3–0. They might have scored again in the third, but Freehan threw Brock out stealing. We came back with two in the fourth with two runs off Nelson Briles on triples by Stanley and Horton and a single by Northrup.

In the fifth, trailing the Cardinals 3–2, Brock doubled with one out. Javier singled sharply to left, and Willie Horton charged the ball perfectly and threw home as Brock raced to beat it. For reasons that he never adequately explained, Brock decided not to slide and Freehan's left leg prevented him from touching the plate. Maybe Brock just had that little respect for Horton's arm. Mayo had replaced Willie in Game 2 when we had a big lead by moving Northrup over from center and putting Oyler at short. But Willie made the play of the Series. Brock was out and it remained 3–2 Cardinals.

We scratched out three in the seventh off Briles and Joe Hoerner on four singles and a walk to take the lead 5–3. Lolich's single had started the rally. The guy was amazing. He shut out the Cardinals the last eight innings, and we were going back to St. Louis trailing 3–2.

I had guys coming at me with needles from all directions. I'd gotten the shot on Monday before Game 5, and on Wednesday, about an hour before Game 6 in St. Louis, Dr. Mitchell loaded me up again. He first shot me with Xylocaine that he said helped sustain the effects of the cortisone. The Xylocaine makes the shoulder feel like dead weight the first 30 minutes before it springs back to life.

He hit the right spot with the Xylocaine because I almost flew off the table. With the shoulder feeling great, I breezed through the first two innings and led 2–0. In the third, we scored 10 runs off Washburn, Larry Jaster, and two other long relievers. Northrup hit a grand slam off Jaster.

The Cards scored a run off me in the ninth, and we won 13–1. It was tied at three each. Game 7 would feature Lolich against Gibson.

Lolich and Gibson traded zeros for five and a half innings of Game 7. Brock singled to lead off the bottom of the sixth, and Lolich picked him off. Two batters later, Flood singled and Lolich picked him off also.

With two out in the seventh, Cash and Horton singled off Gibson, and Northrup hit a shot to deep left center. Flood's first step was in, and by the time he recovered, the ball was over his head for a two-run triple that put us in the lead. Freehan doubled in Northrup to make it 3–0.

Mayo had sent me to the bullpen in the seventh in case I needed to pitch to a few hitters. But Lolich closed it out 4–1. Evidence of how different baseball was in 1968, Game 7 lasted just 2:07. And for his three victories, Lolich got a new Dodge Charger as the Series MVP.

It was a great turnaround for Lolich, who had been in the bullpen with a 7–7 record before rallying to finish 17–9 and then starring in the Series.

Much has been said about the fact that Lolich and I didn't get along, and it's all true. Lolich had this to say decades later in George Cantor's book, *The Tigers of '68.*

> I didn't hate Denny, no. It didn't bother me that he had become the number-one pitcher. I never admitted to myself that I was number two. But I didn't like how he made his own rules and got away with it. I came up with the Detroit organization, and you were taught that there was a certain way that you conducted yourself. It was fairly well regimented. I didn't mind that, and neither did the other guys— just as long as the rules applied to everyone.

Viva Las Vegas

Denny never wanted to go along with the program. He always seemed to be challenging management, flaunting it, seeing what he could get away with.

I think Mayo took out a lot of his frustrations on me in 1968. He didn't dare touch Denny, not with the kind of season he was having. So I became the whipping boy.

Lolich was so miserable in the middle of the '68 season because I was going so well and he was pitching so badly. There's nothing worse than somebody wallowing in his own misery, and Mickey was a miserable guy in 1968. He became Mr. Personality for about four seconds after he won three games in the World Series, and nobody pulled for him more than I did. Lolich saved my season by getting us to Game 6 after I'd lost twice. To have won 31 games and then have been the Series goat would have been beyond awful.

My rivalry with Lolich didn't end in St. Louis. The Frontier Hotel tried to counteract my upcoming gig at the Riviera by booking Lolich for a few cameos. He performed with a Detroit sportscaster, Jim Hendricks, and sang "St. Looee" as a spin-off of "Kansas City."

My agent, Frank Scott, and I had gotten together with the Hammond people and booked a schedule of about 50 dates all across the country to follow my two-week stint at the Riviera. It was a lot of one-nighters and we were everywhere.

It seemed like I had every promoter in America coming at me in '68, and Scott and I were both overwhelmed. Frank's biggest thing to this point had been getting somebody $500 to speak to the Knights of Columbus. We did Ed Sullivan for $10,000 and found out that others got $15,000 or more. I would do engagements for $500 that others were getting two grand to do.

I Told You I Wasn't Perfect

Here are excerpts from the Associated Press report of my Riviera debut a few days after the World Series ended:

> An overflow crowd of about 400 was on hand for the Riviera debut of Denny McLain and his "Denny McLain Trio." McLain, in bright blue slacks and white shoes, shed a $3,000 fur Nehru jacket for a sports coat, calling the Nehru a "helluva warm-up jacket."
>
> The Tigers pitcher sang an off-color version of "Bye Bye Blackbird" that made even the Las Vegas audience blush and afterward quipped, "A Frank Sinatra I'm not."
>
> Comedian Marty Allen walked on stage at the Riviera and broke up the crowd with a sign that read, "Bob Gibson says, 'We shall overcome.'"
>
> McLain told the audience he "would consider quitting baseball if he got a really good music offer." In touching on baseball and the just completed World Series, he said of Series MVP Mickey Lolich, "I wouldn't trade one Bob Gibson for 12 Mickey Loliches."
>
> He will make more [money] at the Riviera than he did during the season.
>
> McLain recently completed his first album and plans a winter tour of one-night stands in Michigan and elsewhere, and since the World Series he has also appeared on the Ed Sullivan, Bob Hope, Merv Griffin, and *Match Game* shows.

I won the MVP and the Cy Young Award in early November. The MVP was a unanimous vote and made me the first AL pitcher to ever garner all the votes and the first AL pitcher to win the MVP since the Athletics'

Viva Las Vegas

Bobby Shantz won it in 1952. *The Sporting News* also named me Man of the Year for 1968.

I was paid a salary of $30,000 in 1968. The Tigers broke 2 million in attendance, an increase of over 25 percent from the best previous attendance in club history.

Jim Campbell called me in that winter to "negotiate" my new deal for 1969. This was pre–free agency, and players had virtually no bargaining power. They were at the complete mercy of the team that owned their rights in perpetuity. A player's only strength was to threaten to deny the team his services, which hurt everybody, especially the player.

I was determined to get what I deserved, even though, deep down, I was pretty certain that Campbell would call any bluff I tried. I expected Campbell to offer me a "generous" $20,000 raise to get me to $50,000 or so, so I didn't want to even let those words flow from his mouth.

I sat down and got right to the point. "Jim, I want $100,000. Mantle, Mays, Williams, and Kaline are all $100,000 players, and I just won 31. You know I'm worth it, and I'll make it real simple Jim—I'm not playin' this year unless I get 100 grand."

Campbell looked passively at me from behind his desk. My heart was pounding because this was big dough at stake and my fighting spirit was fully engaged.

"Denny, you know I can't do that," Campbell gently replied. "I can't give you Kaline money. He's been here since 1953, 10 years longer than you. If I give you 100 grand, then what's Freehan gonna say? What's Cash, Northrup, and all those guys gonna say? They'll be in here wanting their deals tripled. It can't happen, Denny. I've got a ballclub to run, and I won't lose money doing it."

I geared up for another attack. "That's bullshit, Jim, and it's not my problem. You can't win without me, and Kaline was hurt half of last year. I want 100 grand and you know I deserve it."

Campbell stared at me for a few seconds and then quietly said, "Denny, I was going to offer you 50, but here's what I'll do. I'll double you to 60 against my better judgment. But that's it. Take it or leave it."

Now I was up to $60,000 and I figured I had one bullet left. "Jim, that's still bullshit. I'm walking out of here. I'll play the organ this year and make more than that. Good luck with the ballclub."

Campbell started showing impatience and anger for the first time. "Okay, Denny, do what you have to do. But before you walk out, I'll just tell you this. My final offer is 60, and every minute that goes by that you don't sign, it goes down a thousand dollars."

I was cooked. I couldn't live without pitching, and we both knew he had me. I looked at Campbell and muttered, "Okay. Where's the pen?"

Chapter 12

Flyin' High

I wanted the 100 grand because I deserved it and because it was a status symbol in the sport. Carl Yastrzemski was making a major-league high $130,000, and I still wasn't even halfway there. But I'd made a small fortune in the off-season.

We made an album with Capitol Records late in the '68 season. Capitol brought guys in from L.A., and they spent three to four weeks in Detroit putting together the album. I went to the studio every day when we were home, getting in at 8:00 AM and working until 3:00 or 4:00 in the afternoon before going to the ballpark—even on days I pitched.

It was a lot of work, but along with winning 31 games, it set the stage for a huge off-season of fun and big money. The album was the catalyst for our two-week deal at the Riviera that paid $15,000 a week. From then until spring training, I was all over the country with the Denny McLain Trio. I basically made $1,000 a night on a four-month, 100-date Hammond tour that started in Seattle in early November and worked its way down and around the country.

I was really getting into flying, and we leased a small twin-engine Navaho for the Hammond tour. Hammond paid the expenses and arranged the whole tour. It was amazing—flying every day and entertaining every night.

We were flying from New Mexico to San Antonio for a Monday night gig, and Frank Scott told me that a Texas oilman was having a debutante ball for his daughter and was willing to pay us $25,000 to play the party and then join him and his buddies for golf on Sunday morning.

Hell, for 25 grand I would have adopted his daughter, too. His house was as big as any hotel I'd seen at the time, and he had us play in his game room that must have been 6,000 feet. I should have paid him to be there—that's how great a time it was.

When the tour ended, I was so caught up with aviation and the love of flying that I bought a plane just before spring training started. Flying was an addiction, and I couldn't get enough.

Baseball tried to pump up the disappearing offense by lowering the mound from 15 to 10 inches and tightening the strike zone. Instead of the shoulders to the knees, now it was the armpits to the top of the knees. In 1963 they had expanded the strike zone, and now they were shrinking it back. But it was the height of the mound that I noticed immediately. It seemed to make my control a hair sharper, but I lost a little velocity. You needed better mechanics to pitch off a lower mound.

I was really worried about the lower mound. In Minnesota, L.A., and Detroit I'd been king because those mounds were 20 to 22 inches high. Nobody checked back then. The Dodgers had a high mound for 6'2" Sandy Koufax and 6'5" Don Drysdale, and had a team ERA a full run lower at home than on the road.

A lot of pitching has to do with your mental outlook, and when you get on a mound 20 or 22 inches high, the hitter looks so close that it's like you're throwing from the top of the Empire State Building. The ball appears to get there so quickly and you think you can put it wherever you want to.

Mayo Smith and pitching coach Johnny Sain had a meeting in spring training to talk about it. Overhand throwers like Sparma and me were more affected than the sidearm guys. I knew I'd strike out fewer guys in '69, I just wasn't sure how dramatic the drop-off would be.

Flyin' High

My arm hurt a lot in spring training and I thought I might miss the opener. I was quoted in *The Detroit News* a few days before the season started:

> The pain in my shoulder worries me. It's still there. I can't pick up a pop bottle without feeling it. I take lots of heat treatments and doctors say six cortisone injections a year will knock the pain out. My shoulder started bothering me in 1965. It was a Sunday afternoon game with the White Sox. I threw a fastball to Pete Ward and it hurt. Like a dummy, I pitched the rest of the game. I hurt the shoulder again just before the '66 All-Star Game. I've had it off and on ever since. I'll stay in the game as long as I can. But like Sandy Koufax, I might have to quit to avoid permanent injury.

I took a cortisone shot the day before the opener. With a Tiger Stadium record crowd of 53,572 on hand, I beat Luis Tiant 6–2 on a three-hitter, fanning five and walking one. John Sain praised me afterward, "When Denny does well it never surprises me—this boy is a real competitor."

In retrospect, I shouldn't have pitched every fourth day in '69, but we had a great ballclub and we thought we were going to repeat. On April 20 I lost 2–0 at New York to fall to 2–2. I'd gotten great run support in '68, but we had been shut out in both my '69 losses.

Mayo asked if I'd pitch on two days' rest, and on April 23, in 45-degree weather in Baltimore, I threw a three-hitter for nine and a third innings in a 3–2, 10-inning loss. I was 2–3, and my third loss in 1968 hadn't come until July 20.

I took another cortisone shot after struggling in a 7–3 win over the Red Sox on April 27. I gave up 11 hits and walked three in eight innings.

On May 1 we were facing the Orioles at Tiger Stadium when my number one nemesis, Boog Powell, ripped a shot that hit the dirt in the front of the mound and took a wild hop that hit me right in the forehead at my hairline. I dropped like a stone but got up after about a minute and faced only 31 hitters in a 2–0, three-hit shutout. The game took 1:49—the shortest in the majors the last five years.

Winning in less than two hours was the magic number in those days. I didn't walk anybody, and the message was, "Get me two runs early and we'll get out of here in two hours." A two-run lead stopped the other team from running the bases back then. They didn't want to lose an inning by getting picked off or thrown out.

In '68 and '69 all the pitching theories and fundamentals I'd learned came together. Charlie Dressen taught me that if the hitter doesn't hit the pitch the first time, why throw a different pitch the second time? If a guy pops up a fastball, why do I want to throw him a slider?

I fell to 6–4 with a 7–3 loss at Chicago on May 22 and took another cortisone shot the next day because Mayo wanted me to pitch on two days' rest on the 25th against the Angels. We led the Angels 10–0 after six innings in that one, and I had Mayo take me out after the seventh.

I shut out the A's 2–0 on another three-hitter on June 7 and got it done in 1:51. When my arm didn't hurt, I knew I was pitching better than I had in winning 31 the year before. The lower mound may've cut down on my strikeouts, but thanks to the cortisone controlling the pain, I was pitching almost better than I could believe.

I'd ice my arm after I pitched, and for the next day I couldn't even wipe my ass. I'd drown the arm in water as hot as I could stand a few times a day after that. The men in charge of keeping my pitching machinery tuned up never agreed on what the problem was. Tigers team doctor Russell Wright thought my shoulder problem was a muscle thing. Drs. Mitchell and Livingood of Ford Hospital told me that it was my rotator cuff that had been partially torn since 1965.

Flyin' High

They had me take pills for blood flow because blood flow is necessary to repair something that's torn. Back in '67, Livingood explained that there would come a day when the cortisone shots wouldn't help anymore. Throwing overhand goes against nature, and when you have a torn muscle, there were only two cures: stop using it for a very long time or undergo what they called "Billy Pierce Surgery," where they cut through all the surrounding muscles to repair the tear.

The cortisone shots were having diminishing effects—I was getting them on the road a lot more often—and Livingood was getting nervous. Half the time they'd miss the spot, and when they did, the shot was useless. But I wouldn't know it until I went out to pitch the next day. But getting more rest was never an issue. There wasn't any great value put on my arm or anybody else's.

Once I won 16 in '65, they knew I was better than what they'd thought. But they still had 80 arms in the minors. Today a guy can get hurt and take a month off. We got hurt and went to Toledo. The Players Association didn't protect us like they would in later decades.

On June 16 I beat the Yankees 3–2 and moved to 10–5 to become the first in the league to reach 10 wins. I was 25 and it made me the youngest pitcher in baseball history to win 100 games. In the mid-80s Dwight Gooden got to 100 a few months before I did, and he remains the youngest ever.

Detroit News writer Pete Waldmeir never liked me, but he still had to write columns. After I pitched my fourth complete game shutout of the year to beat the Red Sox 7–0 to move to 12–5 in early July, Waldmeir wrote:

> Suffice it to say that Denny McLain is a rare breed even
> among professional athletes: he is a natural-born winner. As
> he grows older, one element of his youth sticks with McLain:
> his cockiness. It's more than walking jauntily on the balls of

129

his feet with his baseball cap pushed forward so that it rides on the bridge of his nose. It's that same intangible something which made him throw that big fat curve to Willie Mays in the 1966 All-Star Game and strike out Mays with it.

And I was having a hell of a time. Mickey Lolich was 11–1, and I loved the challenge. The two of us were vying to be named starter for the American League in the upcoming All-Star Game in Washington, D.C.

Chapter 13

Me 'n' Mickey

The All-Star Game in Washington, D.C., in 1969 sums up the lunacy that had become my life. On Friday, July 18, in my last appearance before the break, I flew my plane to a game in Cleveland and barely got there in time because of a weather problem in Detroit. When I got to the clubhouse, Norm Cash walked me over to Mayo's office and joked, "Mayo, have you had the pleasure of meeting Mr. McLain?" Mayo allowed me to fly my own plane rather than travel with the team. Although it was one thing to stretch the rules for me, it was another to have me stroll in late.

I beat Cleveland and Luis Tiant 4–0 with a seven-hit shutout. It was an awesome night and it was no less than my fifth shutout of the year. I even drove in a run on a two-strike suicide squeeze. The art of sacrifice bunts has faded in the modern long-ball style of play. I had 16 successful sacrifices in '68.

When I think back on it, the worst thing I ever did was buy that airplane. Few things in life can match the control you feel when it's dark and you're flying through the clouds. My mistake was that I kept talking about it and showing off about it. I loved being the guy who could stroll in 30 minutes before game time and spin a shutout.

That's what happened in Cleveland that night, and it was a beautiful thing.

With me at 14–5 and Mickey Lolich at 13–2, our combined 27–7 record made us the league's best one-two punch by a large margin. I'd tried hard to get along with Mickey, but we just never liked each other. Regardless, we were both Tigers All-Stars, and I told Mickey I'd fly him and his wife Joyce to the game. I'd even pick them up at their house to drive to the airport. The plan was to fly in Monday night in time for the 100th anniversary of baseball, have dinner, and then fly back together after the game on Tuesday night.

This was to be the first night game in All-Star history, and the 100th anniversary of the sport made it extra special. And it was special for me, too, because I got the nod over Mickey to start for the AL All-Stars.

It rained like crazy Tuesday night, and we waited it out at the ballpark. While President Nixon visited the American League clubhouse to meet and greet, Ted Williams, in his first year as Senators manager, held court in the dugout with a horde of reporters from around the nation.

Ted was one of Mayo's coaches, and he sat on the bench regaling reporters with his opinions on everything from aviation to interleague play. When I peeked my head out to see how badly it was raining, Ted was into a diatribe about his famous 1941 All-Star home run and about how dumb most pitchers are. He caught my eye and gave me a wink in the middle of the "dumb pitcher" line. I figured this might be pretty good and sat at the end of the bench to listen to his bullshit.

The dugout was almost dead silent except for the sound of pelting rain and 40 reporters desperately scribbling down the gospel of Teddy Ballgame. Meanwhile, the dugout floor was starting to fill with water, and the reporters started kneeling on the bench or standing awkwardly on the dugout steps to keep their feet dry. But no one was leaving—not with the greatest hitter of all time waxing philosophic.

All of a sudden, down the middle of the dugout, came a rat, flailing his legs to avoid drowning. It was as if someone had yelled fire in a theater.

The reporters scrambled to safety, most of them stepping through the rat-infested waters to get to the tunnel leading to the clubhouse.

Ted didn't appreciate being upstaged by a rodent and called the retreating writers pussies and gutless cocksuckers. "Thank God," Ted finally yelled, "you sons of bitches weren't defending our country like some of us had to."

The game was postponed until 1:00 the next afternoon. This presented serious logistical problems for me. I had a major dental appointment at Ford Hospital scheduled for Wednesday morning and felt it was important to keep it. I had horrible teeth because the years of drinking large quantities of sugar-laden Pepsi had rotted them out. The absurdity of it all was that Pepsi was paying me nearly $20,000 a year to promote the very product that was ruining my mouth. I had been getting so many infections from my teeth that at one point they thought my teeth were giving me arm problems. But I loved the damn Pepsi, and I wasn't about to give up it or the money it brought me.

In early July I had 11 teeth filed down, pulled, or capped and had posts drilled into my jawbone to receive new teeth. By All-Star time, the pulling had been done, and this was the appointment where the last nine teeth would be implanted or capped. Mayo knew about it, the league knew about it, everyone who mattered knew about it, and Mayo told the press after the rainout on Tuesday that I had a big dental emergency. Privately he told me, "F*ck the All-Star Game. You go home and get it done. If you're gonna be late, you just better as hell let us know."

His first All-Star experience was turning into a bad dream for Mayo. They had forgotten to include a seat for him on the dais at the centennial dinner Monday night. They remembered to save one for NL manager Red Schoendienst, but Mayo was reduced to sitting off to the side with some baseball writers. When Joe Reichler, the commissioner's assistant, finally realized his mistake and rushed over to get him, Mayo said, "Get lost."

I flew back Tuesday night and got to Ford Hospital at 7:30 AM on Wednesday to meet Dr. McIntosh, the oral surgeon. The plan was to be done by 9:30, get to the plane by 10:00, be in Washington by 11:00, and get to the ballpark by noon for the 1:00 PM start. I certainly didn't need more than an hour to get ready to pitch two innings. Hell, just the other day I'd gotten into Cleveland 30 minutes before the game and shut the bastards out.

Unfortunately, one of the dentures was smaller than it was supposed to be and didn't fit, causing the procedure to run a little longer. We got done around 10:00, and I said, "I've gotta get out of here. If I miss the beginning of this game they'll hang me and Mayo."

Dr. McIntosh said, "It's gonna take me 30 minutes to clean this up and get all the excess particles and cement out of your mouth."

I asked, "Can we do it on the plane?"

"Yeah," McIntosh said after a moment's hesitation. "Can I go to the game, too? Can you get me in?"

I said, "I'll get you the best seat in the park. Let's go!" and raced to City Airport with McIntosh and his dental assistant. We jumped into the plane and were ready to land in Washington by 11:45.

Unfortunately, there was an air traffic controller's strike going on at the time, and the fill-in personnel had slowed the system to a crawl. When we left the Detroit airspace, the controllers were prepared to give us priority treatment, but the message got lost somewhere down the line.

After our pilot was vectored and slowed down, I got on the radio and reminded the controller who we were. After I promised baseballs for him and his entire crew, he said, "Why the heck didn't you say something before?"

We finally touched down at 12:15.

We also should have arranged to have a cop pick us up because we got stuck in traffic outside the stadium. The game had already begun by the time I made it to the locker room at 1:17. Mel Stottlemyre of the Yankees started in my place and had already gotten lit up. Johnny Bench hit a two-run homer deep into the mezzanine in left to put the Nationals in front 3–0.

When I was done dressing, Stottlemyre stepped out of the shower and said, "Thanks for letting me get my balls knocked off out there today." I said, "Hey, if you hadn't beaten me a few times last year, I would have hurried." We both laughed and I went down the tunnel to the dugout. I'd only lost 11 games the last two seasons and Mel beat me in two of them.

Mayo told me to go warm up and be ready to pitch by the fourth inning. As I warmed up in the bullpen, Oakland's Blue Moon Odom was getting rocked. Willie McCovey hit a two-run homer off the top of the scoreboard. By the time I finally took the mound in the fourth, the Nationals led 8–2.

I fanned Felix Millan and Hank Aaron in the fourth and was ahead of McCovey at 0–2. Like Mickey Mantle earlier in my career, I'd been told to never throw McCovey a changeup; but if he can hit my changeup on 0–2, I'll tip my hat to him. McCovey hit it so far and so hard that it sounded like a howitzer going off, and I didn't even turn to look. The Nationals wound up winning 9–3.

The original plan had been for us to fly back Tuesday night after the game and then go to Lakeland after the dental appointment on Wednesday because we were buying an additional piece of property behind our house. I had to get it done, and Sharon was going with me. But because the game had been pushed back to Wednesday, I had to get out of Washington quickly.

Lolich had expected to fly home with us if the game had been played Tuesday night. When Mickey approached me in the clubhouse as I was dressing, he said, "You still gotta go to Florida?" I told him I did and that I had to leave now, before the game was over. He seemed to accept that.

But here's an excerpt from the Associated Press story that ran all over the country and was titled McLain Selfish, Says Angry Lolich:

"Denny pulled a crummy trick on me today," Lolich told *The Detroit News*' Pete Waldmeir. "He buzzed out of here right after he was through pitching and he left me and my wife Joyce without a ride back to Detroit. And all he says is, 'Tough, that's your problem.' McLain does not think about his friends or teammates. All he thinks about is himself. It wasn't so bad that we had to get back to Detroit by ourselves. But Denny's attitude was just beautiful. When he left the game after the fourth inning to get dressed, I stopped him and asked where he was going. He told me that he was in a hurry and had to fly to Florida someplace. I understand he has real estate or a house near Lakeland."

What a f*cking baby, that Lolich. There are a thousand flights a day from Washington to Detroit. The league paid for his first-class transportation back to Detroit, and Mickey should have kept his mouth shut.

Meanwhile, columnists all across the country took their shots at ripping me. Rick Talley, for example, penned a column in *Chicago Sun-Times* titled McLain Puts 'Teeth' into All-Star Test. It read:

Spiro Agnew, members of congress, and David Eisenhower were there—pretty big event, right? Wasn't quite as important as Denny (Sky King) McLain's teeth.

It would seem that on baseball's 100th anniversary, an occasion that drew presidential attention and brought together the greatest array of all-time baseball stars in history, that one right-handed pitcher could postpone saying "ahhh."

Me 'n' Mickey

Had he started and pitched well, it might have been different. It continues to amaze me how some professional athletes live under double standards. They take freely but forget what they owe.

I was pissed at Lolich and saw him in the locker room Thursday night. I read him the riot act in front of half the club and dared him to stand up and fight like a man. I yelled, "Bitch to me. Don't go running and lying to some drunken faggot newspaper guy."

In '68 and '69 when Lolich was running around in his National Guard uniform to stay out of the draft, I either flew him or allowed someone to fly him in my plane to Georgia so he could attend the meetings. Instead of going over to Vietnam and getting killed, I thought Mickey was doing the smart thing by joining the Guard. After all, he couldn't run, so at the very least he was gonna get shot in the ass by somebody.

Lolich apologized and went on the radio before I pitched Friday to explain the "misunderstanding."

It didn't help. When I took the mound Friday night in Detroit to face Kansas City, I got booed like I was a child molester.

I was shutting out the Royals 3–0 when I laid down a sacrifice bunt in the seventh. They gave me a standing ovation. When the night was over, I was 15–5 with a 2.39 ERA and seven straight victories. My six shutouts on the year were as many as I'd had in '68. Shutouts and wins will always win a crowd back.

I told *The Detroit News* that night, "I've had a hectic week, to say the least. I mean, not getting to the All-Star Game on time and then the Mickey Lolich thing. If the All-Star mix-up is why they're booing, fine. I'm sorry about it. If it's the Lolich affair, Mickey and I have everything patched up. He even apologized on the radio. He didn't have to do that. I've been booed by bigger crowds than this. It doesn't bother me that much."

Ultimately, the whole thing was my fault because I shouldn't have bought the plane in the first place, and I shouldn't have been so arrogant as to think I could really get back to the All-Star Game on time. If I had rescheduled the dental appointment to Saturday morning after I pitched Friday night, none of this ridiculousness would have occurred.

But in my mind, the world revolved around me.

It also got me four days of intense attention, and as perverse as it was, I think I enjoyed it.

Chapter 14

Shot Up to Shut Out

The mound was lower, I struck out fewer, my arm was sorer, and I took more cortisone shots than I did in '68, but the best I ever pitched was 1969. I started out 2–3 without much run support but went on an 18–3 roll to find myself at 20–6 by late August.

The game got so easy, I could hit the asshole on a skunk. My control was so good. I could throw sliders, 3 and 2 curveballs and change-ups on the black when I needed them. I had a real high kick, like Juan Marichal of the Giants, and if I didn't kick just right, my entire left side—starting with my butt cheek, would hurt like hell. But I never had an ache in my arm because my mechanics were so good.

Coach Johnny Sain and I worked on stuff and talked every day about being in the right position after I threw the ball. Before you throw is easy, but being in the right position after you throw is what pitching is all about. It's about legs, turn, balance, staying behind the pitch, and final position. If you maintain proper mechanics, you can really protect your arm from damage.

On August 1 I shut out the White Sox 8–0 in 1:59 for my third shutout in four games and seventh in the year. The team record was eight, set by Ed Killian in 1905 and matched by Hal Newhouser during the war in 1945.

On August 12 I took a cortisone shot at Ford Hospital, and the next night I shut out the Angels 3–0 in 1:50 at Tiger Stadium to move to 18–6, tying Killian and Newhouser with shutout number eight.

On August 22 in Anaheim I gave up a first-inning homer to Jim Spencer and cruised in 3–1 for win number 20. It was my 12th win in the last 13 decisions. Cash told reporters afterward, "If Denny writes a book, it'll be called, *How to Win 20 without Really Trying.*"

On September 3 I gave up solo homers to Mike Fiore and Joe Foy in beating the Royals 4–2 for win number 22. Royals manager Joe Gordon said, "What a pitcher. He can always reach back for more."

Sharon suffered a miscarriage with our fourth child, and I lost 5–2 at Cleveland on September 11. My arm was hurting badly and we were both extremely upset at the turn of events. The cortisone shots were really piling up now, and Doc Livingood's prediction that the shots would have gradually diminishing effects was proving true. The injections were coming much more often, and it was taking more and more hot water, rubdowns, Tylenol, and Contac to make my arm feel better.

I shut out New York and Stan Bahnsen 2–0 in 1:58 at Yankee Stadium to break the club shutout mark with number nine. I took another shot before facing the Red Sox on September 19. Reggie Smith hit a two-run homer off me in the first and Ken Brett beat me.

There were two races going on. We wanted to finish in second place behind the Orioles and collect second-place money of $2,300 per man, and I was battling Mike Cuellar for the Cy Young Award.

I won number 24, 2–1 at Boston on September 27. We scored the winning run in the eighth when Sox catcher Jerry Moses couldn't handle a Bill Lee pitch and Northrup came in to score. I was 24–9, and even though I'd gotten a shot two days earlier, my arm was still killing me. The victory put us a game ahead of the third-place Sox.

The *Detroit News* wrote:

Shot Up to Shut Out

Sore-armed Denny McLain pitched the Detroit Tigers back into second place Saturday with great determination and plenty of luck. McLain solidified his American League status as the number-one candidate for the Cy Young Award by setting down the Boston Red Sox 2–1 before 22,459 on a sunny, 65-degree day at Fenway Park.

"My arm felt as bad as it ever felt," said McLain in the Detroit clubhouse. "I didn't throw over 10 fastballs, and every one hurt."

I'd had enough for the year. I didn't say it to the writers, but I'd done all I could to get us second-place dough. There were five games left, and it was up to the others guys to keep it going.

I was 24–9 compared to 31–6 in 1968. I completed 23 games, one less than AL leader Mel Stottlemyre, and led the league in wins, shutouts, and innings pitched with 325—11 fewer innings than I'd thrown in '68. My ERA of 2.80 was higher than my 1.96 the year before, but I allowed only 1.86 walks per game, second among starters to Fritz Peterson.

The only alarming stat was 181 strikeouts, as opposed to the 280 I had in 1968. The lower mound and the chronic soreness hurt my velocity.

Cuellar, who finished 23–11, tied me for the Cy Young Award. Cuellar and the Orioles lost the World Series in five games to the Miracle Mets.

It would turn into a fascinating off-season for baseball. On October 9, the Reds named an obscure career minor-league player named Sparky Anderson as their new manager.

Curt Flood refused to report to the Phillies after the Cardinals traded him. He told Bowie Kuhn, "I'm not a piece of property to be bought and sold irrespective of my wishes. It violates my rights as a citizen."

Kuhn wrote back, "I agree you are not a piece of property to be bought and sold. However, I cannot see its applicability to the situation at hand."

As fate would have it, Bowie would soon find himself in a position to make a major decision about me, too.

Chapter 15

Welcome to My Nightmare

After the 1969 season, Major League Baseball asked me, Mets World Champion hero Tug McGraw, and several other players to participate in a 25-day tour of GI hospitals in Vietnam.

It was a goodwill tour that left me with an overwhelming distaste for U.S. involvement in Vietnam. We spent a night at a so-called "fire base" near the front lines while our helicopter was being repaired. The smell of marijuana was pervasive, but as we heard one horror story after another, I thought, "Who the hell could blame them?" They were fighting a war that no one wanted, and we were in the process of losing 50,000 kids just like these.

About a week into the trip I got a message that Sharon had called because we had an emergency of some sort back home. It took a half-day to get to a phone, and as soon as she picked up she said, "You're not going to believe what I'm going to tell you. We just got a notice of foreclosure—we're nine months behind on our payments."

I said, "That's impossible." She said, "It's not impossible. In fact, our utilities are going off on Friday."

A lawyer named Ed May had been handling our money since halfway through the '69 season. I'd met May through Joe Sparma, whose locker and house were both next to mine, and our kids played together. May represented Sparma, and Sparma convinced me to take him on. Joe was a bright guy who'd played some quarterback for Woody Hayes.

May had stolen every dime from both of us. I found out I was $446,000 in debt and had no reason to be bankrupt. I was making $90,000 as a player, $30,000 playing the organ, and another $30,000 with my contracts with Pepsi and Hammond. May had been sending us a check for $300 a week for essentials and the rest was supposed to be either put away or applied to pay our bills.

By the time the news reached me in Vietnam, Sparma had beaten May within an inch of his life before May then fled with his secretary to Japan. May left me a tangled web of 86 creditors, including himself, for some $23,000 in unpaid fees!

In 1969 Sparma and May had talked me into getting involved with a paint company in Florida. We had taken on a warehouse in Michigan, and May had "managed" the operation. My debt on that one alone was $160,000.

When I got back from Vietnam, I hired Mark McCormack's International Management Group (IMG) to sort out the mess and represent me. IMG was the outfit that Arnold Palmer had helped make famous. I became McCormack's first baseball player client.

Bankruptcy had cleared me of all but $25,000 in unpaid bills, but I needed to build a nest egg while I could still pitch. As '69 turned into '70, I knew I needed to have another great season to help IMG orchestrate my road to financial recovery.

In early February I got a call from Bill Carpenter, who was the agent assigned to me at IMG. He told me that Jim Campbell had called to tell us that *Sports Illustrated* was preparing a potentially damaging article about me that included information about possible mob associations. He told me we needed to fly to New York to meet with the commissioner.

This news, fresh on the heels of the Ed May revelations, was another thunderbolt that shook my entire sense of well-being.

Welcome to My Nightmare

It seems that gambling raids were the rage in January 1970. An FBI crackdown began with New Year's Day raids in five states on a ring that was doing more than $100,000 a day in bets. One of the guys named was a close friend of Dizzy Dean's. Dizzy wasn't indicted, but he was one of five co-conspirators named in a federal investigation that charged 10 others with gambling conspiracy. Co-conspirator means that the grand jury believed the person was involved but not to a sufficient degree to be indicted. It also means that the unindicted co-conspirator was now a snitch for the government.

The grand jury had been in contact with Major League Baseball, and now my name was in the mix. They scheduled me to testify in the middle of February, about a week after Kuhn had told me to come to New York to talk to him. I had no idea why Kuhn wanted to see me because, other than the Shorthorn fiasco and the usual clubhouse activities, I certainly had nothing to do with any nationwide gambling rings.

When I met with Kuhn on February 13, 1970, he started pumping me with questions about my involvement with the Shorthorn characters back in 1967. I was frank with him because I was scared and I didn't think I had anything significant to hide.

Kuhn gave me his assurance that he wanted to help extricate me from any possible mess and that if I told him the truth, no serious harm would come to my career. He told me he could understand why a young player under pressure could get drawn into a lot of bad deals. So I told him all about how Clyde Roberts and Jigs Gazell had successfully played me for the fool.

Kuhn informed me that *Sports Illustrated* would describe me and Ed Schober as "fish" for the operation. But Bowie also told me things that were just too fantastic to believe. He said Flint police chief James Rutherford reported that informants had told him that I'd gone into serious debt with the Shorthorn guys. Then he said, "You were taken to a marina where hoodlums threatened to break your arms but just smashed a few toes."

I told Bowie that was ridiculous. The guys had tried to beat me out of $46,000 after I'd already lost the $10,000 to $15,000 I'd initially put up. But I told him I addressed the phony 46 grand and even paid that off at 20 cents on the dollar.

When I left Kuhn's office with Carpenter that day, I wasn't sure what to expect. Since I'd been a dupe and not a bookmaker, and Kuhn now knew it, Carpenter told me he thought I'd get a short suspension but be reinstated by the opener.

On Thursday, February 19, *Sports Illustrated* began hitting the streets. The cover showed a glowering picture of me, hat pulled down, with the words, Denny McLain and the Mob—Baseball's Big Scandal.

The story was written by Morton Sharnik and started with the bold heading, Downfall of a Hero. Under that it read, "Poor, dumb Denny McLain, the star pitcher of the Detroit Tigers, was a partner in a bookmaking operation during the 1967 baseball season and became inextricably involved with mobsters. Now he is paying the terrible price."

The article accurately uncovered my relationship with Roberts and Gazell, but then veered in such a bizarre, fantastic direction that I started getting hot flashes along with an alarming sense of doom. Sharnik wrote that Ed Voshen, the guy who allegedly won the $46,000 on the Williamston Kid on August 4, 1967, went "from mobster to mobster, seeking influence to enable him to collect his money. He was finally granted an audience with Tony Giacalone, the 'voice in the street'—or enforcer—for Joe Zerilli, the Detroit Cosa Nostra boss."

According to *SI*, Giacalone decided not to intervene because his men had no connection with the Flint handbook. But then Sharnik took the fantasy a step further, saying that Giacalone later went to jail for refusing to talk to a grand jury that was investigating him. Soon after he got out, claimed Sharnik, a teamster lawyer named George Mantho approached Giacalone, again asking the mob boss to intervene. Giacalone then told Mantho to take care of it on his own.

Unfortunately, that wasn't enough for a good cover story—especially one labeled Baseball's Big Scandal. Sharnik related my mound woes in September and went into five "versions" of how I injured my left foot on September 18, 1967, after getting chased by the Red Sox in two innings. Included in the versions was the truth, that I fell asleep watching TV and my foot fell asleep with me. I heard a noise in the garage, woke up, and the ankle bent under me.

The article included a Lolich version that I kicked a water cooler and then brought Giacalone back for another possible version:

> McLain was ordered to report to Giacalone's boat well; Tony wasn't as uninterested in the debt as he had professed. Once McLain was there, Tony Giacalone and his brother Billy, another Mafioso, went into their "angry act." Giacalone is under the impression that he's a great psychologist, that he can outpsych anyone. He gave McLain the full act, including his famous stare. Then he brought his heel down on McLain's toes and told him to get the money up.

After I met with Kuhn, the FBI interviewed me in Jim Campbell's office regarding the national gambling probe. An agent had asked, "Do you know Mr. Giacalone?" I thought he was asking about some guy named "Jack Aloney," and I said, "I've never even heard of Mr. Aloney." These guys had guns and badges on and I was scared to death. They're asking me about Billy Jack, Bobby Jack, Jackie Jack—hell, I don't know. But when I said "Aloney," both agents almost fell off their chairs laughing.

It was all staggering. How had it escalated from getting beaten out of some money by Roberts and Gazell into all this craziness about mob bosses and foot stomping? It was true that Ed Voshen died in a car crash a year later, but Voshen was a sick gambler who had fallen into deep debt. It gave the *Sports Illustrated* piece a final mystery for its readers to ponder, leaving unanswered whether Voshen's death might have somehow been related to all the sordid stuff attached to me.

Who'd given *Sports Illustrated* the story anyway? Sure as shit, Sharnik never hung out at a dive like the Shorthorn. But Doug Mintline did. Mintline covered the Tigers for the *Flint Journal*. Flint is about 70 minutes north of the ballpark, and Mintline's favorite local gathering hole was—you guessed it—the Shorthorn. Mintline was a regular, drinking with everyone from the owner on down to Roberts and Gazell. Mintline chain-smoked, drank, and gambled. These were the good old, "boys will be boys" days, and Mintline was definitely one of 'em.

Mintline was also close to *Detroit News* sportswriter Pete Waldmeir. By the way, Tigers general manager Jim Campbell met very people few he hated. Mintline and Waldmeir were two that he despised—and Mintline the most.

The two drunks, Mintline and Waldmeir, were inseparable in the press box. They concocted this story with allegations they got from another Shorthorn regular, the mentally incapacitated Flint police chief James Rutherford. There was very little crime in Flint in the late '60s. The biggest horror stories would be a white girl dating a black guy, somebody at the Buick plant missing his jumper cables, or people running red lights.

The police chief's original story to Mintline and Waldmeir was that organized crime wanted to break both of my arms, not my foot. I believe that Waldmeir was the one who called *Sports Illustrated* and fed them all of this as they worked a story on the national gambling probe.

Both *Sports Illustrated* and the commissioner's office had told Bill Carpenter words to the effect, "You have two writers in Detroit who don't care much for you." Carpenter's reply was, "Wouldn't that be an upset?"

I met Mintline when I made it to the big leagues, and he loved me when I bought him drinks. But like many of the writers, Mintline eventually stopped liking me because I became arrogant. I know it. I allowed myself to blur the line between media and athlete, and that's exactly why ballplayers should never befriend the media. I allowed myself not only to get involved with the various low-lifes at the Shorthorn, but I also allowed my lifestyle to be exposed to mean-spirited drunks like Waldmeir and Mintline.

In evolving into a young, budding baseball star, I knew I was becoming increasingly boastful, but I saw myself as playful, not nasty. I got up every day thinking of lines to feed the writers. I became the imp Joe Falls called me in a *Sport* magazine article and I loved it. The better I became as a pitcher, the better I could feed my never-satisfied quest for attention.

In 1966 I'd given Waldmeir the quote about the Tigers being "a country club team—the players do whatever they want." My purpose was to direct it at my teammates for having a relaxed attitude. Two managers had died, and players were taking advantage of the situation. It's amazing how guys won't run sprints or work on the sidelines to maintain themselves. I was trying to light a fire, but it came out in print as anti-management.

After Jim Campbell made me deny the "country club" quote, Waldmeir had been understandably embarrassed by my retraction. I had not only impugned his journalistic integrity, but I had also jeopardized his main reason for going to the ballpark—to eat free food and pound down free booze in the press lounge.

After I made my next colossal verbal blunder—the 1968 "Detroit fans are the worst" tirade, ripping me seemed to become a mission of Waldmeir's. There were obligatory things he had to say about me when I was beating everybody in '68 and '69, but he hated my bragging, showboating, flamboyant lifestyle.

Top-level athletes need to be extremely protective and most are. But I didn't understand the meaning of keeping people at arm's length. It was pathetic how I allowed myself to believe that the reporters were my friends and that if I fed them good lines, they'd want to keep me on their side. Now it was 1970, and the realization of how wrong that concept was became more and more apparent and devastating by the day.

On February 19, the day that *Sports Illustrated* arrived in most mailboxes, Kuhn suspended me for half the season—April 1 to July 1—and released this statement:

> I have suspended Denny McLain from all baseball activities pending the completion of further investigation and my review of facts obtained therefrom. I based the initial suspension substantially upon certain admissions made candidly to me by McLain. These admissions related to his involvement in purported bookmaking activities in 1967 and his associations at that time. The action taken today is not based on allegations contained in a magazine article, many of which I believe will prove to be unfounded.
>
> In January 1967 McLain played an engagement at a bar in Flint, Michigan, and there became acquainted with certain gamblers said to be involved in a bookmaking operation…. While McLain believed he had become a partner in this operation and has so admitted to me, it would appear that in fact he was the victim of a confidence scheme. I would thus conclude that McLain was never a partner and had no proprietary interest in the bookmaking operation.
>
> The fair inference is that his own gullibility and avarice had permitted him to become the dupe of the gamblers with whom he associated. This, of course, does not remove the serious dereliction on McLain's part of associating with the Flint gamblers.

Welcome to My Nightmare

There is no evidence McLain ever bet on a baseball game or that McLain ever gave less than his best effort while performing for the Tigers. McLain's association with gamblers was contrary to his obligation as a professional baseball player to conform to high standards of personal conduct, and it is my judgment that his conduct was not in the best interests of baseball.

Under the circumstances it is my judgment that McLain's suspension should be continued until July 1, 1970.

Players Association chief Marvin Miller was furious, telling reporters, "Bowie called McLain into his office and, like a forgiving uncle, said, 'Tell me about it, Denny.' Denny then speaks and discovers he's incriminated himself."

As for Kuhn's "allegations will prove unfounded," *Sports Illustrated* responded, "If it isn't true, then why did they suspend him?" Good question.

Terrified and not wanting Kuhn to slap me again, I flew to my winter home in Lakeland, and a swarm of reporters met me at the airport in Tampa. I was quoted: "I think a few people tried and hanged me. Very few of the magazine's allegations are true. The suspension was unfortunate, but it was all Commissioner Kuhn could do under the circumstances. He did the right thing, but I'm asking for the benefit of the doubt and I apologized to him. I can't go into detail since I'm under supervision of the grand jury in Detroit and also the continuing investigation of Commissioner Kuhn."

For the first time in my life, I was measuring every word. I also told the impromptu news conference, "I have to get a job immediately because of my financial predicament. What am I going to do for money? I've got a family to take care of. The last two weeks has put me under pressure and some of it might be deserved. I'll also tell you again that the *Sports Illustrated* story is just too unbelievable, but I can't say any more at this time."

I Told You I Wasn't Perfect

People like Marvin Miller were harder on Kuhn than I could safely be, but the fact was that Kuhn had taken my information and then stuck it up my ass. I understood that he'd been under pressure. He worked in New York, and the reporters in New York were animals. He felt pressure to do something about me—and he succumbed.

It had been just a year since Kuhn replaced William Eckert, the "unknown soldier" as commissioner. He had already avoided a threatened player strike over the pension plan; seen the Curt Flood case move past him to the Supreme Court; and convinced Hawk Harrelson to "unretire" and accept a trade from Boston to Cleveland. Kuhn had strongly displayed his anti-gambling stance, having convinced the Braves owners and A's owner Charlie Finley to divest of stock in a company that owned gambling facilities in Las Vegas.

In response to my suspension, the level of hysteria surrounding the *Sports Illustrated* article seemed to grow out of control. Fred Down, a writer for UPI, wrote:

> This is baseball's worst scandal since eight members of the White Sox were banned for life for allegedly throwing the 1919 World Series. Denny will not be forgiven because he dragged baseball's name into the gutter from which it was lifted 50 years ago after the Black Sox Scandal. Asked what he wanted out of life, McLain once said, "I want to make a $100,000 salary, and I want yachts and huge houses, maybe palaces. I want all the money I can spend, and brother, that's a lot."

The fantasizing and bragging was coming back to haunt me. And the fact that I hate boats would never get in the way of a good rave, with reporters hanging on my every word.

Welcome to My Nightmare

Rick Talley in the *Chicago Sun-Times* wrote, "Kuhn says he only suspended Denny for 13 weeks because he was duped and really wasn't part of the bookmaking operation he thought he was part of. In other words, since he was such a bad bookmaker, he gets less of a suspension."

Kuhn had determined, at least to this point, that I hadn't booked bets or bet on baseball, yet he was still compelled to suspend the two-time reigning Cy Young Award winner for half a season.

I still believe that the reason Kuhn came down so heavily on me was that a rumor hung out there that I'd fixed a game. Even though Kuhn said in his statement that there was no evidence I ever bet on a baseball game or gave less than my best effort, he was hearing things. One rumor had Billy Giacalone making big bets on the Red Sox and Twins down the stretch in '67 and then betting heavily against me in the final game of the season. It followed, then, that perhaps I faked my injury so "Billy Jack" could win big money against the Tigers.

Kuhn said I'd been a "dupe" and all *Sports Illustrated* could say for sure was that I owed some bad guys some money. But you could suspend hundreds of major leaguers for taking action or betting on sports other than baseball. Gambling is part of the baseball culture. We gambled at cards every day on the road. It just didn't add up to suspend me for half a season.

When Kuhn had asked us about fixing games, Carpenter shot back at him, "Bowie, the guy won 108 games in five years—do you really think he threw a game?" Since the fixing rumor was looking like a bogus witch-hunt, Carpenter thought that Kuhn should have allowed me back for the start of the season.

Mintline was quoted in the *Sporting News*: "In the spring of '67 McLain called in bets from the phone in the press lounge in Lakeland. I was shocked…because he flaunted it before sportswriters while in uniform at the stadium. *Detroit News* reporter George Cantor and a photographer were also in there." Mintline added that he told

153

Mayo Smith and Jim Campbell about it, but neither levied action against me for it.

I may have called in a bet or two when Mintline or Waldmeir were coming around the corner. If somebody heard me make a bet on a game then so be it. I was an arrogant ass, but I didn't go out of my way to announce to people that I was gambling.

A *Detroit News* follow-up to the *Sporting News* article featured the headline, Tiger GM Knew about Denny's Bets. Campbell was quoted: "That's unfair. It sounds like I approved of something. You don't know how it tears me up to have to say 'no comment' every day. Denny is my friend. Don't think this baseball team is bailing out on Denny. Don't think we've washed our hands of him because he's having hard times."

Dick Young ran with the pressroom phone story in the *New York Daily News*: "McLain, using the phone from the Tiger training camp, made sizable bets on basketball games. He made them in the presence of newspapermen. This would tend to support several claims, including the one by McLain that he is stupid."

No doubt about it. I was 23 in 1967 and had put my career in jeopardy. Now it was 1970 and I was in deep shit and also had a bad arm. Even in the best of worlds I didn't know how long I could pitch, and I had no way of knowing where this investigation might still lead. I found myself thinking that a half-season suspension wasn't so bad. There was nothing new to reveal—I'd told Kuhn everything, but I was always expecting that the other hand was coming from around the corner to crack me.

Fortunately, if Jim Campbell hadn't stepped to my defense and helped me out with money from time to time, things would have really been tough. I'd made the club a ton of money both at home and on the road in '68 and '69, and owner John Fetzer had given Campbell carte blanche to come to my rescue.

Welcome to My Nightmare

Although I was suspended without pay, Campbell continued to funnel my salary to IMG to cover my legal fees and basic expenses.

I also retained at least one media ally, TV sportscaster Dave Diles. Diles knew Tony Giacalone and took him to lunch to see where he was regarding Denny McLain. He then brought Giacalone in the studio for a live broadcast and asked him, "Did you ever step on Denny McLain's foot to prevent him from pitching or whatever else?"

Giacalone said, "I have never met, talked to, or had lunch with Mr. McLain. We'll take a lie-detector test to prove it. And just so you know: I don't like baseball—and I don't own a boat."

Spring training began in Lakeland without me, but not without the media working extensions of the story. Some were confused by it all, with Willie Horton saying, "I'm plenty worried. I hope nothing happens to Denny." Gates Brown, another good friend, didn't want to make things worse and simply said, "I just can't understand it all."

Bill Freehan had written a book in the off-season called *Behind the Mask*, and Freehan was dubbed by a UPI writer as "the unofficial leader of the Tigers." Freehan criticized me in the book, saying, "McLain's off-the-field antics split the team in '69. Some of us felt that anything he did off the field was okay, and some felt he should have been held to the same rules. McLain would take off in his plane after a game and wouldn't show up until 20 minutes before he was to pitch. I like to talk to my pitchers before games." Of my current situation, Freehan added, "The players are in the dark about his problems, and I think he owes us an explanation."

Jim Northrup had some fun with it. On the first day of spring training he playfully pounded his bat on the toe of a TV guy and said, "Now give me that $5 you owe me."

Joe Falls covered the opening of Tigers spring training for the *Sporting News*:

155

Opening day at Tigers camp is like a three-ring circus, and McLain wasn't even there. You wonder just what sort of society we are living in when a young man playing a boy's game can command such attention and take such a hold on people as Denny has done these past few weeks.

Never in the history of sports has there been a performer quite like this lad. Even if it kills him, he is determined to live the grand life—to do what no man has done before. He upstaged the (1969) All-Star Game, and he upstaged the World Series by carrying on a running battle with the press of Detroit.

He is as bold and brazen as they come—even to the point of making bets in front of newsmen. Doug Mintline of *Flint Journal* saw him make three bets in the pressroom at Marchant Stadium in '67. He then flaunted them in front of Mintline—even to the point of throwing the phone at Mintline when Mintline couldn't help him with his bets. Mintline told the Tigers to handle it rather than write a story and disappoint kids who look up to McLain. He warned that if it happened again, he'd write about it. The calls stopped.

I had three months to kill and needed to stay in shape and make some extra dough. Carpenter booked me a few speaking engagements in South Florida, and I'd stand there as long as they fired the standard questions: "How do you feel about the suspension? How's your family taking it?" I told them, "We're all living through it—it's been an experience."

Campbell hired Jim Hendley, a former minor-league catcher and the basketball and baseball coach at Lakeland High, to work me out after school. I'd hit golf balls waiting for Hendley to get off work.

Welcome to My Nightmare

I must've hit a thousand balls a day, and it helped my hands, forearms, and arms. I'd get in the sand trap for an hour and hit 200 balls; my short game got really good. Then at about 4:30 Jim would run me up and down the stands and catch for me.

I was due back on July 1, and Campbell told me I'd start that very night. I'd face live major-league hitters with no spring training and no professional hitters to test me. I never got to really exert myself in Lakeland because nobody could hit. Hendley would put his high school hitters in there against me—but am I really in the ninth inning of a game that counts? I'm throwing against a 17-year-old who's never seen a real curveball in his life. The kids had a great thrill, but there was no way I could be ready.

Campbell flew down and took me out to dinner one night in June and asked, "How are you feeling?"

I told him I was nervous as hell and he said, "That'll go away as soon as you step out there." He asked, "Have you pitched to many guys down here?"

I said, "Yeah, but they're all 15 years old." Campbell laughed and said, "This is the Show, and you've gotta go out there and dance for as long as you can."

As I got ready to fly to Detroit near the end of June, Kuhn called and wished me good luck.

On June 30, the day before my return, I still wasn't even allowed to go to the park. A Waldmeir story in *The Detroit News* ripped the Tigers for announcing my return well in advance so as to boost sales. More than 50,000 fans were expected to see me face the Yankees.

"McLain," wrote Waldmeir, "has no more business being out there than Tiny Tim does."

I got to the clubhouse at about 4:00 on July 1, just before the reporters were allowed in. There had to be 50 of them crowded in the hall waiting for me. Somebody had tipped off Freehan that I was about to enter the clubhouse. Trainer Bill Behm came out to help usher me through the crowd.

157

Unfortunately, the Beemer forgot to have me come in first. As the door opened, Freehan threw a bucket of water intended for me that totally doused Behm. It was a great welcome back. We had a good clubhouse in Detroit—always fun, always something going on.

A crowd of 53,863 came to the park that night, the biggest in Tiger Stadium since 1961. When I walked out to warm up about 20 minutes before the game, they gave me a warm welcome. When we came back out to start the game, they cheered wildly.

I pitched into the sixth and left trailing 5–3. They gave me a standing ovation as I walked off, despite having yielded five earned runs on homers by Jerry Kenney, Thurman Munson, and a blast by Bobby Murcer off the facing of the third deck that chased me.

It turned into a great game as my teammates fought back against Gary Waslewski and Yankee relievers Jack Aker, Lindy McDaniel, and Ron Klimkowski. In the eleventh, Mickey Stanley singled to center off Steve Hamilton, scoring Don Wert for a dramatic 6–5 Tiger win.

I waited for the 75 reporters who'd come from everywhere to cover the game. Not surprisingly, they chose to all but ignore the guys who won the game and crowded around me instead. I told them, "I'm very happy. I didn't know what to expect. This whole thing has done some good things for me. I've found out a lot of things about myself. It's evident that my judgment hasn't been very good."

When asked about the ovation that greeted me when I took the mound in the first, I told them, "I'm not an emotional guy, but I got so choked up I thought I was going to swallow my tongue. I didn't realize how big a thing it was until I got out there."

A headline in the *Chicago Daily News* called me "baseball's repentant sinner." Of the 53,000-plus it said, "There is nothing like a little sin to make the turnstiles spin."

I was pleased to see Jim Campbell make a few bucks off the game, seeing as how he had supported me during my exile. Unfortunately, as the season rolled on, Jim could also see that I wasn't the same pitcher who had won 55 games the last two years. Near the end of my time in Lakeland, as I was trying to crank up my velocity, the rotator cuff had popped again.

It took me six starts to get a win. On July 21 we beat the Twins 5–2, and I pitched into the eighth until Caesar Tovar lined one off my shinbone and ended my night.

But most of it was pretty bad. On August 26 I was 3–4 and had a rough night against the Angels and Clyde Wright at Tiger Stadium. I gave up a homer to Roger Repoz in the third and fell behind 4–0. My inability to get people out, throw hard, or put the ball where I wanted it was driving me crazy. Home plate umpire Bob Stewart was calling a tight strike zone, and when he called ball four on Ken McMullen, I went off on him loudly enough for the writers to hear it in the press box.

In the eighth, McMullen hit a two-run homer, scoring Alex Johnson to put the Angels ahead 6–0. Mayo came out and pulled me. As I headed to the dugout, the fans who had welcomed me so warmly on July 1, sang, "Good-bye, Denny." They had done it when I'd gotten pulled in my previous start, and I knew at that point that things would never be the same in Detroit.

I was at a profound career low point, and I couldn't find anything upbeat to say to the writers. One of them felt it important to point out, "There was more booing than in any game since you got back." I answered, "I didn't hear it."

Another genius asked, "Think you can get to .500?"

"I presume so," was my polite response. Then I growled, "What kind of a dumbshit question is that?"

The headline in *The Detroit News* over Watson Spoelstra's game story was, Denny Booed, Cusses Ump. I got to the ballpark the next night and decided to have some fun with the writers. I told Sparma to get the bucket ready, and when Jim Hawkins of the *Free Press* sat down on the stool by my locker, I snuck up behind him and poured the water on his head.

Hawkins took it for the practical joke it was, and we had a laugh. I then sent the clubhouse guy out to the field to tell Joe Falls or Spoelstra, whomever he saw first, that I wanted to see him in the clubhouse. I was sitting on my stool when Spoelstra came in.

I talked to him for a few minutes, shook his hand, and when he turned to leave, Sparma handed me the bucket and I got him, too. There were 15 guys watching, and they all howled with laughter. Spoelstra left the clubhouse and immediately called Campbell in the press box.

After the game, Campbell called Mayo Smith and me into his office and told me he was suspending me for a maximum of 30 days. I was stunned. I said, "Jim, it was a joke—Jim it was a little water. We were clowning around. Everybody was in on it."

But Campbell wouldn't budge.

I was furious and in total disbelief at his overreaction. I got down on my knees and begged him to trade me. I said, "Get me the f*ck out of here. I can't take it anymore."

"You'll get the f*ck out of here when I tell you to get out of here," Campbell roared in return. I got up and slammed the door so hard the stadium had to shake. The next day he sent me a note: "You haven't gotten your trade and, by the way, you didn't break the door, either."

The newspapers went wild with the story, with *The Detroit News* blaring a front-page headline: 2nd Suspension for McLain to Cost Him $500 a Day.

The article, in part, said the following: "The suspension by Campbell was tough action on what was seemingly regarded as a clubhouse prank. Campbell and Mayo Smith were under pressure last spring on charges that they granted McLain special privileges. Favoritism for McLain was spelled out by Freehan in his book *Behind the Mask*. Campbell was challenged last night and dealt a penalty that might change the direction of Denny's career."

Welcome to My Nightmare

The *News* article continued, "McLain has been on the muscle the last few weeks. He had been ejected in Oakland by Russ Goetz for arguing a judgment call in the same game when the organist played during his windup. Soon thereafter, McLain balked home a run and incurred the first ejection of his career."

Spoelstra wrote a separate story: Splashdown—How Denny Tricked Writer.

> Felix (Doc) Mayville, the security man at the home clubhouse door, carried a message to this writer before last night's game between the Tigers and Athletics at Tiger Stadium.
>
> "McLain wants to see you in the clubhouse," he said.
>
> It was 15 minutes to game time and the writer found McLain relaxing on a corner stool.
>
> "I didn't like the headline in your paper," said Denny. "The one about 'Denny Booed, Cusses Ump.'"
>
> "The story said the same thing as the headline," came the reply....
>
> The conversation remained low-key for several minutes.
>
> McLain mentioned that he appreciated the way this writer "stuck with me in spring training."
>
> This was while McLain was in Lakeland, Florida, sitting out the four-month suspension imposed by Commissioner Bowie Kuhn for gambling involvement.
>
> "We've always been friends," said McLain, sticking out his hand. "We're still friends."
>
> "Stay with it, Denny," I said.
>
> As the writer turned, Denny let him have it with the bucket of ice water from about 10 feet. The water found its target on the neck and shoulders.

Anybody can take a bucket of water when the circumstances are right, but this one came with shock and surprise.

The inside hurt was much deeper than the penetration of ice water on a man's jacket.

From the third-deck press box, this writer phoned General Manager Jim Campbell, sitting in club owner John E. Fetzer's enclosed box.

"When did this happen?" Campbell asked.

"Five minutes ago."

"This is terrible. I apologize to you for the club. It's something we can't put up with."

It was here that Jim Hawkins, baseball writer for the *Detroit Free Press*, filled in details on his clubhouse dousing less than an hour earlier.

Within 10 minutes, public relations director Hal Middlesworth announced McLain's suspension without pay for a maximum of 30 days.

"You acted fast," this writer said to Campbell.

"I put the story in front of him," said Campbell. "Denny agreed that was the way it happened."

Campbell phrased the charge against McLain as "conduct unbecoming to a professional baseball player."

This writer told Walter (Hoot) Evers, the new farm director, that he regretted seeing Denny miss any pitching starts.

"Forget it," said Evers. "It isn't just one incident. This thing with McLain has been building up for a long time."

When Campbell calmed down a few days later, he shortened the suspension by seven days. He knew that we had a fun clubhouse, and that had to play a role in his updated decision. Water buckets were only a part of it. A guy would stand in front of one of the big fans with baby powder, and a player or writer would walk by and he'd throw the talcum in the fan and it'd completely cover somebody.

Sure, there were players who didn't always like each other, but that happens when you're together seven months a year. But everybody had a good time, and one thing about our clubhouse was that you never knew what might happen tomorrow.

As I sat at home ready to get reinstated, I was informed that Kuhn wanted to see me in New York. I had no idea what it was about, but I knew it was big because Mayo, Campbell, Evers, and Dr. Livingood were all to meet me in New York for the meeting.

When I walked in and saw everybody looking glum, I sensed that something else big was about to hit me. Kuhn told me he was investigating reports that I had carried a gun on a West Coast trip in August and that he had told the Tigers not to reinstate me.

Bowie relayed one report that I'd carried a gun on the team plane and had also taken it into a restaurant in Chicago. When I had taken off my coat, he said, I displayed that I was carrying a gun in public. Although nobody specifically named him, the indication was that the confidential informant had been our backup catcher, Jim Price.

I said, "Price is my roommate and he knows I didn't have a gun." I owned a gun and owned it legally, but I never packed it.

I denied it to no avail. Kuhn suspended me for the rest of the season and released this statement to the media: "Certain allegations have been brought to my attention regarding Denny McLain's conduct. This suspension takes place while baseball investigators and McLain's attorneys study allegations with respect to the Detroit management and the information that on occasions McLain has carried a gun."

I couldn't understand why Price would do this. He was our union rep, and after the suspension came down, he told the press, "The way

I understand it, the gun story was reported to the ballclub by several people. I don't know if Denny was carrying it around and bragging about it or what. If he was, it was very foolish."

I used to get on Price a lot because he was one of the laziest, most untalented guys I'd ever seen in the major leagues. He couldn't hit or catch, and the only thing he could half-assed do was throw. But he was so slow taking the ball out of the glove that the runner had a chance of getting to third. He wasn't just a no-talent, but I despised people who put their nose up the boss's ass, and that's what Price was when he played. Actually, "played" is a misnomer. I mean when he sat on the bench or was a bullpen coach.

We all knew that Price was a back-stabbing bastard. I used to call him "Hedda Hopper—the rumor starter." He'd be the one to go home and tell his wife the players were f*cking around—while he's getting laid in the hotel every afternoon. Guys on the ballclub eventually stopped going out with him because they knew he was running home and telling people.

Waldmeir had come to New York to cover the story of my third suspension of 1970 and wrote about the vagueness of it all: "(Kuhn) offered the tidbit about Denny carrying a gun and then vanished with no explanation. What gun? When? Did he carry it this year? Last year? Was it a pistol? A rifle? A shotgun? The mysterious aura surrounding the commissioner's statement makes McLain sound like Jesse James in knickers."

The last player involved with a real gun was Frank Robinson, who had brandished one in 1961 in a Cincinnati restaurant when he said that a cook made a threatening movement with a knife during an argument. Robby was fined $250 and court costs, but NL President Warren Giles took no further action.

My world had collapsed. I felt persecuted and under siege from my teammates, the media, creditors—everybody. On top of it all, 1970 had proven my arm was all but dead.

Welcome to My Nightmare

Kuhn told me that the only way they'd reinstate me was if I went through a battery of tests. They all thought I was nuts, and Kuhn indicated that if I didn't get the tests, I might get banned for life. I began thinking of going to Japan for a change of scenery and telling them all to get f*cked.

The long and short of it was that I lacked the tools to understand why all of this had happened to me. I just wasn't mature enough to objectively examine my role in it. Although all three suspensions were somewhat arbitrary, the truth was that I'd allowed myself to get involved at the Shorthorn, and I'd bragged and used my on-field success to bend all the rules and alienate my teammates. I'd flaunted all of it by being a big shot and buying an airplane. And now that I couldn't pitch well anymore, guys like Freehan and Price wanted to see me get what I deserved.

Jim Campbell was my boss and friend, but along with Kuhn, he also thought I might be crazy. The chickens had come home to roost!

When you get punished repeatedly as a youngster, you get used to it, expect it, and in a masochistic way, create it. My dad had been dead for 10 years, but I kept on symbolically getting the belt even though it was no longer Tom McLain wielding it.

My father, mother, and the nuns at school had convinced me that I deserved to be punished, and it looked like I'd lived my life to affirm their assessment. In my house, every error or mistake in judgment drew harsh punishment. Now, even as an adult, I was continually putting myself at risk and then wondering why everybody wanted to beat me.

Since I started in pro ball, I'd pushed the edge—asked for the belt—and I'd gotten it from Glen Miller, Ira Hutchinson, Jim Campbell, and Bowie Kuhn. You could also throw in Doug Mintline, Pete Waldmeir, and dozens of sportswriters around the country who I didn't even know.

Anyway, I agreed to take the psychiatric tests. I didn't think I was nuts, but who knows? Maybe I was. I packed some clothes and prepared to spend three days at Henry Ford Hospital to find out.

Chapter 16

Ink-Stained Wretches

Before going any further, maybe it's time to talk about the media. My mother died in 2004, and when Sharon and I went through her belongings, we were shocked to find several large boxes of newspaper clippings and old magazines she'd saved. The stuff covered almost 40 years, from the early '60s all the way through the late '90s.

My mother had never been able to show me much love or affection, and she had barely acknowledged my career. I still can't fathom what she was all about, but in saving thousands of clippings and old magazines, she must've felt some kind of emotion.

In looking through some of the stuff, an article by Joe Falls in the December 11, 1965, issue of *The Sporting News* caught my eye. It was titled, Denny McLain, King of the Keyboard.

Falls wrote: "What Denny has more than anything else is an innate honesty that sets him apart from any athlete I've ever met…he is the most mature 21-year-old athlete I've ever known; he knows it could all end tomorrow."

Of my 14 strikeout relief performance against the Red Sox in '65, Falls commented, "He did it with poise uncommon to one so young."

But six years later, in an article titled, The Mystery of Denny McLain, written for the 1971 *True Baseball Yearbook*, Falls's prose took on a very sarcastic tone:

Denny, you see, has done it all. He's flown the fastest planes, dated the prettiest girls, appeared in the gaudiest nightclubs, had his picture on *Time, Newsweek,* and *Sports Illustrated.* He appeared on the *Tonight Show* with Johnny Carson, the *Joey Bishop Show,* the *Steve Allen Show,* and the *Dick Cavett Show.* It's been one mad maze of lights, cameras, action. He has upstaged the All-Star Game by showing up late and upstaged spring training by drawing the first of his three suspensions. Denny revels in this. Denny wants it all.

Me? Revel in the media? Damn right, Joe. Baseball was all show biz, and that's why there were writers covering it in the first place. And nobody, including Joe Falls, can imagine how much I craved the attention. Put me, a kid whose sense of worth came from playing baseball, in front of a bunch of attentive, jock-sniffing men with pens and microphones, and you've got all the elements you need for headline-making quotes.

Most people fear public speaking and being under the gun in pressure situations. I'm the polar opposite. I'm unhappy when I'm *not* in the public eye—I'm an entertainer, and performing is where I was always most comfortable with myself.

I wanted the attention of the writers so badly that I'd get depressed between starts because they weren't in front of my locker. I wanted to talk about anything and everything in grand fashion and be the center of attention.

I've been in situations where a writer's pen ran out of ink and I've given him the one out of my pocket.

By 1965, just my second full year with the Tigers, I'd become a caricature of the baseball quote machine that Joe Falls tried to create. Falls had me in his sights my entire career in Detroit.

Ink-Stained Wretches

It was different in the 1960s. The writers ate with us, traveled with us, played cards with us, and messed around with us much more so than they do with players today. People also relied on the papers much more back then, and without videotape, television really couldn't cover us in any kind of depth. The top writers were egomaniacs, just like the players. They were frustrated jocks and wanted their readers to look at them as part of the team.

Back then, there were fewer degrees of separation than you might suspect. Players and writers would loan each other money on long road trips. How about that for a conflict of interest? There's a writer who still owes me money from a card game.

In my playing days, we didn't make much more money than the writers did, which further fueled their imagination that they were a part of us.

But that's where they missed the boat. Not only aren't they in the game, but most players mistrust and even disdain reporters.

Some players learn how to spin the writers as well as the story. No matter what I said or how I said it, they wrote it all down. They would use adjectives to describe how you said it, why you said it, and when you said it. The more sensational the one-liner you gave them, the more pronounced your ability to control them. God knows I love the control of the moment, and when I had writers in front of me, I felt like the puppet master.

I laugh when players who get burned by the media say they don't read the papers. That's bullshit. Every player reads the papers, and any player who says he doesn't is full of it. They sneak it in the bathroom and they may even use it to line the birdcage, like I did with Falls's column for a long time. But before the parakeet shit on it, you better believe I read it.

There's never been a player who doesn't like reading his name in the paper in a positive way, and they all want to be the guy who leads the story.

We had become more open with the media in the '60s than the guys before us in the '50s. I recognized early on that the more I said and the more attention I got, the more I created opportunities outside the game. I knew that if I kept my name in the papers, sooner or later somebody would call to offer me an endorsement, a speaking engagement, or a club date.

But by '69, writers who'd previously sucked up to me started turning on me. I was still winning, but they'd grown tired of my act.

In '69, Bill Gleason wrote a *Chicago Sun-Times* article titled Critics of Baseball as Entertainment Chorus. Gleason said, "What the game needs is a few colorful guys like Ted Williams. Chicago's Dennis Dale McLain is filling that need 365 days a year. But it gets him resentment and ill wishers.

"He pops off, he retracts, and then he embellishes the retraction until it creates a new controversy. Baseball writers should say a little prayer for him every night. Instead, many rap him. That's like punching the mouth that feeds them."

When Gleason interviewed me for the piece, I told him, "I don't think the fans are resentful of me. I think the reaction against me stems from the sportswriters. Some of the writers who praised me a few years ago for speaking my mind are telling me now to shut up."

In the 1971 *True Baseball Yearbook*, when I was no longer "his boy," Falls ranted about all the times I'd been guilty of deceit and fabrication. He wrote of the time I told young Chicago sportswriter Brent Musburger that the Tigers were going to hire Billy Martin. Martin did eventually manage the Tigers, but I told him that three or four years earlier to purposely mess him up.

Falls wrote:

> Musburger went for it, and his paper carried the story big the next day.
>
> It was a flat-out fabrication. McLain even admitted it.
>
> "Why did you do it?" he was asked.
>
> "I don't know," he said.

"Don't you like the guy?"

"I don't even know him," he said smiling.

Of course I knew him.

What happened was that we had a day off, and Lou Boudreau, my father-in-law, was doing the annual Cubs–White Sox charity game at Comiskey Park. I went to see Lou and was sitting in the press box when Musburger, a whiz-kid writer who worked for the *Chicago Tribune*, sat next to me.

Musburger was about 25 at the time, and Lou hated him for being what he called the "biggest backstabber in the country." Lou told me, "Watch out for that son of a bitch."

According to Lou, Musburger started rumors.

Before Musburger approached me, I said to Lou, "Watch me get this prick."

He said, "What are you going to do?"

"You'll read about it."

Musburger came over and said, "Hey, good to see you, what's going on?" and all that kind of stuff.

So I laid a story on him, and he reported it to the world. It was a fabrication. He was a self-endowed I'm-better-than-the-players kind of guy. Musburger was a wannabe and a goody two-shoes who still plays that game. These guys conveniently forget that they ran around and did the same things that we all did, but now they're the judges and juries of sports.

Except for Musburger, I don't recall dramatically misleading anyone. I may have expanded a story a bit, but that was the puppet master dancing over the edge.

In the *True Baseball Yearbook* story, Falls was relentless:

During the '68 World Series, after he'd been beaten in his first two starts, he told me, in no uncertain terms, that he wouldn't pitch anymore—that his arm was hurting and he was through for the Series.... The day after that, with manager Mayo Smith undecided about whom he would pitch in the sixth game—McLain, Joe Sparma, or Earl Wilson—McLain called a Detroit radio man and said: "Hey, I'll give you a scoop—I'm pitching tomorrow. Mayo already has told me." He wanted to put one over on the *Free Press*.

As I explained earlier, I wasn't planning on pitching Game 6. I told everybody that. I'd struggled to throw eight innings combined in Games 1 and 4, and I couldn't lift my right arm. But there were no options back then. You can't call your attorney and say, "This is what they want to do with me." The only guy you can call is Jim Campbell, and he's gonna say, "Take the f*ckin' shots."

I took the shots and pitched Game 6. Had I wanted to burn the *Free Press*? Not really, but I did want to give another guy a scoop. Falls had a right to be pissed off. But I didn't care what he thought. Falls still loved writing about me and was still well paid to fill dozens of pages in national magazines with material about me. The difference was that now it was to point out my flaws and excesses.

Joe and I became close friends again at the end of his life. At some of my lowest points, Joe was thoughtful enough to keep in contact with me. God bless him. Joe died in 2004 and was one of the greats. He was also voted into the Baseball Hall of Fame in 2002.

I hope I had a little something to do with that.

Chapter 17

Teddy Ballgame

Like I said, after the three suspensions in 1970, I had to prove to Bowie Kuhn and Jim Campbell that I wasn't nuts. I checked into Ford Hospital and was put in a room with no TV and sat there while one doctor after another came in to interview me. On the third day, one of the shrinks gave me a bunch of plastic pieces—35 or 40 of them—with the instructions to fit them together as best as I could.

I hate jigsaw puzzles, and after about three minutes it became obvious to me that this pile of parts could never fit together. I thought, "Screw this," and sat with my arms folded. As soon as the guy walked in, I said, "Either this puzzle is total bullshit or I'm an idiot. You decide."

He said, "Good job. You're right. The pieces don't fit," and he went on to tell me that many patients actually see something in the puzzle and that can indicate a degree of insanity. I was released and flew to my winter home in Lakeland to wait out the off-season and see what the baseball powers had in store for me.

I found out later that the hospital reported directly to Kuhn and sent him this statement: "For three days Dennis McLain underwent tests from three eminent psychiatrists. We see no reason for McLain to undertake any further psychiatric treatment. He is not ill, although he has been subjected to emotional stress from his various involvements."

I was still just 26 and it had been a really rough year. Was I unsettled? Sure. But was I clinically nuts? I didn't think so, and thankfully they didn't either.

Kuhn explained to reporters that my suspension was purely gun-related, keeping the psychiatric testing a private matter. "It was typical flamboyance for McLain to do a thing like carry a gun. Also, the FAA is satisfied that McLain did not pilot a commercial flight without a license. McLain had boasted that he made money piloting private planes. It came down to the gun. An $11,000 loss in salary was adequate punishment for that."

A few days later I was playing golf at Lone Palm Country Club, a beautiful course in Lakeland, and was on the farthest hole from the clubhouse when a kid in a golf cart drove up to tell me I had an important phone call. I hopped in his golf cart and, when I finally got to the pro shop, whoever had called was still on hold.

I picked up the phone, said hello, and heard a booming voice say, "Denny McLain, this is your new manager in Washington, Ted Williams."

After the initial shock and realization that I was headed to the perennially worst team in baseball, Williams added, "I'm not entirely convinced that this is the right thing for our ballclub, but now that you're here, let's try to do what's best for the team."

In other words, "I didn't want to make this trade, but…." I found out later that Ted had also trashed the deal in the papers and that he and Senators owner Bob Short almost went to blows over trading for me.

Great way to start, huh? You've got a manager who doesn't want you and a club that's destined to lose 100 games!

When I got to my house, the phone was already ringing and didn't stop all day, as one reporter after another wanted the story. I was as gracious as I could be regarding all involved in the deal. I was quoted in *The*

Detroit News, "I want to thank everybody from the clubhouse man to Mr. Fetzer. I mistreated my friendship with Mr. Campbell near the end. I'm sad about leaving Detroit. The majority of the fans were behind me."

In the *News* article, Campbell said, "We've had Denny for seven years. He's a great pitcher and we wish him well."

I later learned that when the 1970 season had been winding down and I was on suspension, Campbell had begun talks with Short about moving me. Williams had been fishing at his home in Islamorada in the Florida Keys when Short called to tell him that the "Tigers wanted Ed Brinkman, Aurelio Rodriguez, and Joe Coleman for McLain."

Williams told Short to tell the Tigers to "go f*ck themselves." Brinkman was a great fielding shortstop, and the 22-year-old Rodriguez had already been called the next Brooks Robinson.

When Short made the trade despite Williams's warning, Ted told the writers, "I told Bob all year, 'Don't trade Brinkman and Rodriguez.'" Short not only traded them but also threw in pitchers Joe Coleman and Jim Hannan. Along with me, the Senators got outfielder Elliott Maddox, Don Wert, and a pitcher named Norm McRae.

The genesis of the deal on the Senators' end had taken place a year earlier when I had flown on Short's private plane. We had both been at a dinner together in Minneapolis and, knowing I was going to be one of the speakers at another dinner the next night in New York, Short asked me if I'd like a ride rather than fly commercial.

Short was a delightful guy with a dynamic personality and on the flight had said, "I'd love to have you in Washington someday." I told him to wait until I got to the back end of my career and maybe I'd hang my hat with a club like the Senators. He said at the time, "You never know."

What Short did know was that he wanted to move his team to Texas. He was thinking ahead and wanted a big name to help sell tickets in

Washington and then set up lucrative radio and TV contracts in Texas. In Washington, Short had the worst radio and TV deals in all of baseball.

The Senators were an expansion team that came into existence as a replacement for the old Senators, who moved to Minnesota in 1961 to become the Twins. The old Senators had been perennially pathetic and the new Senators kept the tradition alive, losing 100 games or more in their first four years.

In December 1968, Short sold his Los Angeles Lakers for $5 million to Jack Kent Cooke, borrowed $7 million more, and paid $9.4 million for controlling interest in the Senators.

Short then lured Williams from his boat in the Florida Keys with a big salary and set him up, all expenses paid, at the Shoreham Hotel in D.C. With perhaps the greatest hitter in baseball history making his managerial debut, Short presented his '69 Senators with the phrase, "It's a whole new ballgame."

The hiring of Williams had been a surprise because Williams had always said that he didn't want to manage. But he came back because Sears Roebuck was threatening to pull his endorsement deal. Teddy Ballgame hadn't played for a decade, and too many kids didn't know him.

Sears had been paying him $100,000 a year, and it was the best endorsement deal any athlete ever had. All he had to do was hang out in the Keys and fish and make the occasional personal appearance. When Ted put himself back in the spotlight with the Senators job, Sears re-upped him for even bigger money.

Right on cue, Williams led the 1969 Senators to an 86–76 mark, a 21-game improvement, and the best record a Senators team had enjoyed since World War II. Attendance rose by almost 400,000 to 918,106, and things looked promising.

With the club apparently reenergized, Short's marketing people raised the ante with, "'70 belongs to the Senators."

Teddy Ballgame

Alas, the team fell to last in the East in 1970, losing their final 14 games. Attendance plummeted, and after the 10th consecutive loss as the season wound down, pitcher Dick Bosman said, "Five, maybe six key guys weren't putting out and they should be ashamed."

The Williams magic was long over by that point. The players had tolerated Ted's sharp, witty barbs in 1969, but when reality set in during the '70 season, Ted became unbearable. Bosman was Ted's boy and tried to put it all on his teammates instead of pointing the finger at his utterly miserable manager.

To make matters worse, Short was upside-down financially. In September 1970 he had to sell pitcher George Brunet to the Pirates just to make payroll.

The oil crisis had hit in 1970 and that, coupled with a tanking ballclub, prompted Short to tell *LOOK* magazine, "It's more of a pain in the ass (owning a team) than it is fun. It's drudgery to be in over your head—and it's just because of the whole goddamn economy."

Short had tried everything in 1970—even a promotion called "Sweetheart Night," where he gave away free panty hose to every woman in the crowd.

Going into '71, Short was desperate. In two years of owning the club he was already $2 million in the hole and needed to make the franchise more attractive to pull off his secret plan to move to Texas. He needed assets in place, and I and a few more stars would help grease the move.

On November 3, 1970, Short sent three nondescript players to the Phillies for Curt Flood, one of the game's great outfielders. Flood had sat out the 1970 season while courageously taking his challenge to baseball's reserve clause all the way to the Supreme Court. The case was still pending, and Short convinced Flood that it wouldn't hurt his chances if he played at the same time.

Short also signed third baseman Joe Foy, who had played with Boston in the '67 World Series. "The book on Foy," Short said, "was that he drank, caroused, and associated with questionable people. Nothing else. They didn't say he couldn't play ball. And if he can't, what did I lose—$25,000."

Short now had his new "name" players: Flood, Foy, and me.

Flood had also just written a book called *The Way It Is*, in which he'd said he liked white girls and that they liked him, too. One newspaper headline called us: The Bob Short Freak Show. That one didn't bother me. The headline that did bother me was the one that called the deal with the Tigers: The Worst Trade Ever.

In regards to the three of us, Short told *LOOK*, "If these players weren't tainted, then how could I get them? Don't forget, I own an expansion club. I'd rather have a team with no stars, but until you can build a decent team, you'd better have stars."

The only other well-known Senator was left-fielder Frank Howard. Frank was 6'7" and showed up for spring training at 296 pounds, the heaviest player in baseball history. Nicest guy in the world, but Frank couldn't move 15 feet for a fly ball.

It *was* a freak show, starring Ted Williams as the biggest freak of all. I was standing on a platform with Flood and Williams at a photo op in Pompano Beach, Florida, that spring, when the photographer said, "Okay, guys, look serious."

I said, "What's it gotta be serious for?"

Flood says, "Don't you know, Denny? We're supposed to be mad at the world."

Truth is, we weren't at all mad at the world. And if we were, it still wouldn't be nearly as mad as all of us would quickly become with the great Ted Williams.

Since Ted had hit .406 in 1941, he had been one of the most powerful forces and personalities in all of sports. In *The Teammates*, David

Teddy Ballgame

Halberstam's story of a dying Williams being visited in his Florida home in 2001 by his former Red Sox teammates, Halberstam described the young Ted Williams that I came to know decades later. Halberstam talked of "the sheer force of Ted's unyielding personality," of Ted as "ever tempestuous, the man-child who dominated every conversation, who shouted others down, who never lost a single argument to anyone… because he shouted all the time and appointed himself judge and jury at the end of each argument to decide who won."

As a manager Ted was still the same man, certain that he had all the answers, assured that he didn't need to listen, and always displaying an attitude that he was on a pedestal and everyone else was looking up at him.

Early in spring training, Short took Ted and me to dinner in Pompano and said, "I like you both a lot. But you can't lose sight of the fact that you have roles here for me. I have to sell tickets to make this organization go. We need cash flow. You have to say the things I need said to generate money."

Ted and I came away all but hugging and kissing each other, determined to establish rapport. We shared conversations regarding our mutual love of aviation, and Ted captivated me with stories about being a fighter pilot in World War II. I listened in awe as he told of volunteering for the Korean War, willingly passing up the opportunity to earn one of the top salaries in the sport. He'd gotten shot down in Korea, yet came back to play some of his best ball ever. I told him, "You've got the biggest balls in the world for going back to Korea and doing what you did."

I'd just gotten additional aviation ratings, and a friend of mine owned a Twin Commander. One night I flew Ted to Orlando for a dinner, and we had a great time flying that night.

I wanted to play well for him, and I wanted to do everything I could for Short. I made all the appearances and said all the right things. But as time went on, I couldn't for the life of me understand what made the great Teddy Ballgame tick.

One day in spring training he said to me out of the blue, "McLain, what's dumber than one f*cking pitcher?" After I said, "Geez, Ted, what?" He bellowed, "I'll tell ya what is—it's two of you dumb f*cking pitchers." It wasn't a joke—the son of a bitch was serious. Not only was I in Washington, D.C., with 24 guys who couldn't play, but I had an uncouth manager who was the most ill-tempered human being I'd ever met.

One day early in spring training he came up to Flood and me in center field after our pictures had just appeared together on a magazine cover. He pointed his finger at us and said, "Let's never forgot who's running this club." Curt and I looked at each other, and Flood gently said, "Ted, we understand. You don't have to tell us that."

Williams desperately needed to be the center of the universe. It always had to be in the papers, "Ted said this," "This is what Ted's thinking," "This is what Ted did." And when Denny and Curt came on the scene and briefly moved him off the front page, he got all insulted and put off.

Sometimes it's 80 degrees and sunny in early March in Florida, and sometimes it's 50, windy, and cold as hell. On one of those nasty, bone-chilling early spring training days, a 20-year-old named Pete Broberg was pitching batting practice. Broberg was a typical young kid trying to make the team the first hour he puts on a uniform. He was throwing bee-bees on the second or third day of spring training. None of the hitters wanted to get in there because he was wild and balls were banging all over the cage.

Mike Epstein reluctantly stepped in and got hit right in the ass as he tried to turn away from one of Broberg's pitches. All the veterans were bitching and whining while Williams was behind the screen listening to all of it. Finally he says, "Give me a f*cking bat, you motherf*cking, syphilitic cocksuckers." His language was the worst. "Motherf*cking syphilitic cocksucker" was his favorite phrase, and he used syphilitic so often that I assumed he must have had syphilis at one time.

Williams grabbed a bat, told the "syphilitic cocksuckers" at the cage to get the hell out of the way, and stepped in against Broberg. Understand that Ted was 52 at the time. He took a wide one, and then Broberg threw his first strike of the day right down the middle. Ted hit a line drive over the right-field wall into the wind.

I was standing in right field shagging flies as the ball sailed out. We were all in awe. I yelled in to Williams, "Now get a f*ckin' glove and come play right field."

Williams was rough and gruff all the time. There was never, "Hey, Denny, how are ya today?" Obviously, Bob Short catered to his whims and allowed him to be this way with no recrimination. Not only did Williams live for free at the Shoreham Hotel, but Short paid for his hookers, the best-looking hookers in the league, too. Williams had both sides covered: he also had a young, gorgeous wife who stayed in Florida all season.

The story went that Williams met her in the first-class section of a flight. The guy was huge—6'4"—and he stretched out his legs under the seat in front and accidentally kicked her with a cowboy boot. She got up and said, "Would you mind taking your boot out of my ass"? It was the start of a perfect relationship. She was a beauty all right, but she was never around.

Another strange thing was that Williams always wore his Senators warm-up jacket. Not only did he never take it off—even in 90-degree weather—but he also never showered at the ballpark. He'd go back to the hotel in his stinking uniform and jacket, shower there, and then wait for the hooker to come over.

It didn't take me long to realize that there was total solidarity in the dislike of Williams. Ted just had no clue how to be nice. Most of his coaches couldn't stand him, either, with the exception of pitching coach

George Susce. Susce had played with Ted in Boston in the late '50s when he was coming up and Williams was nearing retirement. George had become Ted's lackey back then and was still trying to stick in the majors by catering to Ted's needs and whims.

If Ted sneezed, Susce would reach down and hand him his Kleenex. If Ted had ever stopped quickly, Susce's dick would've wound up in Ted's ass—that's how close they were to each other.

The saddest case of player abuse—and there were many—involved Flood. Williams was a racist, and Flood was too proud and too troubled at the time to tolerate his abuse. Flood hadn't played in more than a year while taking on the baseball establishment and needed some time to round into shape. He was still just 33 and had won the Gold Glove Award for National League outfielders every year from 1963 to 1969. The guy was a proven star.

But Flood got off to a slow start and, about two weeks into the season, Williams started platooning him. Just to make Flood more miserable, one night Ted had the gall to take him out in the seventh inning for a defensive replacement. A seven-time Gold Glove winner was removed for defensive purposes. It was ludicrous.

In Williams's old-guard mind, Flood was an ingrate who had insulted baseball with his lawsuit, and Ted would show him up despite the fact that Bob Short had brought Curt in to give us some profile and sell some tickets.

Flood grew up in Oakland and began his career in 1956 as an 18-year-old playing 3,000 miles from home in the Carolina League. He was demeaned and humiliated by teammates and animals in the stands who called him "nigger" and impugned his manhood. As a lonely teenager, the team bus would drop him off at the edge of town to stay in a fleabag black hotel while his white teammates all went to stay together.

Teddy Ballgame

Now at 33 and having come so far, Flood had too much pride and too many important issues to have to put up with an insensitive boor like Williams. Flood had a guaranteed contract for $110,000, and he needed it after being jobless in 1970. Our lockers were adjoining, and I tried to commiserate with him as best I could. But after 13 games, 35 at-bats, and 7 hits, Flood walked away from Williams, the Senators, and baseball. By the way, 7 for 35 wasn't all that bad on that club.

To make matters worse, a few weeks later, on June 19, 1971, the Supreme Court upheld a federal court judge's earlier ruling and denied Flood's injunction against Major League Baseball as well as denying him any damages.

We started the season 12–8 before losing four straight at home to the White Sox. That was all it took to send Ted into a full-fledged panic. He started platooning like crazy, and that's around the time Flood realized he just couldn't play for the guy.

A few weeks later, we were on the road and in the midst of an eight-game losing streak when Williams told us that there would be a 10:00 AM workout the next day. It was a bullshit move, especially because we had to play another game that night.

We were all pissed. I'd found a kindred spirit in Bernie Allen, a 32-year-old veteran who had the most tenure on the team, and the two of us took charge on this one. When Ted announced the morning workout on the bus back to the hotel that night, the revolt was underway.

Bernie and I told all the players to take a cab the next morning. We said, "Don't get on the team bus. If you can't afford the cab, we'll pay for it. But nobody is gonna take the goddamn bus." So the next day Ted, Susce, and the other coaches rode alone on a 40-seat bus. Ted went berserk, and for a few days he went around like the ship captain looking to string up the culprits who organized the mutiny. He called me into his office and said, "If it was you, I can't waive your ass, but if I find out there was anybody else, I'll get the motherf*cking syphilitic bastard."

Williams then got on an everybody-is-undermining-my-authority kick and stepped up his intimidation tactics. We'd read quotes in the paper like, "Half this club is over the hill, and the other half isn't ready for the big leagues." He was right. But you just don't say it. I wanted to throw it back in his face by telling him, "Some people also weren't ready to manage in the big leagues."

A leader can shit on somebody in his office, and it's not necessarily a big thing until it gets in the papers. In the 20 minutes he gave the writers after every ballgame, Ted would throw out cutting, counterproductive statements while telling the writers, "It's off the record." Then it becomes identified as "rumor has it," or, "a reliable source tells me." But it was Ted all the time.

We just couldn't accept Ted's egomania and the fact that he didn't give a shit about anybody. He always had to be the feature in everything written or said about the team. He wanted it to be known that Ted was the team, not the players. It was easy to understand why he had battled with the Boston writers his entire playing career.

We had a 29-year-old infielder named Tim Cullen who Williams demoralized when he told Cullen to quit "because his career was already behind him."

Williams loved to humiliate people in front of others. He said to Elliott Maddox before a game, "Do you think we can take a chance on you for defensive play?" Elliott assured him he could, so Williams said, "That's great—too bad you can't hit."

We tried to enjoy ourselves and remain focused despite our lack of talent and Williams's woeful leadership. The pitchers formed a club where we'd fine each other for walking the opposing pitcher or not backing up play. It was fun and good for morale—but Williams quickly intimidated us into stopping.

With Ted in a constant state of anger over all the undermining, we formed a group dedicated to his overthrow. Somebody then painted

Teddy Ballgame

"Bernie Allen—Imperial Wizard of the Underminers" on one of the bathroom stalls. The three stalls next to it read, "Denny McLain," "Tom McCraw," and on the fourth one, "Dick Billings and Tim Cullen." Cullen deserved his own stall, but there were only four of them.

Around the All-Star break, we had a team party at my place after a Saturday afternoon game. All the players were there with their wives, and at end of the night when everybody was sauced, the Grand Wizard, Bernie Allen, suddenly appeared with his court. They had the sheets and hoods on, and Bernie proceeded to read a long proclamation about what a rotten, no-good SOB Ted was. He finished by shouting: "This pledge of solidarity will remain in place forever."

We all raised our glasses and roared in approval. To this day, Sharon says it was one of the funniest things she's ever seen.

Bernie was traded to the Yankees after the season and told reporters about a confrontation he'd had in July with Williams. One day, according the Bernie, Williams had actually brought himself to say, "How are you?" Bernie answered, "I'd be better if I were playing more." The Great One never spoke to him again. New York writers quoted Bernie as saying that Ted was "the most egotistical man I've ever met in my life."

One day Ted called on Don Mincher to pinch-hit, but Mincher didn't hear him right away. Williams began bellowing, and Mincher never got out of the doghouse. After a series in May, Cullen threw his spikes into his locker and yelled loud enough for the coaches to hear, "There's just no way I can play for this man."

I went on the disabled list for a few weeks in July because my shoulder was aching so much that even cortisone wasn't helping. It was actually a relief because I hated going to the ballpark by then.

You couldn't have gotten close to Ted if you'd wanted to. He hated bad players and he hated stars. Who was left? In fact, at the end of his career, my father-in-law, Lou Boudreau, played with Ted in Boston in

'51 and '52. Lou commiserated with me, saying of Ted, "He was a great hitter but never gave a shit about anybody but himself."

One day outfielder Dick Billings made a comment on the bench like, "Just because you read a medical book it doesn't make you a good surgeon." The analogy to Ted as a manager was obvious. Williams charged over and cut loose on Billings. He was screaming, "That's what's wrong with you guys. You don't believe you can do anything. You don't believe you can hit a ball on the outside of the plate for a double down the right-field line. You don't understand what a cutoff man is." I tried to play peacemaker by saying, "Ted, you fail to realize that you had so much ability that you can't overlook the shortcomings of a normal ballplayer."

He yanked me in the third inning of that one, and I blew up on him after the game. He threw me out of his office and said, "It'd be best to sever our relationship."

Bob Short tried his best to keep the peace between us and called me into his office because word of the clubhouse war had reached him.

He asked, "How bad is it?"

I answered, "How bad is it? You should fire him. You can't believe what goes on. But I know you can't fire him, and other than that, there's nothing you can do."

It never got better because it couldn't.

By that point, anybody who came near me was in trouble, and I think that's why he cut loose on Billings. Guys used to stay away from me on the field. Even Frank Howard, who steered clear of the "Underminers" would say, "Denny, you get away from me."

On top of it all, Williams over-managed to an absurd degree. He'd order a guy with a good fastball to stick to the slider and curve. All Ted believed in were curves and sliders and more curves and sliders. Ted didn't want you throwing a fastball. He thought anybody could hit a fastball. I thought I'd done pretty well with mostly a fastball, but since Ted could always hit them, he didn't want us throwing any.

Don't get me wrong—no manager was going to win a pennant with this club. It was a great group of guys, but about the worst group you could put on the field. Except for Flood, Howard, and myself, this was a low-paid team, with most guys making $15,000 to $20,000 a year. But with Williams you couldn't even enjoy the game, and that made everyone play worse than they otherwise would.

It wasn't Williams's fault that the Senators were the worst team in baseball. No one who'd ever owned them had any money. And if the Senators did sign a guy who had potential, they'd trade him to make payroll. Bob Short had some wealth, but not enough to make a difference.

Still, you've got to work with what you have, and a good manager would have told his players that if they hustled and played hard, they wouldn't hear criticism from the manager's office. These were guys either trying to hang on in the majors or just become a team guy. But Ted thought that everybody should be able to hit like him, and he lacked the patience to teach anybody.

I'd laugh years later when I'd see him sit down and do a TV special with George Brett or Rod Carew and philosophize about hitting. But would he sit down with less talented players like Jim French or Tim Cullen, who needed the help? He was too intimidating to help a young player. And if you could find pictures of the Senators dugout back then, you'd see that nobody ever sat near him—except for Susce, of course.

The 12–8 start had been a positive thing. Ted should have just left everybody where they were and not over-managed. There was no reason to jump off the bridge, but the worst thing that had happened to Ted was 1969. He had that big winning season in his first year and believed he actually had something to do with it.

Ted was also small-minded enough to reveal his obsession with Red Sox star Carl Yastrzemski. If the situation demanded he walk Yaz with men on base, Williams would insist we pitch to him so as to embarrass him with men in scoring position. He wanted Yaz to look bad so that Red Sox fans would never forget the great Teddy Ballgame.

Williams had a hard and fast rule against golf. He said, "It's a thousand bucks if I even think you're playing golf." Needless to say, we defied him with a group called the "Touring Pros" and played every day on the road. He never got a dime from any of us.

I don't think I pitched that badly in 1971. Although I had 15 losses by the All-Star break, the most by any pitcher since 1960, I finished 10–22 with a 4.28 ERA, which was pretty good with that club. If I'd been with Detroit I might've won 20 that year. But nobody could hit or catch a ball. I had 300-pound Frank Howard playing left field for me. Bernie Allen used to say, "If it was to Frank's left we're okay because we have Flood or someone else in center. But anything to Frank's right is a ground rule double."

We lost 19 of our last 25 to finish 63–96, but not without some final drama. On September 14, in Cleveland, against the only team in the league that would finish with a worse record than ours, we were tied 5–5 when the game was called after 16 innings because of the 1:00 AM curfew.

The Indians came to Washington six days later and, after we completed the suspended game, I was scheduled to start. My record was 10–20, and I swear that Williams wanted me to become the first starting pitcher in 50 years to be charged with two losses in one day. The suspended game was to resume in the seventeenth inning, and Ted told me that the night was all mine.

I pitched three scoreless innings before we scored three in the top of the twentieth on an error, an infield single and a fielder's choice to take an 8–5 lead. Since the game had begun in Cleveland the week before, the Indians batted last and scored one off me to make it the 8–6 final.

I was credited with the win, and Ted's plot was foiled.

In the 20 innings of the suspended game, there were 30 walks issued, a new AL record for an extra-inning game. I pitched the nightcap, losing 3–1 for my 21st defeat. All of the exciting festivities that night were viewed by a listed attendance of 1,743. I didn't mistakenly leave out a digit. It was 1,743 fans. Don't laugh yet. The next day Bosman beat the Tribe 9–1 before 1,311 thrilled spectators.

The following day, September 22, 1971, Bob Short's wish came true. The American League owners, by a 10–2 vote, approved the move to Texas. In the media, Short said that the Senators had lost $3 million over the last three years. He was gracious in adding, "I wasn't able to do in Washington what I tried my best to do. I apologize to Senators fans for having to shift the club."

Commissioner Bowie Kuhn said, "It's a sad day for Washington, but the Texas area has long deserved major league baseball."

Even President Nixon piped in, saying, "It's very disappointing to lose the Senators."

Short, meanwhile, had negotiated the best stadium deal in history—$1 rent per year in Arlington. He appeared to undersell the Ranger's radio rights for just $10 million for 10 years, but got the cash up front. It was obvious that all he wanted to do was get to Texas, take the money, and then sell the club.

His other immediate order of business was to put the disastrous 1971 behind him and start selling the product in Texas.

The people he promoted heaviest were Howard, Dick Billings, and me. Frank had led the league in 1970 with 44 homers and 126 RBIs, and although he had fallen off in '71, he remained the team's high-profile hitter while I was the most promotable pitcher.

Bosman had a good year as the number two starter, but he had no personality and wanted to be left alone. Billings, Frank, and I began the job of going to lunches, talking to clients, and doing whatever we could to move tickets. Short even got me a radio show in Dallas after the season and paid me $800 a week plus hotel and food to keep pumping the product. He also helped me get an endorsement deal with a food supplier. I gave him what he wanted—a 31-game winner telling stories and hyping for him all over town.

Early in spring training, I read an article where Williams said that he'd sort of wished I'd lost 30 in '71. Quite the sarcastic humorist, he said, "It would be a nice touch if the same guy who won 30 also lost 30." I will say this—if I wasn't on the disabled list all of July when my shoulder was killing me, I could've come close. No one enjoyed the game more than I did when I was pitching, and I made 32 starts in '71 even with the trip to the DL.

Two weeks into spring training, on March 4, 1972, Williams called me into his office and said, "Bob Short's on the phone." I asked Ted what the matter was, and all he said was, "He wants to talk to you."

I was thinking somebody died or something.

"Hi Bob."

"I've got good news and bad news," Short said. "You and Ted are never ever going to get along…"

Before he could finish, I said, "Where are you sending me?"

"That's the good news. I made a deal with Oakland."

I perked up. "You gotta be kidding." Oakland was the club everybody wanted to play for.

And that was that. The Rangers got two pitching nonentities for me—Jim Panther and Don Stanhouse.

The Rangers would go 54–100 without me in the strike-shortened 1972 season, which was also Williams's last year as manager.

Teddy Ballgame

When Williams died in 2003, I thought back to when Ted and I had first spent time together, talking aviation and flying to Orlando—before the strains of the season pushed us apart.

It was sad and humiliating to see his name and legend tarnished when his children fought over his dead body. If Ted had wanted to be frozen that way, it should have been in writing. Obviously, his son, John Henry, who died of leukemia in 2004, was as goofy as Ted was.

I guess the bottom line for posterity is that Ted Williams was a Hall of Fame player and a great patriot. It was unfortunate that the one thing he was awful at, managing, is where our paths had been destined to cross.

Chapter 18

All Good Things...

I flew to Scottsdale to join the A's the night I was traded. Oakland had won the AL West with 101 wins in 1971 and got swept by the Orioles in the playoffs. The first guy I saw at the hotel was Ken Holtzman, who the A's had acquired from the Cubs in the off-season. As our eyes met, Kenny's face lit up and he shouted, "My new roomie!"

Ken told me they were putting the two new pitchers together. I thought, *If everyone around here is as warm as this guy, things will be good.*

He helped me find the traveling secretary, who set me up with meal money, and I ran into manager Dick Williams, who was situated at his favorite table in his favorite place, the hotel bar.

Williams frankly told me they'd brought me over because they weren't going to be extorted by Vida Blue. As a 21-year-old rookie in '71, Blue had won the Cy Young Award with 24 wins, a 1.82 ERA, and 301 strikeouts. He had also angrily turned down Charlie Finley's contract offer for 1972.

Williams said of Blue, "He's such an asshole for playing that Sandy Koufax shit. He's gonna be a good pitcher, but he sure the f*ck isn't Koufax. He can rot in hell as far as Charlie and I are concerned."

I thought, *Does this man get this drunk often?* I'd never met Williams before and after a quick hello, he's telling me the A's front-office strategy.

Blue had informed Finley that he was going to work for a company that made bathroom fixtures rather than play for the bullshit money

Finley was offering. It was okay with me—Finley was paying me $75,000 with the hope that I could still get the ball up to the plate.

Kenny walked me to our room and sat on his bed while I unpacked. The place looked like an airplane crash. We would've needed a full-time staff to keep it clean. I'd just met my bookend, and it figured he was left-handed.

Unfortunately, I still had to prove I could pitch in order to complete the pretty picture. The air was warm and dry and the ball carried a lot in Arizona, but it still shouldn't travel all the way from Scottsdale to Phoenix. I was giving up homers that no one had imagined before.

Milwaukee bombed me in my first outing, and I blamed it on the air. I followed with a few decent performances, and then the Padres lit me up for about 10 runs in half a game. Home plate looked like the launching pad at Cape Kennedy.

Williams came out to the mound at one point and said, "How do you feel?"

"Don't ask me," I said. "Ask the outfielders. They're the ones taking all the abuse."

"Just don't get anyone hurt out here—I may have to take out the married guys." At least Williams was showing some humor and giving me some veteran's respect.

Spring training had just begun, and my arm was already killing me. I thought about Ted Williams pitching me 12 innings in one night against Cleveland and how much trauma that had dealt my arm. I'd had at least 20 cortisone shots in Washington, and now it was only March and I needed a shot every time I pitched.

The A's sent me to a chiropractor to manipulate my back and give me acupuncture treatments. When that didn't solve the problem, they sent me to a doctor who injected cortisone in my shoulder and spine. The theory was that the shot in the spine would help eliminate my shoulder pain. But the shot in my spine hurt so badly it made me scream, and while I was screaming I threatened to kill the guy. Trying to get my arm to work again had become outrageous, but I was willing to try anything to keep my career alive.

I resigned myself to a cortisone shot after every outing. It took a few days to reduce the inflammation, and I'd pitch again and repeat the process. Twenty minutes before I warmed up it was the old hot shower routine I'd been doing the last four years.

Aside from the pain, it was great being with the A's. It was a veteran club, and I happily found myself in the middle of a gambling haven. The A's bet on everything. They'd play a buck or two a point in pinochle, and that's a lot of money for pinochle. They called me "Dolphin" early in my career when my old Tigers teammates suckered me at cards. But after watching some of these guys play, I knew there were some easy pickings on this club.

We'd bowl for $5 a pin. Every day. It was always Holtzman and me against Brant Alyea and Rollie Fingers. Golf was $20 a hole with automatic presses, and it would get up to $400 a round. Seven or eight guys were betting college basketball in the clubhouse, and Williams was one of them. Dick fit in perfectly because he was as big a drunk and gambler as any of his players. The A's had an alcohol problem equal to the Tigers in the '60s.

Holtzman was the biggest habitual gambler I ever met. We laughed, drank, and gambled together. But he was many degrees sicker than I was when it came to gambling, and he got hurt badly by it. He eventually lost everything he had, and he made a lot of money. His wife, Michelle, divorced him over it.

As for Fingers, to this day Mr. Hall of Famer owes me $15,000. Of course, I don't believe a relief pitcher should be in the Hall anyway. Alyea settled with Holtzman, but Rollie never paid me. And it was always

Rollie who wanted to play more golf or bowl some more. When you are getting your ass kicked, you always want to deal one more hand or roll one more game, and Fingers was the champ at that. As his debt grew and grew, I even started calling him "one more" to grind his cheap ass just a little more.

There was labor strife in the air in the spring of '72, and the players were threatening to go out. Although Curt Flood had lost his court battle over free agency the summer before, the issue now was pension money.

We held a team meeting in Scottsdale, and the older players explained the need for solidarity and to not be intimidated by Finley and the owners. There were a lot of educated guys on the A's: Mike Epstein, Holtzman, Sal Bando, Rick Monday, and Reggie Jackson had all gone to college.

We had good meetings, but the next day everything we talked about was in the local paper, along with quotes from Finley about how foolish we would be to carry out our threats. With great solidarity throughout the entire Players Association, on April 6, 1972, Major League Baseball experienced its first general strike.

We had to pay our own expenses to get from Scottsdale to Oakland, and we held another meeting a few days after we got there. Reggie and Blue Moon Odom told us that Finley had okay'd use of the clubhouse.

After the second meeting, Finley called. "What do you want to do, Denny," Finley asked, "end your career this week? This game is bigger than Denny McLain."

I fired back. "Charlie, this has nothing to do with me. And I'm not sure if it's got anything to do with Charlie Finley, but some things have just got to get better. We don't have to scream and kill each other. Let's just make it fair—what the hell's wrong with that?"

Finley yelled, "Watch me—I'll define what's f*ckin' fair!" And with that idiotic statement, he slammed the phone down.

The next day there was another article relating everything that happened in the clubhouse, and the witch-hunt began to find the rat. Turns out it was "rats." A rat of course is a snitch, and I've met my share of snitches. But why would you snitch out the guys trying to get you a better pension and better working conditions? Apparently, Blue Moon and Reggie hadn't been able to get to a phone quick enough to let Finley know what was going on.

Odom had slipped to 10–12 with a 4.29 ERA in '71 and probably felt the need to suck up to Finley. Reggie had a few good years under his belt and was starting to make relatively good money. Thinking 30 years down the line to his pension obviously wasn't a top priority. Reggie became antiestablishment later in his career, but at that time, like Odom, he was going to do whatever he could to ingratiate himself with the man.

Holtzman told me he wanted to kill both of 'em. We were concerned that once the first star crossed the line, the whole situation would collapse.

In Detroit, Al Kaline crossed within 48 hours, and it didn't surprise me. After the '68 season, Kaline refused to accept a raise to $100,000. He had made $94,000 that year and had been injured a good portion of it. Had it been up to guys like Kaline, we would have given money back to the owners in the spring of '72.

The strike was over in 10 days after we pressured the owners to put an additional $500,000 per year into the pension fund. The season would be shorter, and it began on April 15. On that day Reggie became the first major leaguer with a mustache since Wally Schang of the Philadelphia Athletics wore one in 1914. Finley had encouraged him to do it and told the rest of us that anyone who grew a mustache by Father's Day would get a $300 bonus. The race was on—$300 was a great bonus back then.

Blue was still holding out, and I became the fourth starter behind Catfish Hunter, Holtzman, and Odom. The few weeks' rest had done me good—I beat Kansas City 3–2 on April 18, allowing just two unearned runs in seven innings.

I pitched four more times, with each outing worse than the last. With or without medication, the pain in my shoulder was awful. On May 12 against the Red Sox, Rick Miller and Tommy Harper homered off me in a four-run second inning, and Williams pinch-hit for me in the bottom half.

I was done. Blue came back a few days later, and Finley didn't need me anymore. I was 1–2 with an ERA just over six runs per game. But it was past the May 15 cut-down date, and if I went to the minors, Finley was on the hook to me for $45,000.

I reminded Finley that my contract called for the club to pay for my housing in the minor leagues as well as airfare for my wife and children. "Charlie, my arm is killing me," I admitted, "and what I really want to do is just quit."

Of course, Charlie quickly shot back, "So, you're turning in your resignation?"

"No, I'm not that stupid." If I quit, he owed me nothing. "Why don't you just give me $60,000, and I'll announce my retirement and move on." He told me he'd think it over.

He came back the next day with an offer of $25,000 and I said, "F*ck that, Charlie. I'll pitch in Guam if I have to get the $45,000 you owe me."

If Finley had a team in Guam, he would have sent me there. Instead, the A's shipped me to Triple-A Birmingham, which might have been hotter than Guam. Charlie was on the hook for the $45,000 along with major league meal money. I also charged everything I was allowed to that cheap bastard.

Finley had a great eye for talent, and people never gave him the credit he deserved for building those great A's teams and for trying to bring the game into the 20th century with innovation and daring marketing.

From the mule mascot he had in Kansas City to experimenting with orange baseballs to having his players grow facial hair, Finley was way ahead of his time. He was the first to have ball girls, one of whom made news by getting pregnant and having to retire.

The A's went on to win the West again in '72 and began their run of three straight World Series victories. They beat Sparky Anderson's Big Red Machine in seven games and were great for baseball with all their personality and color.

Finley set the tone that allowed the A's to become the rowdiest group I saw in all my days in baseball. They played hard on and off the field, and Williams was right there with them. If we had cell phones with cameras in the clubhouse back then, Williams could have never released anybody without getting extorted.

I never played for a guy who drank, gambled, and f*cked around with his players like Williams. I ripped Williams when I wrote my book, *Nobody's Perfect,* in 1975, and when he wrote one some years later, he ripped me for "bringing gambling" to the A's clubhouse. I didn't bring the gambling. I just joined in the festivities of baseball's only traveling casino, although Holtzman and I might've kicked it up a notch.

Williams took the credit with the we-win-because-I-pull-the-right-switches attitude. He never did anything as a player, but he had the same sense of self-importance that Ted Williams had. Dick acted as if the A's success had little to do with Vida, Reggie, Catfish, and Bert Campaneris. Molly Putz could have filled out a lineup card and won with that club.

Meanwhile, I took my medicine and went to Birmingham. At least I was going to play for manager Phil Cavarretta, one of my boyhood idols as a Cubs fan in Chicago. When I arrived, Chuck Dobson met the plane. I'd beaten Dobson for my 30th win in 1968. Chuck and I were both 28 now, and we were in the same boat, trying to recapture our form. Chuck had gone 15–5 for the '71 A's, but an arm injury put him back in the minors in '72.

We went out for a few drinks and came back to the hotel at about 2:00 AM and woke up Cavarretta. Cavarretta played an incredible 22 seasons with the Cubs and White Sox and hit .293 for his career. We rousted him out of bed and shot the shit for a while. It was obvious that Cavarretta was as disappointed to be managing in the bush leagues as Chuck and I were to be pitching there.

There were many times when Phil, Chuck, and I would jabber away the long nights on the road in the Deep South, pounding down beer and turning the routine story into the sensational as the hours ticked away.

Sadly, neither Cavarretta nor Dobson ever made it back to the majors. But Chuck was a kindred spirit and kept me laughing and sane as I tried to make the best out of a very depressing time in my life.

I stayed in Birmingham long enough to pitch in eight games and put together a 3–3 record. I played a lot of pepper with Dobson and got in great shape running in the outfield. I was also a big name in the league, and when we hit the road our opponents would sell out by promoting the 31-game winner coming to town.

We were in Chattanooga to play the Lookouts, and the club had sold out the final game of the series that I was scheduled to start. But my arm was killing me and Cavarretta pushed me back two days when we were due back in Birmingham.

The Lookout's GM approached me in a panic when I got to the ballpark. I told him my arm ached and that "there's no way you can hope to comprehend what the f*ck it feels like."

"But I've got 5,000 people coming tonight," he wailed, "and they'll kill both of us if you don't pitch. Denny, if the owner finds out, he'll fire me. I'll give you $2,000 cash if you'll at least start the game and go a few innings."

"This is my career we're talking about," I said. "Don't you get it?"

"Okay, I get it. I'll give you $5,000."

All Good Things...

"All right," I relented. "Gimme the ball." I pitched, won the game, and slept like a baby on the bus ride home.

On June 29, 1972, the A's traded me to the Braves for Orlando Cepeda, an aging, former star. I sat around for a few days in Atlanta and was scheduled to pitch the second game of a July 4 doubleheader against the Cubs, my first ever in the National league.

The Braves had been on a two-week road trip and came home to a crowd of more than 50,000 for the twin bill. Understand that the Braves were an under-.500 team that drew a pathetic 752,973 fans for the entire season—50,597 represented a considerable chunk of their entire year's attendance.

When I walked with the bullpen coach from the dugout to the bullpen to warm up between games, I started hearing all this noise and cheering. I looked around to see what the hell was going on, and the bullpen coach, whose name escapes me, said, "That's for you, big fella."

It was totally unexpected, and at that point in my career, it was so nice to be appreciated. It was a wonderful five minutes. I tipped my hat time after time, and many of 'em stood and applauded for the duration. I had goose bumps, and I still had goose bumps when the game started.

With the big crowd on hand and my arm feeling pretty good, I took a 3–2 lead into the seventh inning and faced leadoff hitter Ron Santo. I jammed him, and his bat splintered into a hundred pieces. Unfortunately, the ball went about 105 feet over first baseman Earl Williams's head, hit the chalk line like a dying quail, and rolled 50 to 60 feet farther into foul territory. Slow as he was, Santo steamed into third base.

Two batters later, Randy Hundley knocked in Santo with a sacrifice fly to tie the game. In the eighth, Jose Cardenal and Don Kessinger singled to start the inning before the rain came and eventually ended it in a 3–3 tie. But I'd pitched well, and for the time being, felt like a big leaguer again. Like the old days, I entertained a large media throng at my locker with a special bonus—in among the reporters was my father-in-law, Lou Boudreau, who had broadcast the game for the Cubs.

The Braves were an interesting group. After Phil Niekro, Rick Reed, and Pat Jarvis, we had no pitching, which explained why they were desperate enough to get me. We had two terrific position players in Ralph Garr and Dusty Baker, who both hit over .320 that year. And we had the great Hank Aaron, who was 38 years old and would finish the season with 673 homers. Man, he was something to watch in batting practice. He had the most effortless and smoothest swing I had ever seen, and his wrists were still lightning quick.

Hank was closing in on Babe Ruth's record 714 homers, and people were pulling and tugging at him every day. Although many fans revered him, others were resentful and cruel. Hank was bright enough to recognize all the bandwagon jumpers who had never paid attention to him and now acted like they were his best friends.

He became socially alienated in his total obsession to get to 714 and seemed to be bracing for the torrent of resentment that would become almost unbearable as he narrowed in on the mark. Aside from the "Dear Nigger" letters he later revealed receiving, Hank was also tired of playing with a loser with almost no one in the ballpark.

Meanwhile, my ability to pitch quickly diminished as my shoulder hurt beyond belief. I was scheduled to throw in Pittsburgh when Paul Casanova, one of our catchers, approached me in the clubhouse before the game.

Casanova said, "Listen. I can see how each time out you short arm it just a little more. I've got something for you that gets me up every f*cking night to play this game."

"Tell me more," I said.

"The only problem is that you probably won't sleep much tonight. But tomorrow you'll catch up."

All Good Things...

He showed me a paper cup with maybe an ounce or two of liquid in it. "Take it about 10 to 15 minutes before you go out. Don't take it any earlier because you can get a little nuts, and I don't want to see you running around the clubhouse like a lunatic."

I drank it about 15 minutes before I went out to warm up. It tasted like pure whiskey, bitter and burning, and I almost threw up. But by the time I got to the bullpen, I didn't know who I was. It had taken me to 35,000 feet immediately. Normally, I'm in so much pain that I gotta start warming up 10 to 15 feet from the catcher to get my shoulder loose. By the time I got to the pen, I felt like Superman, with a high energy buzz like nothing I'd ever experienced. I threw about 10 pitches from 60 feet and I was loose and ready to go.

I knew about greenies and amphetamines in pill form that were everywhere and had always been easily available. But this was a much more potent version of amphetamine.

I pitched a strong first inning, but the game got rained out after the inning and I was up for days. I drank the stuff again before the next time I pitched and, although it helped mask the pain, I still got my brains beat out. I said to Casanova, "If it's not gonna give me better stuff, I'm done. I've been up since last Tuesday."

Shortly after my unsuccessful encounter with liquid speed, manager Luman Harris asked me to go to the bullpen so that the Braves could look at others as potential starters. I took it as a compliment. It's amazing what the mind will do when it desperately starts looking under rocks for assurance.

Luman was fired in the beginning of August, a few days after I went to the bullpen, and they named first base coach Eddie Mathews as manager. A lot of first base coaches are lucky if they can keep track of the outs. But before Mike Schmidt came along in the 1970s, Mathews was the greatest power-hitting third baseman in baseball history. He hit 512

203

homers and was a Braves legend. The club needed a big name to boost attendance until they could build a better team.

Mathews had also been my teammate in Detroit in '67 and '68, and unfortunately, I knew him too well. When he was winding down as a player, Mathews had a crappy attitude, resentful of younger players, thinking that the game had turned to horseshit.

Like many others, when Mathews's career went to hell, he became an uncontrollable drunk and degenerate. I knew right away that this was not going to be a good time for Eddie Mathews and me. He didn't like me and I didn't like him.

When he was in Detroit in 1968, a back injury effectively ended his career. Mathews was in Henry Ford Hospital recovering from surgery when he was visited by two local TV personalities, sportscaster Al Ackerman and weatherman Sonny Eliot from the local NBC affiliate. After a few minutes, Mathews struggled out of bed and said, "Guys, let's get a drink." He proceeded to put his street clothes on and asked the stunned TV guys to drive him to the Lindell, a popular sports saloon in town. Mathews just walked out with the reporters and didn't bother to tell anybody.

Ackerman was looking at the Associated Press newswire a few hours later and saw a bulletin come across: "Tigers infielder Ed Mathews has been reported missing…"

Ackerman raced to the phone to call Lindell owner Jimmy Butsicaris. "Jimmy, where's Mathews?"

"Relax, Al, he's right where you left him at the end of the bar," replied a calm Butsicaris.

There's no soft way to put it: Mathews was a drunk. He'd come to the ballpark everyday in Atlanta either with a few Bloody Marys in him or with a hangover. As a result, Eddie was never balanced and never gave himself a chance to be a good manager. He certainly knew how to play the game and had played on some championship teams. But he was bitter and an alcoholic. How could he be happy?

The best thing that could happen to Eddie was that the Braves would win a ballgame and he could go drink and laugh. If he lost, he could still drink, but he wasn't as happy. It's an awful disease, and Eddie would die of complications from it in 2001 at age 69.

On September 12, 1972, with fewer than 4,000 fans in attendance, the Braves hosted the eventual National League champion Cincinnati Reds. Our starting pitcher was a 21-year-old rookie named Jimmy Freeman, who would compile a 2–4 career record before going on to find his real life's work. Pete Rose singled, Joe Morgan walked, and Bobby Tolan loaded the bases with another single before Johnny Bench belted a grand slam off of young Freeman.

The Braves managed to tie it with four in the fifth inning, and after eight innings it was still a 4–4 game. Mathews called on me to pitch the ninth. I dished up a homer to leadoff man Cesar Geronimo. Joe Hague pinch hit for Red's reliever Pedro Borbon and ripped a single to right. Pete Rose came up next and singled to right center. I was done. Tom House relieved me, the two men on base eventually scored off House, and I took the 7–5 loss. It was the last time I pitched all year. I sat in the bullpen the final few weeks of the season and ended the year 4–7 with 76 innings pitched and an ERA in the sixes.

Less than three years earlier, I was the back-to-back Cy Young Award winner. Now, I sat in the bullpen as the Braves staggered to a 70–84 record, 25 games behind the Reds.

After the season, Mathews and general manager Eddie Robinson brought me into the office and told me I should come to spring training in '73 ready to pitch as a relief specialist. It was as much as I could have expected. I had developed a terrific forkball, but the problem was it only went 55 feet. At 55 feet it would dive hard and was amazing. But when I had to throw it 60 feet, it wasn't as effective.

I told them I'd get the extra five feet worked out and we'd go from there. I also willingly took a pay cut from $75,000 to $50,000, which was larger than the rules allowed. But it was either take it or get released.

Near the end of spring training in '73, we'd driven across the state from West Palm Beach to St. Petersburg to play an exhibition against the Mets. I was relaxing in the locker room and reading an incredible story in the *Tampa Tribune*. Yankee pitchers Fritz Peterson and Mike Kekich had announced to the world that they were switching families. Susanne Kekich was going to take the kids and the dog and go live with Fritz, while Marilyn Peterson was going to live with Mike. Amazing.

It was my turn to pitch and I went out to take batting practice with the other pitchers. I'd been on the field a few minutes when the clubhouse guy told me Mathews wanted to see me in his office.

I sat down at his desk. "Whassup, Ed?"

With the ever-present booze on his breath Mathews said, "I've got some bad news."

"What's the matter?" I had no idea where he was going.

"The organization," he said flatly, "decided to release you today."

That was it. Like my mother saying, "You're father died; go have dinner."

I felt my body flush with heat. "You gotta be kidding."

He wasn't. I'd had no inkling it was going to happen. They'd given me the rah-rah speech last September and I hadn't pitched that well, but on this club you didn't have to.

That was it. I wasn't going to stand and defend anything. I just turned away, took a shower, and walked out. No one was in the clubhouse and it was just as well. I wasn't in the mood for good-byes and I couldn't get out of there quick enough.

The real bitch of it all was that it was the end of March, and most clubs had gotten down to where they wanted to be. If it had happened a week or two earlier, I could have tried to hook up with somebody else. But with Opening Day just around the corner there was no place to go.

There was no class to it at all, but that was Eddie. If he even had the decency to tell me in the morning, I could have gone home from West Palm. They must have known what their plans were. But now I was across the state with none of my stuff. Besides ending my career, the ultimate indignity was leaving me in a logistical predicament.

I walked into the corridor wondering how I was going to get to the Tampa airport in order to fly home to Atlanta. It struck me that as recently as 1969 I couldn't go out of a clubhouse door and not be swarmed. Now it was 1973 and not a single fan recognized me. I may have been a few pounds heavier, but wasn't I still 31-game winner Denny McLain?

The first hour after getting released was the ultimate definition of rejection and depression rolled into one. Out in the corridor, I ran into Detroit radio reporter Pete Sark, who asked me where I was going. I told him, "To the airport and to Atlanta."

Sharon had already left West Palm because spring training was almost over, and I couldn't bear the thought of trudging back there to get my stuff. Sark drove me to the airport and got a nice little story for his radio show.

I had almost no money. I had a couple of restaurants in Atlanta that spun off about $800 a week, and when they release a veteran they give you $5,000. Aside from whatever piano gigs I still might be able to generate, that was it.

In my era, 1950 to 1970, what did guys do when they got released and didn't have anything going? They struggled or starved.

In a strange sense, as I flew to Atlanta, I felt a tinge of relief. The concept of not going to the ballpark the next day started to sink in, and deep down, I knew it was time to give it up. I could have conceivably done a contract for somewhere above the major league minimum and pitched relief, but I wasn't getting anybody out anymore, and that really didn't appeal to me.

My last official game had been that one inning of relief in September 1972 against the Reds. I thought back to the night the previous September when Ted Williams had me pitch 12 innings against Cleveland. My career really had really ended in 1971 when I went 10–22 in Washington.

I had lots of people to blame, but I decided not to be resentful. The cold truth was that I just couldn't pitch anymore.

It was March 27, 1973, two days before my birthday. I was soon to be a 29-year-old washed-up baseball pitcher.

Chapter 19

One Last Fling

I owned two bars in Atlanta and, since they were now my main source of income, I had to make sure they succeeded. I was there five to seven nights per week and often wouldn't get home until 4:00 AM. After a while, Sharon just couldn't take my schedule and threatened to leave me.

Looking back, I don't blame her. But I felt stuck. I had two locations: one was across from the Georgia Tech campus and catered to the college kids. The other was a lunch, 5:00 cocktails, and dinner place where the working Georgia Peaches would look for men. It was all about keeping it crawling with lovely ladies because where the ladies were, the men would follow, paying for drink after drink.

I quickly learned that if you owned places like these, you had to physically be there or get robbed blind by your employees.

Whether it was all the beer you could drink for $3 a night, there was always something going on, and I needed to be there to guard the till. They were both great places for action and intrigue, but being on duty 15 hours a day caused some serious issues in my life.

My brother Tim was the manager of the Georgia Tech bar and had his hand in the cookie jar. We had an electronic system that counted shots, and every time you squirted a shot, it dinged and counted it. My shots and my dings were way off, and it ended in an actual fistfight between us before I fired him.

Like my dad, Tim was an alcoholic and died of complications from alcoholism in his mid-fifties. But unlike Tom McLain, Tim McLain was a lightweight thief all his life. It was both depressing and pathetic to watch him in action. Free booze was like a gun to his head. Tim's shtick to get laid was to drink with women and then hire them. When the "new employee" came to work the next day, no one knew she had been hired, including Tim, more often than not. He must have "hired" 50 women who never got to put an apron on.

◆ ◆ ◆

One night Sharon called around dinnertime and said, "If you're not home by midnight I'm leaving."

I said, "Sharon, it's Wednesday night, 50¢ beer night. I've got a thousand kids coming. How do I get out of here? There's a ton of cash in this building."

"You've got 'til midnight."

I got home at 4:30 in the morning and everything was gone except my bed. Tim had moved her to Chicago to get even with me. I was deeply hurt by it but couldn't really blame her. I'd get home late, sleep 'til noon, and go back to the bars at 2:00. I wasn't with the kids and I wasn't happy. It was a smoke-infested den and I hated smoke. I grew up in a tiny house with a chain-smoking father and felt like I needed an oxygen mask in those bars.

It was the spring of 1973. Not long after Sharon left, my old friend and general manager Jim Campbell called to tell me that a guy named Ray Johnson was looking for me. Ray owned the White Sox Triple-A Iowa Oaks team.

I hadn't called anyone in baseball to beg for a major league job, but since I had him on the phone, I asked Campbell, "You need a former great pitcher?"

"No, Denny," Campbell laughed. "But I do need a great pitcher. The last couple years have really been something, huh?" Campbell said with some compassion.

"Jim," I said, "I've learned the hard way that fame comes and fame goes. And there's one thing you can be sure of—it'll go no matter who you are."

I called Johnson, who had attendance problems in Iowa, and he offered me $2,000 a month with a $10,000 bonus if I made it back to the big leagues. I told him I was in but that he had to give me a week or so to get organized. Sharon had already served me with divorce papers. I flew to Chicago to beg her to take me back and give baseball another go.

I arrived in Chicago the morning she was going to court to file for separate maintenance. I caught her as she was going into the courtroom and talked her out of it right then and there, 15 minutes before the hearing. I'd never come out of a bullpen to put out a fire that quickly.

Within hours, we were driving to Des Moines with the kids.

Living with her parents and four kids hadn't worked out very well, and she said she'd try again as long as I was out of the bar business. I sold the bars to a guy who worked for me and got enough of a down payment to get a decent place for us in Iowa.

I had no idea if I could get Triple-A hitters out but suspected I couldn't.

When I showed up, I saw two familiar faces I'd played against: Tom Egan and Joe Keough who, like me, were both on the downside of their careers. Egan was a 27-year-old catcher. You could tell him what was coming and he still couldn't hit it. Keough was a 27-year-old outfielder with no power. I was 29, out of shape, and couldn't reach home plate anymore.

I looked at the two of them and figured that, at the worst, it would still be a good time.

The manager was a guy named Joe Sparks who never played an inning in the major leagues and was suspicious of me even before I showed up in Des Moines. Sparks immediately told me that my reputation preceded me and he didn't want any trouble.

Sparks was prejudging me, and his less-than-enthusiastic greeting reminded me of my experience with Ted Williams. But Sparks had no baseball credentials and, with such a demotivating style, stood no chance of ever making the big leagues. Predictably, he never did.

"Sparks is so paranoid," Egan explained, "he thinks any time a former big leaguer comes here, he's been sent to take his job. He even suspected that of me!"

Sparks resented me even more when a local car dealer offered to let me drive an AMC Gremlin if I did a radio commercial for him. It may have been the ugliest car in the history of the auto business, but it was free. And needless to say, Sparks was never offered one.

I think Sparks was also jealous that the older guys like Egan and Keough hung out with me instead of him. And Keough, Egan, and I had a great time. We played golf and cards and had dinner together every night.

Before we'd visit a city I'd call a veteran I knew or the manager of the other team to find the best place to play golf. Whether they made the arrangements or told me who to call, the 30-game winner was on his way to play at their club for the next few days. It was the Denny McLain dog-and-pony show. The only drawback was that Keough and Egan didn't have enough money to gamble the way we would have liked to.

As for baseball, my routine was:

Day 1: Pitch and then ice my arm afterward.

Day 2: Get a cortisone injection and ice my arm until my skin froze.

Day 3: Run gallons of hot water on my arm, throw for five or six minutes, and ice it again.

Day 4: Pitch and start the process again.

The good news was that there was no shortage of cortisone in

This is me and my father enjoying a light moment when I was 10, but times weren't always so happy around the McLain household. *Photo courtesy of the McLain family.*

Baseball was the only thing that my father and I shared, and he would have loved to have seen me pitch in the big leagues. He was gone by the time I signed my first contract with Ed Short of the White Sox.

The White Sox sent me first to Harlan, Kentucky, then here to Clinton, Iowa, where I rode the roller-coaster in Class D Midwest League. *Photo courtesy of Wilber M. Kirby.*

I was only 21 years old when I had my breakout season in the big leagues, going 16–6 in 1965 and being selected "Tiger of the Year."

Kristin during the magical 1968 season, when she was just approaching three years old.

Kristin (left)
and Michelle.

That's my brother Tim (second from left), wife Sharon, and my mother Betty in the stands cheering for win number 30 in 1968. *Photo courtesy of Dick Tripp.*

My other passions were music and the Denny McLain Quintet. I was probably a better pitcher, but I could also play the organ pretty well.

Horsing around with Mickey Lolich at Tigertown in Lakeland, Florida, during training camp before the 1969 season.

Sharon and I share a moment at her father's induction into the Hall of Fame in 1970.

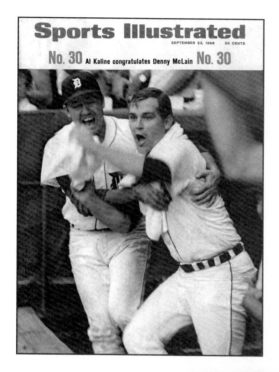

Sports Illustrated

SEPTEMBER 23, 1968   50 CENTS

No. 30 Al Kaline congratulates Denny McLain No. 30

One moment I'm celebrating my 30th victory in 1968 with Al Kaline (left), and the next, it seemed, I'm at the center of baseball's biggest scandal since 1919 (below).

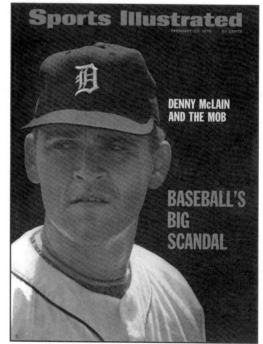

Sports Illustrated

FEBRUARY 23, 1970   50 CENTS

DENNY McLAIN AND THE MOB

BASEBALL'S BIG SCANDAL

Leaving the court-house in Tampa to serve my first sentence in 1985.

Exhibit 1
McLAIN

NEWLY
DISCOVERO

New evidence that was disclosed while I was in jail for the second time (right). The time stamp on the fax shows I was on the air at the time Egan claimed I was with him and I signed this document (above).

February 15, 1994

Mr. Michael Zimmerlin
Trust & Investment Services
Mail Code 10-79
Michigan National Bank
27777 Inkster Road
P.O. Box 9065
Farmington Hills, MI 48333-9065

RE: PEET PACKING RETIREMENT RETIREMENT INCOME PLAN

Dear Mike:

Upon receipt of this letter please wire transfer $3,060,000.⁰⁰ from the Peet Packing Retirement Income Plan Account # 1571809306.

WIRE TO: VANGUARD INVESTMENTS, INC
COMERICA BANK
ROUTING/ABA # 072000339
ACCT. # 1033108499
FBO Peet Packing Ret. Income Plan

Thank you.

Sincerely,

Roger Smigiel
President
(517) 845-3021

Dennis D. McLain

GOVERNMENT
EXHIBIT
27

1151

America. The bad news was that even massive doses of it no longer helped. I would get a good stretch of a few innings, but the pain returned and I couldn't let the ball go freely like I once did. I kept trying, but I knew I was kidding myself.

In eight games, I was 1–4 with a 7.55 ERA. Johnson also owned a Double-A team in Shreveport, Louisiana, and suggested I go there to get in shape and work the kinks out. I had put on some weight and I told him I'd do it. Ray had treated me well, and I had honored every request to entertain his clients and advertisers. But 30-game winners who get their nuts knocked off each time they take the mound can only last so long, even in Triple-A.

Shreveport was 145 degrees in the shade with humidity to match and featured the biggest mosquitoes on earth. The manager was Gene Freese, a good guy but another degenerate. At the risk of making it sound like every manager I had was a degenerate, I'll try to do a better job of defining it.

Every manager back then was from the old-boys school. They all drank, and none of them ever made any money. Freese played 12 years in the majors and had been the starting third baseman for the 1961 National League Champion Cincinnati Reds. But he was 40 now and stuck managing a Double-A team in Shreveport.

The reason he was in the minors was because nobody really liked him that much as a manager and he needed to make a living. There are some tough ways to make it in America, but it doesn't get much tougher than trying to make it as a big league manager coming out of Shreveport. It's an insecure role to begin with, and the major source of camaraderie is that everyone—managers and players—are broke and desperately hoping to catch lighting in a bottle with a big league job.

Each all-day bus ride served as a harsh reminder. I was on a bus again, as I'd been in Duluth 10 years previous—before all the good things happened.

I was on the bus with 24 people, half of whom were on their way up, and the other half, like me, were done but too proud, too stupid, or just too scared to stop lying to themselves that they still had a shot.

Hell yes, it was depressing.

Freese drank all the time. He was Ray Oyler, Ed Mathews, and Mayo Smith rolled into one, starting the morning with a beer, going to bed with a beer, and drinking beer whenever he could in between. It's pathetic to see a guy buzzed or drunk all the time.

Freese and I lived at the same Holiday Inn in Shreveport, ate some great crawfish together, and shared some laughs about old times. Although we did learn how to get along, his paranoia was still a pain in the ass much of the time. Like Joe Sparks, Freese probably worried that I was there to replace him. He knew that Ray Johnson really liked me, and the media was always talking to me because I'd been such a big name a relatively short time ago. And yes, I could have managed in Des Moines or Shreveport if I'd wanted to.

I finished the 1973 season in Shreveport with a 6–4 record and an ERA in the mid-fours. But this was Double-A and that wasn't good enough. With a week to go in the season, I told Ray Johnson I was done. I took my clothes off the hook in a cramped, lockerless minor league clubhouse and, once and for all, said good-bye to the stench of sweat and urine and headed off to civilian life.

Chapter 20

Knockin' Around

With a ruined shoulder and my baseball career dead and gone, I was 30 and unemployed. Money was suddenly a serious issue, and I needed to find something productive to do. I had lived through the disappointment of being a baseball vagabond for four years, but now I was completely out of the spotlight and off the public radar screen.

I figured that Detroit held out the most hope and opportunity, so I headed back to the city of my greatest playing days.

I'd always been pretty good at talking, so I began hosting a daily talk show on a new UHF station, Channel 20. My old catcher Jim Price, who had squealed on me for carrying a gun back in 1970, became my Ed McMahon on the show.

I didn't particularly like Price, but he had a "money guy" behind him named Don Nick, and I was willing to put up with Price's bullshit to have Nick finance the effort.

I also hosted a daily radio show on WEXL, an AM station, and doing both shows was a very tough gig. Getting guests was always a problem, and there wasn't a hell of a lot going on in Detroit in the mid-'70s.

Next up was a quasi shopping mall that I went in on with an attorney friend, Mike Schwartz. I bought an old department store on Detroit's east side called the Trading Post. The concept was to break it up into smaller stores and lease space. We called it the International Mall and found some people to rent the shops.

We wanted to attract kids and created a huge pinball gallery with hundreds of machines, and we booked rock acts on a stage we built. We actually got some major acts to come—Kiss and Rush played there in 1974 before they became big stars. But we couldn't control the kids who used the place to hang out all day, smoke weed, get into fights, and hide in cubby holes to make out.

It didn't take long until we had a disaster on our hands. When we hired security to clean up the drugs and other wayward activities, the traffic decreased. Then we had major trouble getting the lessees to pay. Our best tenant turned out to be a head shop. They sold a shitload of pot-smoking accessories, all totally legal, and paid their rent on time. Mike and I sold our interest to a guy who turned it into a skating rink, and I was on to other ventures for the brave of heart.

Beaten up as a talk show host and entrepreneur, Ray Johnson called me in early 1975 and offered me a job broadcasting games back in Iowa for the Oaks. Ray indicated that the parent club, the White Sox, would hear me and maybe give me a shot. We gave it a shot and moved back. But between the travel and the White Sox passing on me, by the end of the '75 season I was looking to move on when I got a call from the owner of the Triple-A Memphis Blues.

The owner, a doctor named Bernard Kruass, had suffered a heart attack a few months previous and wanted to unload the team. The club was more than $300,000 in debt and wanted me to use my high profile to find investors and pump up sales so he could eventually dump it.

The Blues's biggest problem was that they had jumped from Double-A to Triple-A, and their expenses had gone through the roof. You had to fly now because the cities were too far away to take a bus. We did a good job—built a sales staff and moved 80 percent of all the tickets before the '76 season began. We sold billboards and traded old debt for season tickets. We had country music festivals and had companies buy sponsored evenings.

Knockin' Around

The season started out well and attendance was up, but by mid-summer we were getting rained out a ridiculous number of times. We had 11 or 12 rainouts and lost the gate each time. When it rained in Memphis that summer, it rained forever. I've never seen so much f*cking rain in my life.

On top of all of that, the club was awful and interest waned. Typical of poor, dumb me, when the creditors came calling again and the Blues went under, my face was on it. A lot was said and written about me ripping off the ballclub. My salary had been a whopping $500 a week. I had my house paid for and I left there with no dough at all.

Badly needing to bring in cash, I took a job selling radio and TV advertising at William B. Tanner Co., a Memphis ad agency. I got a break in early 1977 when I was awarded $31,500 in a workman's compensation settlement with the Tigers and several other clubs for having poked me full of cortisone all those years.

The money helped, but it really didn't make a dent. Creditors were breathing down my neck, and by July 1977, I was back in bankruptcy court. I had debts of more than $1 million and assets of less than $1,000. Ed May had gotten me in 1970, but this time I'd done it to myself with bad planning, bad decisions, bad deals—just bad everything.

Before I left Memphis in '77, Elvis died. I didn't think I had anything to do with it, but at that point, how the hell did I know?

It was then that I got a call from a friend in Lakeland named Merle Dixon, who had made a ton of money in the insurance business. Merle was all excited about something called a "projection TV," a giant-screen TV that he thought I could help him market across the country. He had a company named Viewpoint and figured that I could attract some attention for the new TVs.

So I left Tanner and we moved to Florida to sell TVs.

God, those TVs were ugly contraptions. They had cone-shaped lenses that were hooked up to your regular TV and projected the picture onto a seven-foot screen. The picture looked great—until you turned the lights on or unless you didn't sit directly in front of it. It was also a ghastly piece of furniture—a cone connected to a TV that had to be put in the middle of the room so you could project the picture onto the screen.

We sold it with a 30-day, money-back guarantee. Sure enough, after the guy's wife realized it wasn't a piece of furniture she wanted dominating her home and the customer realized it was better suited as a boat anchor than a theater, they'd ask for their money back. It didn't take Dixon long to lose $50,000 or $60,000 and bail out on the business.

I still liked the concept, and in early 1978 I found a technical wizard named Jack Swallow to become my partner. We imported cheap TVs from Korea for less than $150, and Jack figured out how to place a power unit in them and attach the screen right on the TV. That way you didn't have to put the damn thing in the middle of the room and project it onto the screen.

All we needed to get going was cash, and the way I knew how to get it was golf. I was pretty good, and I got to a minus one or two handicap at my peak.

I played with a steady group of guys and traveled all over the state playing in amateur tournaments and hustling. Guys wanted to beat the fat pitcher, and I got a reputation of being willing to take on anybody. I'd spend a week or two at a time in Ft. Lauderdale playing 36 holes a day.

I knew my game, and I was very good at sizing up the competition. Let's face it, I was a novice in a lot of things, but playing sports was my world. I'd run into some good players from time to time, but I always figured, *How much better than me can they be? The guy's not gonna win 9 and 18 when the real dough is on the line.* I was accustomed to performing under pressure and they weren't, and it always comes down to that.

The game I played was a one-down press. That means that every time a player falls one hole down, another bet is automatically created. If you were playing $50 a hole, by the time you got to 15 or 16, you had 10 or 12 presses going.

I wouldn't play a guy for $1,000 a press if I didn't know him, but most of these guys wanted a shot at the baseball player and would start at $10 or $20 a hole. They'd lose or win a couple hundred and want to play another 18 the next day.

Excuse me, but this is hustling, and hustlers make sure that they know when to lose. When somebody would beat me, either legitimately or with a little help from me, the next 18 holes were mine. I was hustling, winning, and I was having a ball.

Jack and I called our company Projector Beam, and we sold the units for about $900 each. We had really good years in '78 and '79. I even leased a Swearingen Merlin IIB, a twin-engine prop-jet. I'd fly from city to city, selling the Projector Beam and hustling golf.

It wasn't long before Advent, RCA, and Panasonic created their own line of big-screen TVs. Not only did their TVs work better, but they also looked a hell of a lot nicer than ours.

Jack and I couldn't compete.

I was on the road in August '79, near the end of Projector Beam's run, when the phone in my plane rang. A neighbor in Lakeland was calling to tell me that my house was burning down as we spoke. My 11-year-old son, Denny, had found an emergency flare for the plane in a closet and had lit it by pulling the cord. He threw water on it, but the flares are designed for use at sea and water doesn't faze them.

Luckily, my family made it outside and watched from across the street as our house burned down. Making a bad situation worse, I'd failed to make my insurance payments and we also lost all of our possessions, including my MVP plaque and the Cy Young Awards.

I was at another low ebb in my life. No money, no house, no business, no new bright ideas.

We leased a house in St. Petersburg because the teachers at Denny's school thought that he was depressed and shouldn't have to deal with living near the "scene of the crime." We all felt the same. We needed a fresh start and were ready to go.

For the next few months, I continued to hustle golf. Because I made enough to pay the bills, Sharon was okay with it.

Chapter 21

First Fidelity

In the summer of 1980 I was hustling golf in the Tampa area and was introduced to a guy named Barry Nelson at an amateur tournament.

Nelson didn't seem particularly different from most of the other jock sniffers I'd met, and a few months later I came home to find a phone message from him.

Nelson was operating a mortgage business in South Florida named First Fidelity Financial Services and had a partner named Stanley Seligman. Nelson told me they had four offices and were thinking of opening a new one in Tampa. They were using Johnny Unitas as their spokesman, and it all seemed legitimate enough to me.

Nelson and Seligman told me that if I got a mortgage license, they'd have me run an office for them. They said they'd send somebody up to show me how to get the license and would pay me $50,000 a year plus commissions and give me a chance to make some real money.

I thought it over for three seconds and said, "Sounds good to me!"

The guys who owned First Fidelity were part of the so-called "Jewish Mafia" in Florida. Seligman was an attorney and could be a real nasty son of a bitch. He looked like the guy in the black stovepipe hat in the old movies that threw the mother and children out in the cold at Christmastime because they missed a payment.

Nelson was about 5'5", 240 pounds, and wore perennially food-stained shirts under ill-fitting jackets. He looked like a guy who'd hide wristwatches under the coat to go sell them on the sidewalk or at the bus station. And he was always sweating, even in his air-conditioned offices.

One of the main guys was Sy Sher, a former accountant for the infamous mobster Meyer Lansky. Sy was right out of a Jimmy Cagney movie. In fact, he loved Cagney and Humphrey Bogart and was a caricature of both. Sy would say, "Hey, how ya doin'?" in his New Yorkese. He honored the Jewish holidays just like the Italian Mafiosos followed Catholic customs. Sy liked wearing a jogging outfit and looked like a larger version of Danny DeVito. He always carried a small satchel filled with stacks of $100 bills because he was also a major bookmaker.

There was a pervasive smell of cash and an aura of intrigue around these guys, and I was drawn to the excitement of it. I was especially enthralled by Sy, who might have been the largest layoff bookmaker in the country. Bookies have to keep their bets balanced and need to lay off bets on other bookies. Sy was huge.

The First Fidelity boys had observed my style on the golf course, and although they considered me a bit naïve, they felt I was a kindred spirit. I hadn't had a real job since I pitched, and I wanted in on the action along with a regular weekly income and a steady lifestyle. I allowed myself to think that I'd find some stability amid this set of characters.

First Fidelity had begun as a legitimate mortgage company but took a turn when the oil crisis of the late '70s and early '80s wreaked havoc on Florida real estate. Interest rates had shot sky high and market prices had shrunk. Homes weren't selling well, and First Fidelity started to become what the industry would later call the "lender of last resort."

Credit had very little to do with qualifying a guy at First Fidelity. He could be the worst stiff in the world, but as long as he had equity in his house, First Fidelity would loan up to about 80 percent of it. When no one else would listen to somebody in trouble, First Fidelity was there if he'd pay 28 percent interest. People with money go to banks. People panicking about losing their house or business go to the First Fidelities of the world.

Besides charging unconventional interest, First Fidelity also got lawyer fees, title fees, and appraisal fees. It was greedy and usurious as hell, but being a lender of last resort was legal.

In addition to selling loans, I also got involved in bookmaking with Sy. I'd had my ill-fated bookmaking fling back in '67 with the thieves at the Shorthorn but saw Sy as the real deal. He had guys all over the country running bets for his operation. He probably only had a few dozen bettors in each city, but they all had to bet at least $1,000 a game.

Sy said, "If you find a guy or two who'll play for at least a dime a game ($1,000), take the action, and I'll give you a third. When you lose, we'll put it against what you've won."

I'd been in the habit of going to the dog track near my office on Monday and Wednesday and would see the same guys there all the time. One of them was a stockbroker named Larry, who later went to jail for stock fraud. It turned out that Larry was a compulsive gambler who stole from his client's accounts to pay off his losses.

I wanted Larry's action to get me started, and the first thing he asked was, "Will your guy pay?"

I said, "Sure, he'll pay. But my question is, will you pay?"

He said, "Of course I will." And I called Sy, who asked, "Do you know him real well?"

"Yeah, well enough."

"Okay." But Sy warned, "You know you're on the hook for the money if he doesn't pay, right?"

After a few basically uneventful weeks of offsetting wins and losses, Larry told me he wanted to put down 10 dimes on the *Monday Night Football* game. He wanted to bet the spread, bet the over and under, bet this, and bet that.

I made one quick phone call and he was booked.

The Raiders were playing at Minnesota in the second Monday night game of the 1981 season. The Raiders had won the Super Bowl in 1980 but had just lost the '81 opener at Denver. Larry liked the Vikings to win at home over Oakland and spread his 10 grand on them in every imaginable way.

Oakland clobbered the Vikings 36–10 and took Larry to the cleaners.

When guys lose, they have to pay on Tuesday. I went to see Larry at his office, and I was pleasantly surprised when he pointed to an envelope sitting on his desk with $11,000 in it—$10,000 for the bet and $1,000 for the juice. When a bettor loses he has to pay the book 10 percent on top of the bet. I took my third and delivered the rest to Sy.

After a while, I was taking bets for five or six guys in Tampa and made more than $50,000 on the '81 football season alone. As I put more and more cash in my pocket, my swagger and desire for more and more action also influenced my mortgage dealings.

When I first came on board with First Fidelity, there were some loans even they wouldn't touch. But as we ran into more desperate people, we dug even deeper into the bowels of unconventional lending. First Fidelity preyed upon people's weakness. They especially liked dealing with self-employed guys who owned cash businesses like stores and gas stations. They'd do the loan if the guy agreed to kick back $5,000 under the table. Someone who desperately needs money says to himself, *I don't care; I'll do whatever it takes.*

An upfront fee is legal. Hiding it from the tax man isn't. The interest rate was also usurious and very illegal if the customer had to pay an under-the-table bribe to get a loan. So First Fidelity was beating the tax man and enjoying great walking-around money. We'd refer to the under-the-table money as "Benjis," as in Benjamin Franklin $100 bills.

I'd get a call for a tough loan—a guy with little or no equity—and Barry would say, "Get at least 50 Benjis up front."

Sy Sher was the king of all the loan sharks. He'd even loan money to mob guys who'd pay Sy a point a week and then loan the money to somebody else for two points.

First Fidelity had given a legitimate loan of $150,000 to a guy named Dale Sparks, who had responded to the Johnny Unitas ad. Sparks operated a disco in Sebring, Florida, but was having problems with the city of Sebring, as well as his partners.

He came back to me in a state of desperation and told me that if I went on the hook for him for $40,000, he'd let me drive his new Lincoln Continental as collateral. I introduced him to Sy in Ft. Lauderdale and told Sy that Sparks had made all of his payments on the $150,000 loan and I'd vouch for him.

Sy gave Sparks $40,000 in $100 bills with no paperwork to identify the loan. The terms were $1,000 interest every week (two and a half points) and $10,000 off the principal every two months. Sparks made his first eight interest payments, but the disco went under and he couldn't come up with the $10,000 that was due.

This was clearly a bad situation because I was on the books to Sy for $40,000. What the hell was I thinking to back this loser for $40,000?

Sy and I met with Sparks and told him that we didn't want this to get ugly. When he still failed to pay, Sy arranged another meeting and introduced Sparks to Frank Cocchiaro, a guy he called the "General." Cocchiaro was a New Jersey mobster who told Sparks that if he didn't pay, "I'll cut your ears off and hand 'em to ya."

I wasn't invited to that meeting, and when Sy and the "General" told me about the threat to Sparks, I couldn't believe what I was hearing. I felt like I was in a "B" movie sitting across from George Raft and Sy, who was playing his Cagney role.

Sparks couldn't sell his house because it looked like somebody had shit all over it, and he wound up settling part of the debt by handing it over to First Fidelity. The house was in the middle of nowhere, and judging by how Florida real estate has shot back up, it might be worth a few million today for all I know.

Since I'd recommended the loan to Sy, I had to pay off the balance. I was lucky to be able to scrape up the cash. One rule was imperative in the loan sharking and bookmaking businesses I was in: Sy must always get his money.

Another character was Paul Higgins. He was a decent guy who was already in to us for a few loans and was frantic for another $30,000. Higgins actually got down on his knees and begged me for the money. He had a wife and four kids, and his world was collapsing because a business partner had absconded with his dough. He was about to lose everything, including his home, and I gave him $500 just to buy groceries.

I told him that borrowing money from a guy like Sy Sher could have horrible repercussions. But Higgins was so desperate that the stern warning couldn't deter him.

Sy lent him the $30,000 at $900 a week interest.

What was I thinking? How can a guy who can't buy groceries pay that kind of interest? It was another loan that shouldn't have taken place and put Higgins and me in a very uncomfortable position. Predictably, Higgins ran through the money, and I had to start pressuring him to pay.

I tried to impress upon Higgins that these were serious people, and if he didn't pay, I'd have to pay for him. When he inevitably defaulted, I went to see him at his house that had been on the market for months. It was a pigsty. I opened the fridge and the stench was so awful—it smelled like a dead body was in there. I almost puked, thinking, *How can people with children live like this?*

With his home and place of business unsellable at the time, Sher and Cocchiaro made me responsible for his loan. I paid it off, less some interest.

First Fidelity

I was on a roll, losing money left and right. Between greed and stupid decisions, I was destroying my mortgage business and desperately trying to keep my head above water.

The shit hit the fan on April Fool's Day in 1982. The state of Florida controller's office raided the offices of First Fidelity and closed it down. Barry Nelson and Stanley Seligman were accused of racketeering, usurious loans, fraud, extortion, money laundering, and under-the-table kickbacks. The government also charged them in a Ponzi scheme, which is taking money from new investors to pay old investors—pretty soon the money runs out.

I didn't see what we were doing as a Ponzi scheme because there were real property and real assets involved. Until the Feds shut it down, there was never a payment missed to any investor. I certainly understood the illegality of the kickbacks and the bookmaking associated with First Fidelity, but the government was just charging Nelson and Seligman with everything you could pull out of a law book.

Nelson still owed me $95,000 in commissions, and that created a real problem for me. I was tapped out from paying off the loans for Sparks and Higgins, and now it looked like I'd also get stiffed on the $95,000.

Needing a new gig quickly, I quickly hooked up with a guy named Felix Bertucci, who was in the real estate business. Felix was a lefty golfer, and we had made some money together playing in a few lefty-righty tournaments. We started a bookmaking operation together in Tampa that quickly ended when one of our clients beat us with some huge wagers.

I've always said, bookmakers always win unless I'm the bookie. The mortgage business was all but dead because of the sad state of the Florida real estate business, and now my latest bookmaking operation had also been beaten to a pulp.

Felix then came up with an idea. We were attempting to finance some walk-in medical clinics, and he suggested we lease a Cessna Cheyenne twin-engine turbo-prop to help chase down investors with a real dog-and-pony show. I'd been flying since my big year in 1968 and naturally thought it was a brilliant idea.

At the same time, Nelson, who still owed me the $95,000, said he could help make it up to me if I was willing to lease him the airplane for a trip or two. Nelson had a cocaine-dealing nephew named Todd Siegmeister who sold the stuff in New Jersey. Felix got three kilos of cocaine fronted to him, put it in golf bags, and told me that he put Siegmeister on a train to go to Jersey and sell it.

Felix told me that the plane would only be used for him to fly to New Jersey to help complete the deal and then bring Siegmeister and the money back. Again, my ability to rationalize and justify the use of my plane while disregarding my participation and the consequences was typical for me. The law calls it "deliberate indifference." And once again—what the hell was I thinking?

Not surprisingly, Siegmeister not only failed to complete the deal but also managed to steal about eight ounces of Felix's coke in the process.

There were other deals, but none that would haunt me like this one.

At the risk of sounding Clintonesque, as in, "I never inhaled," I never had the slightest curiosity to use cocaine. For me, the exhilaration was in the action and the money, not the drug itself. My drug was the adrenalin that flowed through me when the action got hot.

I met another of Felix's associates, a drug dealer named Larry Knott. Knott bought his coke from a major dealer named Jim Pritchett.

Pritchett, as I later found out, claimed the dubious distinction as the only man to ever be convicted of manslaughter while flying a plane. In 1980 Pritchett was high on coke, flying his private plane on autopilot while he was getting oral sex from his girlfriend. Automatic pilot is supposed to be used at altitude, but Pritchett was making circles dangerously close to the water while his girlfriend worked him.

First Fidelity

His right wing clipped the water, and the plane caught fire and started doing cartwheels. His girlfriend was killed on impact, and Pritchett was convicted of manslaughter. Low-life that he was, Pritchett bragged that as the plane hit the water he was in mid-orgasm.

Pritchett appealed, and on July 12, 1982, the state mailed Pritchett a letter that told him he'd lost his appeal and ordered him to begin serving a five-year prison term in a Florida state prison 15 days later.

Knott told me that Pritchett wanted to flee and would pay me handsomely if I could smuggle him out of the country in my plane. Knott arranged to have me meet a few of Pritchett's friends at a location north of Ft. Lauderdale.

In a scene right out of a spy movie, I was asked to lie down in the back seat of the car and remain covered by a blanket so Pritchett could keep his whereabouts secret as we drove to his place.

Only when the car arrived at Pritchett's house was I allowed to emerge from under the blanket. Pritchett asked me if, in addition to smuggling him out of the country, might I also have a place where he could hide for a few weeks. I told him that, as luck would have it, I could probably put him in a friend's place on an island. I asked him what he was willing to pay for the flight and a place to stay.

Pritchett showed me a suitcase with $320,000 in $5,000 stacks all rubber-banded together. My eyes bugged out and I tried not to stare too hard. I'd never seen anything so incredible in my life. I could have had a row of naked Playboy bunnies in front of me and not been so totally turned on. I was scared I would hyperventilate and pass out.

Pritchett told me he had a brother who'd been busted and needed to get him released on bond. He figured that bond would cost $250,000 and told me he was willing to give me the other $70,000 for the flight and a month's room and board at Stan Myatt's island hideaway.

I agreed. I'd fly him out, give him the place to stay, and use the remaining $250,000 to take care of his brother. I told Pritchett he needed to give me the $320,000 up front and consider it done.

Pritchett handed me the suitcase, and I could've shit right there. He said, "Do you want to count it?"

I gulped and managed to say, "No, but if it ain't 320 you got an issue. My partner will be pissed off."

His guys put me under the blanket and we drove back to Ft. Lauderdale.

When I got in my car, I was shaking uncontrollably. I was terrified that I'd get stopped for some stupid traffic violation and be caught with the money. I drove right to a gas station, filled the tank, and made sure all my blinkers worked. I was staying in a Ft. Lauderdale hotel and drove there never exceeding the speed limit or rolling through any stop signs. If they were going to stop me for anything, it would be driving too slow.

I need to introduce one more player in this drama. Through Barry Nelson, I had also met a character right out of central casting named Stan Myatt. Myatt claimed to be a former CIA agent and told me that he owned a three-mile-long island in the Bahamas called Great Harbour Cay.

We later found out that Myatt was a government informant who knew how to work both sides of the street. When it benefited him to work with the cops, he did; and when there was a profit to be made from illegal activity, he'd grab the money and then give up his partners to the authorities.

When I got to my hotel room, I called Myatt and said, "I've got a big-time guy looking to run and needs to stay somewhere for a few weeks before he finds a more permanent place to hide."

"What's he willing to pay?" Stan asked.

"He's got $320,000 in cash and he needs $250,000 of it to bail out his brother." I explained to Stan who the brother was, and Myatt said he'd look into it.

Myatt called later and told me that Pritchett's brother wasn't going anywhere. He explained to me that even though Pritchett was thinking like a fugitive, he wouldn't legally qualify as one until he was due to report 15 days later. Therefore, if we moved him at this time, it was technically not a criminal act. He said, "My guy who handles these things tells me the brother's already got a slew of drug convictions and they caught him this last time with enough snow [cocaine] to cover the Olympic alpine competition."

Myatt then asked, "When will he pay?"

"He already has," I said. "I've got the cash in my car."

"You have what in your car?" he said, astonished.

I stated once again, "The cash is in the car," in a much firmer voice to disguise my huge smile and pounding heart.

"Then have your pilot fly him to Great Harbour Cay, and we'll give him the bad news later."

"What bad news?" I asked.

"The news that his rent has just jumped to $320,000 a month. We'll take 160 each, and he'll have to be okay with it."

The excitement was nothing short of spine tingling.

I hooked up with Pritchett's drivers to tell Pritchett where to meet me at the Ft. Lauderdale airport and that we'd fly him right out. Pritchett met us at the airport with his wife and kids, and off we went. Myatt had cleared Pritchett's family with Bahamian customs, and when they arrived they walked right through customs en route to Myatt's house.

I flew back to Ft. Lauderdale, and the next day Myatt and I flew back to Great Harbour Cay to tell Pritchett that the terms of the deal had changed. Myatt said he knew how to handle all this—he understood the mind of a dope dealer—and that Pritchett would believe us when we told him that springing his brother was a long shot.

"You've done all the talking so far, so you should tell him the bad news," Myatt said. "If he doesn't like it, tell him to enjoy swimming back to Florida. All I have to do in two weeks is tell customs he's a fugitive and he'll wind up rotting in a Bahamian jail."

I walked down the beach with Pritchett as Myatt, with a gun under his shirt, trailed behind. I had the uncomfortable thought that I was the only guy in this equation who wasn't carrying a gun. I knew I was in way over my head, but it had come this far and there was no turning back. Pritchett was clearly a guy with little regard for human life and already had one manslaughter conviction under his belt. Hell, if he didn't kill me, then Myatt could kill both of us and swipe the money from my car at the airport.

I told Pritchett that we couldn't get his brother out of jail, even with all the connections that Myatt had. I was stunned when Pritchett believed it and reluctantly said he understood.

Then I told him that the rent had gone up. I sounded like a damn travel agent by listing everything: the arrangements with customs, the round-trip flight, the food, and that the fabulous 5,000-square-foot house was gonna cost him $10,000 a day—the whole $320,000.

He rammed both his hands into my chest, almost knocking me over, and yelled, "That's bullshit. I trusted you f*ckers by fronting the money, and you're f*cking me over."

We eventually calmed him down and got him to admit that money wasn't the issue—maintaining his freedom was. It was obvious there was more money where that came from.

Myatt and I flew back to Ft. Lauderdale and split the money. Then I flew over to Tampa and had Sharon meet me at the airport.

When we got to the house I took a shower to cool off and then asked her to come in the bedroom. I opened the suitcase and dumped $160,000 on the bed.

Sharon put her hands over her mouth and said, "Oh, my God."

Sharon's human, too. We needed the money to cover any number of debts I'd run up since First Fidelity had been shut down. The walk-in medical clinics in Lakeland were in the hole, and the $160,000 also allowed me to keep the Cheyenne. Sharon and I never discussed the nature of the money, and I rationalized that no matter where it came from, it wasn't going to be used for drugs.

♦   ♦   ♦

A short time after the Pritchett affair, Myatt introduced me to a character named Earl Hunt, who was in the marijuana business. I liked Hunt and got too deeply in bed with him. Hunt was also a pilot, and when the Feds busted a cohort of Hunt's, we all became marked men.

Hunt got set up and then busted in Alabama with a planeload of grass and actually tried to run the cops over when they approached him on the tarmac. Shots were fired at Hunt as he tried to get airborne again to escape.

Hunt told them I wasn't involved in his busted deal but that I had agreed to do another deal with him. That was all the Feds had to hear—that the 31-game winner was doing drug deals. When all the dots were connected, enough of them led to me.

The government made a great case against all of us and, fittingly, my little lefty golfing buddy Felix Bertucci, the first to suggest that I loan out my plane for drug transportation purposes, became the star witness.

The investigation had begun with the demise of First Fidelity, and all I'd done since that time was to leave a neat little trail of clues, just like Hansel and Gretel going up the hill.

Felix came off as a sweet and sorry government witness. I could see that the female judge, a former Catholic nun, also took a liking to him. She just couldn't believe that Felix sold and used drugs even though he had a nose on him like the Swiss Alps. Felix took every drug he could buy or steal, but he denied it on the stand, lying piece of shit that he was. I doubt they ever even bothered to give him a drug test.

Barry Nelson, Sy Sher, Larry Knott, Frank Cocchiaro, and I were indicted. Curiously missing were Stanley Seligman, Earl Hunt, Todd Siegmeister, and Felix, all the guys who supplied the government with information. And whether it was accurate or just plain bullshit, the government used it.

I was charged with racketeering (illegal collection of money), conspiracy (that we planned these things together), extortion (threatening with bodily harm), possession of cocaine with intent to distribute, and conspiracy to import cocaine. If I was convicted on all counts, I faced a $90,000 fine and 90 years in prison.

The government went so far as to have a Colombian kid named Jose Rodriguez in the same trial with me, alleging that he and I were going to ship 400 kilos of cocaine per week to south Florida.

On Saturday, March 16, 1985, after four days of deliberation, the jury announced they had reached a verdict.

Chapter 22

Judgment Day

I had felt the pressure of being on the mound in the World Series, knowing that 50 million people were watching my every move. I'd also been able to tell a gun-toting Jim Pritchett that we were keeping his $320,000. I thrived on pressure like that—putting myself in risky situations and rolling the dice. It wasn't the money, it was the win—knowing that you had outsmarted or outmaneuvered the other guy.

I could count on my own skills and wits in situations like those, and the pressure only served to make the experience exhilarating. The polar opposite is to be in a risky situation and have no means of changing the outcome.

When jurors had entered the courtroom during the trial, I would get the occasional smile or head nod. But now, on March 16, 1985, all the heads were down and no one looked me in the eye. I sensed that the outcome was going to be awful and there was nothing I could do about it. They looked like they were going to announce the death penalty for me.

Getting hit with the first count, racketeering, was a crushing blow because I knew it meant eight years. With eight years, you do 30 months and go home on parole.

When they hit me with counts two and three for loan-sharking, extortion, and cocaine possession, it's difficult to put into words the physical and emotional shock that coursed through my body. I had been standing for the verdict and, as it came down, my legs went out and I had to put my hands on the table to stay propped up. I began sweating profusely and shaking heavily. I could actually feel and hear my heart thumping, and I thought I was having a heart attack. My lawyer, Arnie Levine, muttered in disbelief, "What did you do?"

The cocaine trafficking charge was coming up next on count four, and I was thinking, "If they hit us with this one, I might as well jump out the window." Count four was the most serious and preposterous—conspiracy to distribute 400 kilos of cocaine a week with the Colombian kid, Jose Rodriguez, who I had never met.

After the "not guilty" on count four was announced, there was a little lull as the judge reviewed the paperwork. I sat back down.

In those immediate and awful moments, I saw my family sobbing uncontrollably in the courtroom and realized that my life as I had come to know it would never, ever be the same. My thrill-seeking lifestyle had finally caught up with me. I had destroyed my family and all I had stood for and accomplished in my life. How would Sharon and the kids survive?

My life wasn't over; it just felt that way. I could still feel my heart pounding, the sweat was pouring off me, and I began passing gas. Arnie got a whiff, looked at me, and said, "Is that you? Are you okay?" I wasn't certain which bodily function might break down next. I grabbed onto the table, fearful that I was also losing control of my kidneys.

Arnie put his arm around me and whispered, "It could be worse—she might have locked you up today. We'll have a month or two to put our heads together on what to do." I whispered back, "We haven't figured out what to do yet?"

The prosecutor, Ernst Mueller, jumped to his feet and said to judge Elizabeth Kovachevich, "The government has one more request."

Judgment Day

"Yes, Mr. Mueller," she replied. I thought, *He just won a six-month trial for crissakes—what the hell does he want now? My arm, my legs, my children?*

"We want all of the defendants taken into custody immediately," replied Mueller, "because they're flight risks."

I wanted to pick up a chair and whack Mueller in the face. "Why?" I asked Arnie in my shock and fury.

Kovachevich immediately concurred with Mueller, calling me a "danger to the community" and saying, "Marshals, please take them into custody." It was shocking beyond description. Arnie leaped to his feet and asked for an immediate bail hearing.

"No, Mr. Levine," Kovachevich calmly replied, "but when would you like to schedule one?"

"Right now, judge, but tomorrow will be fine."

"Tomorrow is Sunday, is that alright?"

"Absolutely, your honor." She set the hearing for early afternoon. Kovachevich's game was to make it appear that she was bending over backward to accommodate the defense.

In those few moments I went from a ballplayer and family man to a convict. I was put in handcuffs and leg irons and, in front of my family and friends, was led out of the courtroom to be held in the county jail until they brought me back for sentencing.

Sharon and the kids were still crying, all reaching out to me, but the marshals wouldn't let them get near me. I was a prisoner now, a marked man at their mercy.

What was I gonna do—run outside and kill somebody? Suddenly I'm an animal? I'd been on trial for a year and didn't flee. When they put me in handcuffs and leg irons and marched me out of the courtroom, it was the most devastating moment of my life.

On the way out, my 13-year-old daughter Michelle called out, "Daddy, where are they taking you?" My shame and embarrassment ran so deep I was unable to answer her, and when I got to the hallway, I could no longer hold back the tears. I started bawling and started peeing in my pants before regaining some control.

As the marshals walked me to their van, dozens of media people were waiting. I had plenty to say, but with my pants wet and the cuffs and shackles on, I was too humiliated to stop.

They could have taken me out through the garage and avoided the degradation of a public display, but they forced me to shuffle down the sidewalk in cuffs and leg irons for all to see. It was a complete dog-and-pony show for the cameras, like I was an O.J. Simpson who was going to try to run down the block and escape.

We drove an hour or so to the county jail in Bradenton, where they would hold me overnight. While processing my paperwork, they took the cuffs and leg irons off, and I sat there with the guards, signing autographs and baseballs. I was allowed to use the phone and spent an hour trying to calm Sharon down. I figured I'd make it through the night here and then we'd win our bond hearing in the morning. I kept telling her I'd be home the next day because there wasn't any reason to hold me while our appeal was being processed.

Then reality struck like a sledgehammer again. Apparently I wasn't going to sit there and shoot the shit all night with the guards. The mood quickly changed as they took my tie and belt and led me down a corridor to a one-man cell that had a bare bulb hanging from the ceiling that you couldn't shut off. There were no books or newspapers—nothing at all to occupy my mind. They'd taken the belt and tie because inmates can use them to commit suicide, but did they think I was gonna to kill myself by eating a book? I was also planning on getting out on bail in the morning, so why would I commit suicide?

I was so angry, aghast, and ashamed that I might have taken my life that night if there was a way to do it in the cell. At 2:00 that same day I could have gone out for lunch, hugged my wife, or seen my kids play ball. All of a sudden, that was gone. It was the ultimate despondency. My life was no longer mine. I was awestruck by the power of a system that allows a judge to suddenly decide that I might hurt somebody, so boom—just like that—she makes me public enemy number one. I still didn't know how many years I would get, but the first 15 minutes were torture. Thank God they did take my tie and belt.

All my life I've needed action. I can't just sit and relax, and I began to pace the cell to try to power down and avoid hyperventilating. I need people around me, and the concept of isolation and loneliness day after day was terrifying. I couldn't process living like this, and I prayed that I'd die in my sleep.

Sy Sher was in Bradenton also, and they brought us back to Tampa for the bond hearing the next morning. I had nine character witnesses, including a judge, a sportscaster, a minister, and Jim Campbell. But their words fell on deaf ears. Mueller called me a second-degree sociopath and suggested I'd even flee in my plane—as if I'd abandon my wife and four kids. The lies and expansions of truth the government resorted to was amazing to me.

I was transferred to the Seminole County Correctional Facility the next day. Frank Cocchiaro and Sy were brought there also. Frank had been in prison before and warned me not to be intimidated. He said that once people know you're scared, you might as well be dead. He also warned me that rats are everywhere looking to please, and that I shouldn't tell anybody anything.

Sy and I shared a seven foot by 10 foot cell with a solid steel door. There was a sink, toilet, and a concrete slab with a mattress for the bed. I got to put the second mattress on the floor with my head about a foot from the toilet. Sy agreed to my one and only rule: he would never pee when I was sleeping because I was too close to the pot. There were 12 of these two-man cells on the upper level and a community room down below where the 24 of us in the pod would spend most of our time.

Sy was a great cellmate because I was broke and he had the money to keep the cell brimming with commissary goodies. I may have been contemplating suicide, but I was at least going to die with a belly full of Hersheys.

I broke down again when I called Sharon that night. The crying was becoming epidemic now. The loss of freedom and separation from my family was crushing. Sharon told me to get it together and not make any assumptions until I was sentenced next month.

Arnie told me to prepare myself for an eight- to 25-year sentence with up to a $75,000 fine, but he guessed it would be 15 years at the most.

"At the most?" I asked.

"Don't get ahead of yourself," Arnie warned. "We have a great appeal, and if we get it on the fast track, you'll be out in a year. And with 15 years, even if we lose the appeal, you'll only do five."

"Only five?" Easy for him to say.

The thought of five years of this caused me to start mentally discounting the value of my life. I had no income, and Sharon and the kids had no means of support. Since my life insurance policies also covered suicide, I figured I was worth more dead than alive.

◆   ◆   ◆

There was a big black guy called Bubba, believe it or not, who thought he was running the pod. Bubba was about 6'5", maybe 300 pounds, and was in terrific shape. He was a street-dealing cokehead who thought he was King Kong.

Bubba would feel free to grab the TV remote or go over to a card table, snatch the cards, and tell everybody to get the f*ck away from the table. I was in such a suicidal mode the first few weeks that I decided to challenge the obnoxious son of a bitch. I took Frank Cocchiaro's advice in deciding that no inmate was ever going to push me around.

I steered clear of Bubba until I had the TV remote in my hand one night. He demanded it, and I refused to give it up. I said, "You come near me again, and I'll take this chair and stick it up your ass."

Bubba never laid a fist on me. He was an angry and violent man, but I was a high-profile inmate and there were cameras. If he beat me up, he would pay for it with more years. And it made no difference to me if he killed me because I knew I couldn't go on for at least five more years of this anyway. The concept was inconceivable.

After a few more weeks, I started becoming more rational regarding my desire to survive. I held the TV remote one afternoon when Bubba entered and announced he wanted to watch cartoons. He had just gotten his ass kicked again in court, failing to get some evidence against him thrown out. He was raving about "those dirty motherf*ckin' white bastards. They're no f*ckin' good, none of 'em."

There were half a dozen guys watching with me when Bubba demanded the remote. I said, "Sorry, we're watching the news. When it's over, you can do what you want."

I'd embarrassed him and he was pissed.

"If you don't give it to me, I'm gonna break every f*ckin' bone in your body."

Apparently I hadn't effectively intimidated Bubba in our initial encounter.

"I'm in deep shit now with this coke beef," Bubba continued, "so what the f*ck do I have to lose?"

I decided to see if I could give up the remote and still save face with a verbal barrage.

I slammed the remote on a nearby table and yelled, "F*ck you, asshole. Watch your two-year-old cartoons. That's why you're here anyway, for being a stupid jerk-off."

Bubba moved toward me, screaming, "Who you calling stupid, motherf*cker? You're here, too."

My flight reflex kicked in, and I ran to the stairway and bolted up the stairs to my cell and stayed put. I had Sy bring me my meals the next few days, peeking out the window of our cell to make sure it was him. Sy and I even had a secret knock. Some irony, huh—an inmate with a secret knock trying to get into another jail cell. Sy successfully played peacemaker for me and got Bubba to give his word that he wouldn't be the first man in history to kill a 30-game winner.

The food was inedible in this jail, and I gave most of it away. I called the punch "Jim Jones Juice" and told Sy that if Jones had served shit this bad, most of those poor people would have survived because Jones would have run out of bullets.

I was brought back in cuffs to the courthouse in Tampa for sentencing on April 25, 1985, about six weeks after the conviction.

Frank and Sy went first and got 20 years each, but their sentences were classified as "B-2." That meant that they were eligible for parole and had the chance to convince a parole board to free them. What I didn't know at the time was that Sy had already become a government "rat," giving up information on other "wise guys." In other words, his freedom was already being negotiated.

But seeing as I had been portrayed as the bad guy during the trial, Arnie and I now figured we were looking at 35 years. We were allowed to plead our side before sentencing, and Arnie spoke eloquently about the disreputable government witnesses who had perjured themselves and why, as a first time offender, I should be allowed to perform community service.

I had my turn to speak, and as Sharon and the kids quietly sobbed in the background, I talked about the shame I'd brought to my family and myself—the greed and selfishness I'd displayed—and that I didn't know how I got to where I was today from where I had been 17 years ago in 1968.

None of it made a difference. She gave me 23 years with no chance for parole until November 1992. By then, my daughter Michelle would be 20, and all my kids would be grown and gone.

I had been guilty of enough things—aiding and abetting, extortion and gambling, and making usurious loans. But to give me more years than Sher and Cocchiaro was crazy. They'd been criminals almost their entire lives. Cocchiaro was a known mob enforcer, Sy a money-laundering agent for the largest mob bookmaker in the United States. And they got less time. Go figure.

I also owed $8,900 in fines and $200,000 to Arnie in legal fees. I had no money and was looking at a prison salary of 11¢ an hour.

Chapter 23

The Big A

I was held in the filthy and cockroach-infested Hillsborough County Jail near Tampa before my more permanent destination was determined. Within a few days, I was picked up in a van and told I was being transferred to the federal prison in Tallahassee, which I took as good news—it was only four hours from Tampa, and Sharon and the kids would be able to visit. I had heard that the Bureau of Prisons tried to keep you close to your family, and I assumed that was why I was heading to Tallahassee.

Aside from the barbed-wire fences and the reality of what the place was, the check-in area was clean and they gave me a few sandwiches that were actually worth eating—two pieces of baloney, mayonnaise, and lettuce on some pretty fresh bread. There's nothing like enjoying a good sandwich in leg irons and handcuffs.

I also endured my first strip search. A guard looked through my hair, under my armpits, up my nose, and had me bend over to see if I had anything hidden in my ass. The only explanation for such a thorough perusal is to degrade and dehumanize you more than you already have been.

I wondered what guys had historically stuffed up their assholes to necessitate this part of the procedure. Food, knives, guns—was it maybe a getaway car? They do it to remind you who the boss is.

As fate would have it, one guy blew a large fart in the cop's face as we were checking in to Tallahassee. He was thrown to the ground and handcuffed and we never saw him again. So much for practical jokes in the penal system, huh?

I was soon informed that I was only passing through Tallahassee and would be taken to the federal penitentiary in Atlanta. While the prisoners who were staying lived in dorms, I and another guy were held in a claustrophobic six foot by eight foot cell that had a bunk bed, toilet, and sink. In other words, there was no room at all, and I'd have to endure this confinement until they moved us. We'd have no privacy, and the only activity outside the cell was to take a shower every morning.

My bunkmate was a guy named Frank Smith, a 77-year-old bank robber who began his criminal career at age 17 in 1925 when he held up a poker game. Frank spent 35 of the next 60 years in prison and showed me newspaper clippings that detailed his various capers and convictions. The events that brought us together were two 1984 bank holdups in Daytona Beach that netted him $8,000.

Frank told me that he would have gotten away with them in the old days, but the new-fangled surveillance cameras led to his capture after he returned to his trailer to count the dough.

Frank liked life on the inside. The jobs he had in prison seemed fair exchange for the free food, clothes, medical care, and TV. He also got to shoot the shit all day, talking "shop" with his peers. Many of the elderly in this country don't enjoy the care that Frank received for free from the Feds.

By the second day in Tallahassee, I would have jumped for joy at the opportunity to go outside and break up rocks with a sledgehammer. Give me a mop and a pail—anything—to end the monotony and escape the ridiculously close proximity to Frank.

After an agonizing month at Tallahassee, I was transferred with six other guys to the U.S. Penitentiary in Atlanta, about a four-hour Bureau of Prisons bus ride away.

The Big A

The Big A, as it was affectionately called, was built around the turn of the century and was surrounded by a concrete and steel wall that reached 37' at its highest. It had been the world's largest piece of masonry until the Boulder Dam was built in 1936. This was a bona fide prison, not some little house of detention. You expected Edward G. Robinson to greet you at the door. Al Capone, in fact, had been housed here a half century previous.

They led us off the bus to walk up about 20 steps into the Big A. Armed cops stood on guard as they led us to a holding cell down a long shiny hallway. Inmates wax the hallway all day, and it sparkled like the Halls of Congress. We walked through what they called "sally port" doors. When you get through the doors, they lock behind you and the doors on the other side open. You go through those and the same thing happens. After three of them, you're released into the penitentiary and they take off your cuffs and irons.

By the time we reached the cell blocks, the quiet, clean hallway was a thing of the past. The Big A was not only filthy, but the noise level made it sound like there was a riot or a wild sporting event going on.

We were put in a holding cell, and the powerful stench in it seared my nostrils. We waited in that cell for more than three hours, and with no urinal, guys had no choice but to piss in the corner. It was pathetic and demeaning, and you certainly couldn't holler for a guard to give you a bathroom pass.

This was June 1985, and of Atlanta's prison population of 2,200, 1,900 were Cubans. Back in 1980, when President Jimmy Carter offered asylum to all Cubans who wanted to flee the dictatorship of Fidel Castro, Castro trumped Carter by emptying his prisons and mental institutions and dropping those dregs of his society at the port of Mariel, where the so-called Freedom Flotillas departed for the U.S.

More than 120,000 Cubans swarmed our shores. Most blended nicely into our society—in fact, the Tigers signed Barbaro Garbey right off the flotilla, and he played for the '84 championship team. The Big A was used as a holding tank for the undesirables. The jail had been condemned for being outdated and dilapidated, but now it was apparently just fine to put Cubans and others like me in there.

The Cubans in the Big A were in limbo—with no rights, no legal standing, and unable to return to Cuba. Those who were deemed good security risks were allowed to mix with the American prisoners and work in the kitchen, but most were quarantined in subhuman conditions—locked up 23 hours a day with eight men jammed in a 10 foot by 21 foot cell. They had no privacy, ate awful food, and were given virtually no medical care.

There were two facilities in Atlanta—the maximum-security prison and a camp for nonviolent offenders. I was certainly nonviolent, but it became apparent that they had no plans to move me to the camp. I lived in a dorm in the basement of the prison hospital. My room was 12 feet by 20 feet, with five bunk beds for 10 guys. Unlike the Cubans, we only had to cram in there to sleep. We shared community TV rooms and toilets that were stopped up with sewage spilling on the floor half the time.

Five of the 10 guys in my cell did nothing but smoke cigarettes, and one of them puffed, coughed, and gagged all day. You were free to smoke anywhere in the prison, and here I was in a condemned building full of chain-smokers. I've hated cigarette smoke since my earliest memories of my father, and there was no escaping it in Atlanta. Like my old baseball roommate, Ray Oyler, these guys would wake up at 4:00 AM for a cigarette. Every time somebody lit up, I'd also wake up and wouldn't get back to sleep until he snuffed it out. Like with my dad, I was fearful that the dormitory was going to burn down with me in it.

Then there were the cockroaches, spiders, mosquitoes, flies, rats, mice, and asbestos. I had an upper bunk, and my face was about a foot from an open ceiling tile filled with asbestos. I imagined thousands of cockroaches emerging at any moment to attack my face and wondered how much asbestos was finding its way from the ceiling to my lungs.

The Big A

There was also the phone situation. There was one phone for the 78 inmates in my wing, and it was in constant use from noon to midnight. Telling grown men when they could talk on the phone and having only one of them in operation was typical of the dehumanizing nature of prisons. The phone was the only real way to touch the outside world, and we groveled like dogs to get at it.

The phone caused more fights than anything in the prison. There was constant unrest caused by jockeying for the use of that single phone. To keep the carnage to a minimum, there was a sign-up sheet, where inmates could reserve 15-minute blocks. As it was, that still left almost half the guys without the opportunity to use the phone on a given day.

Some guys had nobody to call but would trade their phone time for cigarettes or food. I signed up for the 8:00 to 8:15 block one night and noticed that the phone was on the hook at 7:45. The name on the sign-up sheet was Joe Marrow, a small-time organized crime gopher who was running the projector for a movie that had run a little long.

I called Sharon at 7:45, hoping that I would have a full half hour to talk to her and the kids. I was engrossed in conversation at 7:55 when Marrow tapped me on the shoulder to say, "Hey, motherf*cker, this is my time you're using."

"I'm on my f*ckin' time," I growled back, "and don't call me motherf*cker, you old asshole."

Marrow wasn't physically intimidating, and at 55 was almost 15 years older than me. But he didn't leave, pointing his finger in my face and ripping me with every profanity in the book. Sharon was shocked at the language she was hearing, so I put the receiver to my chest and bellowed to Marrow, "Go f*ck yourself and get the hell outta here."

"F*ck you, cocksucker," Marrow yelled back with equal intensity, and stomped off.

Having stood my ground with Marrow, I tried to regain my composure and reengage Sharon in some civilized dialogue.

Within seconds I felt a sharp pain in the back of my head and dropped to the floor. I put my left hand on my head and my fingers were soaked with blood. I saw Marrow quickly walking away and put the phone to my ear to hear Sharon screaming, "What happened? What's going on?"

I felt faint, like I was going to vomit and pass out, and as nicely as I could I said, "Honey, I'll call you back. Everything is okay."

Everything was hardly okay. I had blood all over my head and my face. An inmate came to my aid and said that Marrow had clobbered me with the fire extinguisher. Had it not glanced off one of the wooden extensions on the sides of the wall phone as he brought it down on my head, it could have crushed my skull. The wooden extension was on the floor next to me.

I asked a cellmate named Doc to look at my head, and he said there were two deep gashes a few inches long that needed stitches. But I knew that going to the hospital wasn't an option. If I took the problem up there it would get written up; Marrow would likely be thrown in the hole and I'd be put in segregation for my own protection. Marrow deserved more than the hole—he was guilty of assault with a potentially deadly weapon. By the same token, I'd risk the reputation of being a snitch, and in prison, that's a label that can get you killed.

Unless the gashes in my head became infected and I had to go to the hospital, the prison powers would only find out if a rat gave up Joe or me. Going to the cops wasn't an option either.

But getting even didn't defy any unwritten codes.

Doc helped me find a towel and ice, and I took four Tylenol that I had in my bunk. A couple of the guys worked it out to get me some phone time a little later, and I called Sharon to tell her that it was no big deal.

Frank Cocchiaro, my convicted co-defendant, all but ran the Big A and was the final word for most of the prisoners. He sat me down and said he was proud of me for not running to the cops. But he also told me that I had to settle the matter, and he would make sure I had the chance.

It took a few hours for the bleeding and throbbing to subside, and I was able to fall asleep by around 3:00 AM.

The very next morning, a Saturday, Frank told me to go to the weight room. The place was usually jam-packed on a Saturday, but I walked in to find it totally empty except for Joe Marrow, sitting on a bench. Frank had made sure there would be no witnesses to whatever was going to happen.

Before I could open my mouth, Marrow stood up and said, "I'm sorry, Denny. I didn't mean it."

"Didn't mean it?" I said, my fury rising. "You almost killed me, you f*ck."

"Look, asshole," Marrow said, his contriteness quickly disappearing, "if you won't accept apologies, then f*ck you."

The words were barely out of his mouth when I wound up and nailed him with my right fist between his cheek and nose. Marrow dropped like a stone, rolled over, and tried to stand up.

"Joe, get up and I'll f*ck you up real bad," I said, my heart pumping and adrenalin flowing.

He got up and said, "F*ck you, asshole. I'll take the phone from you next time."

I hit him again, harder than I'd ever hit anyone in my life, and Marrow sank to his knees and then fell on his side. He was bleeding from his nose and mouth and I wanted to kill him. I said it again. "If you get up, I'll break your f*ckin' neck!"

He sat in silence. It was over. Prison justice had been served.

As I left the weight room, guys appeared from all directions and walked in as if it were business as usual.

Think of the pettiness and the code of conduct that arises when men are stripped of their freedom and dignity. Marrow could have killed me with the fire extinguisher, and I could have killed him with my fists and whatever else I could hit him with. And it all happened over a phone call. And if it wasn't a phone call, guys might throw haymakers because one was watching a cartoon and the other said it was time to watch *The Price Is Right*.

◆   ◆   ◆

A while later I developed a severe numbness from my right knee to hip and went to the prison doctor. He told me a neurosurgeon would be on hand in two to three months.

"In two or three months," I said incredulously.

He had an attitude like I should understand. In other words, you're a convict, and why should you expect any better?

I had a cellmate named J.C. who had a growth the size of a baseball on his chest that was the most unsightly thing I'd ever seen. A cop who we worked with in the kitchen was from Detroit and asked the medical staff to help. He was told to butt out. J.C. waited five months for a biopsy. Sure enough, he had cancer and didn't last the rest of the year.

Not all the guards and administrators were pricks. There were some very decent people working in the prison system. But the abuses were such that it almost didn't matter.

I worked in the kitchen for a few months, where some of the Cuban inmates thought it was hilarious to drop rats or mice in the food. One guy mashed a huge vat of tuna salad by taking his shoes off and doing it with his feet. The guys who made salads never wore gloves and didn't bother to wash the produce. One night a rat ran across the preparation table and leapt off the end before disappearing from sight. They were ladling gravy and sending it out to the tables. When they got to the bottom of the vat, there was the rat, scalded to death. Out in the mess hall, they poured gravy over the mystery meat like nothing had happened.

The Big A

I told the guys in the dorm about the rat incident and vowed I would never again eat any food that I didn't personally see come out of the cooler.

♦   ♦   ♦

Early on at the Big A, somebody suggested that I manage the Cardinals, the prison baseball team. I offered my services, but the reigning manager said, "We don't want any outside interference." As a fellow convict, I wasn't sure what "outside interference" meant.

About a week later, a Cuban inmate named Juan told me that there were a dozen other guys who had been excluded from the team for one reason or another who wanted me to manage them to challenge the Cardinals. I was 41 and weighed about 275, but said, "Sure, I'll even pitch for you guys." Thirty minutes after I said "yes," I started kicking myself for succumbing to the temptation to play baseball again.

Our team was immediately named the "Detroit Dennys," and we practiced for a few weeks on one of the two diamonds in the prison yard. After a week, my arm felt like it was going to fall off. I hadn't thrown a ball competitively in a decade, and I didn't have any doctors around to shoot me up with cortisone.

Luckily, the game was rained out and rescheduled for the next week. I rested my arm and took the mound on July 14, 1985, before a large crowd in the prison yard anxious to see what a former major league pitcher looked like in action. Every inmate who could make it was there, along with every cop, the warden, and his staff.

The wagering was enormous. One of the bigger bettors offered me $1,000 dollars to throw the game. Shit, I didn't do it in the real world, and I couldn't do it to a bunch of guys who were depending on me.

I gave up a three-run homer over the prison wall in the first inning but struck out six batters in the next three innings and left the mound with the score tied 4–4 in the sixth. I played shortstop the rest of the way and even managed to hit one off the left-field wall. But we had no backup pitching and were mauled 25–5 by the Cardinals.

My arm hurt so much that I could barely raise my hand. To make matters worse, I slipped in the shower afterward and hurt my back. The good that came out of it was that our prison bookmaker made out well and gave me $200 in commissary after the game.

Once again, I was washed up as a pitcher and looking for something new to occupy my mind.

Chapter 24

The Hole

I had to get out of the Big A. It was a pigsty, one of America's most violent penal institutions, and I needed to be close to my family. I wanted to go back to Tallahassee and stumbled upon a plan that I thought might work.

There was an Atlanta attorney named Herbert Shafer who represented Jack Hanberry, our warden at the Big A. I learned through the grapevine that for $5,000 Shafer could get Hanberry to transfer you almost anyplace you wanted to go.

Shafer had represented Hanberry in a criminal case when Hanberry, an ordained Baptist minister, had been arrested for shoplifting a $1.10 hairbrush from a grocery store. Shafer got him off, and now the two were in the prisoner transfer business.

I arranged to have Shafer meet me at the prison and asked him what it would cost to get me to Tallahassee. "It's five grand for low-profile guys," Shafer said. "You pose more of a problem. Ten grand will get you in Tallahassee in 60 days."

"Ten grand?" I said. "That's ridiculous."

I couldn't afford it. Sharon and the kids were barely getting by. Back to the drawing board.

Frank Cocchiaro had a female attorney who was doing some post-conviction work with him. I joined Frank for one of his sessions with her and shared some of my knowledge about the Big A, including the ridiculous phone situation. I also mentioned the Herb Shafer thing and her eyes lit up.

She confided that the FBI was looking into the transfer scam and wanted to know if I'd consider talking to an FBI colleague of hers. I told her that I'd work with them on the outside, but if word leaked on the inside, I could get hurt badly.

She visited me a week later and brought along her FBI friend. I freaked out until the FBI friend assured me that she had just been transferred to Atlanta and no one in the prison knew who she was.

She promised me a transfer if I cooperated by wearing a wire to nail Shafer or have Sharon go see him wearing one. But if either Hanberry or Shafer caught on, Sharon's life would be in danger and God only knows how badly I could have gotten whacked on the inside.

It was all too risky, and I decided to look for a different way out.

To keep myself busy, I started taking notes so as to document all the dirt going on in that rat hole of a prison.

Many inmates were worried about AIDS, which was already a big epidemic in 1985. There were a few inmates in the hospital who we figured were dying from it, and homosexuality was rampant in the Big A. Lots of the Cubans were gay, and we didn't know how it was transmitted. Hell, if you shook hands with one or sat on the same toilet seat, would you get it?

I found a private memo written to hospital employees detailing how they should be careful handling things around AIDS patients. But no literature, condoms, or anything was distributed to educate the inmates.

I found a 1984 report on asbestos that detailed how 50 percent of the material in the walls was asbestos. The whole damn prison was lined with

256

asbestos. Every time the light came through the window, you could see the shit flying in the air. Lawsuits had been filed against the Bureau of Prisons, but the judges also work for the government, and nothing had been done about it.

I heard from a few inmates that guards would supply answers to the Graduate Equivalency Degree test because the prison got paid for every inmate who passed.

I wasn't looking to go after the warden or the cops, but once I started looking for stuff, it was a joke how easily things fell my way. I found purchase orders for dozens of X-rated tapes, like *Emmanuelle* and *Little Miss Innocence*. There were scores of other videos, like all the Dallas Cowboys Super Bowl tapes. But the prisoners only saw 35-millimeter movies, meaning that somebody had spent $2,300 of prison cash to stock his personal video library.

The holiday season of 1985 rolled around and I became very depressed again. Sharon and the kids had eaten hot dogs for Thanksgiving dinner, and Christmas was now approaching. My old Tiger boss, Jim Campbell, sent them a check for $1,500, and a few other friends came through with smaller amounts.

Around this time I met with Gary Leshaw, an attorney with the Atlanta Legal Aid Society who was helping the Cubans with a class-action suit. I gave Leshaw the X-rated tape story that he relayed to a reporter at the *Atlanta Journal and Constitution*. An article ran under the headline Porno Tapes Ordered at Atlanta Pen.

I was working in the kitchen two days after the article ran when a guy with a captain's badge grabbed me and told me to come with him. The cop running the kitchen asked him where they were taking me, and the captain said, "Shut up. You haven't been working here long enough to ask questions. Replace him. He ain't coming back."

The captain and a few of his men walked me to the segregation unit and then took me down some very dark stairs to an even darker hallway.

He opened a door to a pitch-black room and stood me in the doorway. "Can you see anything in there?" he asked sharply.

I said, "No. What's in there?"

"There's nothing in there. No toilet, no chair, no water, no nothing. And if you don't stop the bullshit, here's where you'll spend the next 23 years."

This part of segregation was for the lowest, most out-of-control scum in the prison. You are at their mercy. I asked the captain what the point was in showing me this awful cell.

They had found about half the stuff I had written because I had smuggled some stuff out to Sharon. The prison goon squad had torn my room apart and found all of my notebooks.

"You want to expose people you have no business talking about?" he said evenly and coldly. "We'll put you where you can't do nasty to anybody. Do you get the f*cking message?"

I had been so angry and pissed off at the system that I'd lost sight of the reality that I had no rights and options. This was the worst hole you could imagine, and they made their point with me.

People do their time in different ways. I did my time writing down what I heard. "Yes, sir. I get the message." It didn't matter that I was thinking, *If I'm in jail for doing what I did, why aren't these people in jail? They're doing things worse than some of the people doing time in this place.*

They marched me back my cell and the captain said, "Pack up your shit."

I packed it up and they took me to a more populated segregated area with about 15 other cells and locked me down 24 hours a day. From that point on, I kissed any ass that needed to be kissed to get out and stay out of the black box.

I had no phone privileges in lockdown, so one of my guys on the cell block told Sharon that she might not be hearing from me for a while. In the meantime, she went to Senator Laughton Chiles from Lakeland and told him about the transfer bribery scheme.

The Hole

Chiles told her, "He's in an awful place, and he better be careful because that's how the system works." He essentially shrugged off her pleas to get me transferred with the attitude, "He's in jail—what can we do?"

They had sent me to Atlanta instead of Tallahassee because they felt I knew a lot about organized crime and were trying to squeeze me to tell them all about Sy, Frank, and their organized crime buddies. But it was a fruitless enterprise. Sy was my friend and coworker at First Fidelity and in his bookmaking operation, but he would never bring me into his inner circle. That's how he survived all those years. FBI agents visited me in Atlanta and kept pounding me for information. I told them about First Fidelity, but they said, "We've already got you in jail for that shit."

I told them honestly that I didn't know who Sy's guys were. Hell, I'd have given up Santa Claus if I had had the stuff on him.

Sharon quickly became desperate to get me out of the hole and went to the female FBI agent who had talked to us months earlier about exposing the transfer scheme. Somehow, I suspect that that did the trick.

It was March 6, 1986, and I'd been locked down for two days when they came and got me at 6:00 AM. It was obvious I was leaving when the cop slapped the cuffs and leg irons on me and brought me to a waiting van.

A marshal in the van said, "How do you feel now?"

I said, "I'll let you know when you tell me where I'm going."

"You're going to Talladega, and you'll be much better off there."

Chapter 25

Talladega

We headed due west on I-20 to Alabama. Although Talladega was also maximum security and no closer to Sharon and the kids than Atlanta was, I knew it had to be an upgrade.

A pair of 20′-high fences surrounded the prison, with barbed wire filling the space between them. Absent were that awesome wall and the gun-toting guards in the towers at Atlanta.

I had to complete my 15 days in segregation and was pleased that the hole wasn't as awful as the one at the Big A. My cell was a spacious 10 feet by 14 feet and clean—anything looks clean compared to the Big A. The men's room at a Mobil station looks like a hospital operating room compared to the Big A.

There were a few small gaps in the walls of my cell that allowed some dialog with my neighbors on either side. One of the guys seemed to have his head screwed on right.

I was confined 23 hours a day with my books and thoughts, and I was given a half pencil to write with—apparently, you're less likely to kill yourself with a half pencil. I was allowed to shower every other day, but they even managed to take some of the pleasure out of that. I had to back up to the food slot to get cuffed behind my back and then do the same in the shower—back up to the slot to get the cuffs undone and then the same to get cuffed up to leave.

When my time in the hole was up, I was moved to an eight foot by 15 foot two-man cell. The dimensions were acceptable because we used a community bathroom out in the pod.

It was April 1986, and I'd been in prison for almost a year. I hadn't seen Sharon and the kids since a Christmas visit in Atlanta. Sharon had moved again to less-expensive housing in Tampa, and I started to sense that she wanted out. She started talking about moving in with her parents in Chicago, and the thought of losing her was too much to bear. I'd already missed Denny Jr.'s high school graduation, and Sharon was losing hope that I could win an appeal and get out anytime in the not-too-distant future. I couldn't blame her. She was poor, lonely, and bearing the full burden of raising our kids.

I was given a job as a dormitory orderly for the standard 11¢ an hour and fell into a relatively livable routine. I'd scrub and mop the floors in the halls and TV room for about half an hour and was still being paid the full 88¢ a day. What a deal, huh?

I'd watch *Donahue* from 8:00 to 9:00 AM and then CNN news for an hour. The law library was decent, and I'd work on my appeal and help other prisoners with grievances and various typing projects. I was managing to keep my mind occupied and even got a little physical exercise by playing some tennis in the afternoon before getting back to the cell for the 4:00 PM body count.

I went to a Monday-night chat session with the prison priest, Father O'Reilly, who then invited me to play the organ at Sunday mass. There'd be 40 to 50 guys in the chapel, and I'd play "How Great Thou Art" and "Amazing Grace." I'd play them a second time so that the Latin inmates could sing in Spanish.

I started writing a few columns for two Detroit sports publications and predicted a Red Sox victory in the '86 World Series. The Sox led 3–0 in the sixth inning of Game 7 when we had to get to our cells for the 9:30 body count. By the time we got back to the TV room, the Sox had blown the lead and the Mets went on to win 8–5. Most of the guys were Mets fans and, with all the hooting and hollering, you'd have thought they had just won their appeals.

I stayed out of trouble in Talladega and benefited from another idiotic TV room incident. I was watching the news after dinner when a guy named Gerald walked in and changed the station. I switched it back to the news.

Gerald got up, changed it again, and announced, "This TV is mine. Don't f*ck with it again."

Guys were starting to arrive after their meal when I got up, turned it back to the news, and planted myself in front of the TV. When Gerald took a step toward me, I said, "One more step and you'll wish you'd gone to dinner with everybody else."

Gerald lunged and threw a wild punch that spun him around. I grabbed him and threw him to the floor. He reached up, trying to grab me by the balls, and I whacked him twice, splitting his lip.

"If you get up," I said, "I'll kick your f*ckin' ass."

It was an important confrontation. If you don't stand your ground, you'll soon become somebody's wife.

Homosexuality and sex are rampant in prison. But rape is a rarity and falls out of the sex category into violence. I knew of only three rape incidents, and two of them stemmed from a guy stealing and then getting beaten up. Part of the punishment was rape. The third incident happened when a slightly built white kid, a new arrival, happened to be alone in the TV room when three black guys came in and raped him. If anyone else had been in the room, it wouldn't have happened. But the kid was alone, frightened, and made an easy target.

My family visited me at Christmas in 1986, and the sight of them blew me away. In the year since I'd last seen them, Denny and Tim had each grown four or five inches and my girls looked like starlets. Sharon looked tired but struck me as being more beautiful than on our wedding night.

We had a great time in the visitor's room, and I told them that I was optimistic that our upcoming appeal on January 15, 1987, would be successful. We would be heard in the 11th Circuit Court of Appeals in Atlanta.

Our main argument was that a fair trial had been impossible because Judge Kovachevich allowed a wholesale lack of decorum. Prosecutor Ernst Mueller had continually impugned the character of my attorney, Arnie Levine, and hearsay evidence from Barry Nelson and Stanley Seligman had been allowed on the record. When Arnie told the appellate judges that Kovachevich had even allowed a lighted Christmas tree in the courtroom, the judges stared down at their bench, as if they'd heard it all before. Kovachevich had more cases overturned than any judge in the history of her district.

The wheels of justice turn in agonizingly slow fashion. At 2:20 in the afternoon of August 7, 1987, nearly seven months after the appeal and 28 months since I was first taken into custody, I was told that Arnie Levine had called and I was to call him back immediately.

I got him on the phone and said, "Level with me."

"We got the whole thing reversed," he said gleefully.

"The whole thing?"

"The whole thing."

"Meaning what?"

"Meaning you can go home soon. You're about to become a free man."

I thanked him for the great news and instantly called Sharon. Neither of us could calm down over the incredible news.

The 14-page written judgment called the trial, "A classic example of judicial error and prosecutorial misconduct combining to deprive the appellants of a fair trial.... [Kovachevich] allowed the proceedings to get out of hand, seriously impeding the appellants' rights to a fair trial. This case was deserving of more patience and care than the judge gave it, and the appellants' case was prejudiced by this lack of care."

That was the crux of it, but it included Mueller's outrageous conduct toward Arnie and addressed the use of testimony that was clearly false.

The only hitch was that the government could still retry me and file motions to keep me in jail until a new trial began. Four weeks later my bond appeal was heard and granted. A New Jersey memorabilia dealer I knew named Walt Olender put up $200,000 to release me on bond.

On September 5, 1987, 902 days after I had been put in cuffs and irons and led out of the courtroom in Tampa, I walked out of Talladega.

A throng of reporters awaited me outside, and an hour later, Sharon and the kids arrived from Tampa. I'd arranged an exclusive interview with a Tampa TV station in exchange for my family being flown up on a chartered plane to take me home.

I waited on the tarmac as the plane arrived. I hadn't seen them for eight months. Denny and Tim were both in college, but as Sharon, Krissie, and Michelle walked down the steps and into my arms, the feeling was as indescribably wonderful as the degradation and loneliness of prison had been horrific.

We flew home and Sharon made pork chops, my favorite meal. In my 28 months away, Krissie hadn't permitted Sharon to serve pork chops until I was back home to share them.

Freedom. What an amazing concept.

Chapter 26

Freedom

I was free, and I was a big old papa bear again with my kids. I wasn't out of Talladega for more than a week when Arnie Levine called to say he was being pestered by a guy named David Welker, who owned a minor league hockey team called the Fort Wayne Komets.

Welker wanted to take advantage of the publicity that a just-released Denny McLain could produce, and he wanted me to do what I'd done in Memphis in the '70s—talk it up, be visible, and sell tickets. "When Denny McLain shows up in Fort Wayne," Welker said, "will there be another story for a month?"

I took the job. Minor league hockey is tough to sell, and we did our best by giving away cars, trips, and anything else we could. We paid Pete Rose $10,000 to come in for a game and sign for three hours. People lined up all around the rink to get at Rose. It was before Commissioner Bart Giamatti suspended him from baseball, and he was fabulous with the fans.

I worked out a promotion with a local supermarket to give away almost 3,000 turkeys for a Thanksgiving promotion. I also arranged to get a dozen live ones and offered prizes to anyone who could get on the ice and catch one. We had more than 7,000 people that night, and the hilarity of seeing people and turkeys slip and slide on the ice was better entertainment than minor league hockey. The animal rights people were irate, but everybody else got their money's worth.

Unfortunately, Welker was mentally unstable and kept hitting on Sharon. After three months, he fired me over a meaningless dispute. But I'd had enough of him by then. The good news was that I'd been practicing the organ extensively and started to make some inroads in that area.

I got a regular gig at a bar and restaurant in suburban Detroit called Mr. B's. Mr. B was a sports nut and liked guys who were a little off center. He even brought in the down-on-his-luck former heavyweight champion Leon Spinks to tend bar. While I played organ, Leon made drinks and suffered through an endless string of fools who'd put their hands up in a boxing pose and say, "C'mon, champ!" Everyone was buying Leon drinks, and he had already lost his driver's license because of drinking issues. Leon got smashed every night and had to be driven home.

Leon's tenure at Mr. B's came to an end on a 90-degree July night when he attempted to leave work with his trench coat on. A suspicious maître d' stopped him at the door and discovered that he had stashed 50 lamb chops in the pockets and under his arms.

Mr. B fired him when he came to work the next day. "God, Leon," Mr. B. said to him, visibly hurt and upset. "All you had to do was ask and I would've given you a thousand of 'em." Leon had also been pinching booze and pulling some cash from the register. Mr. B told me he'd been aware of that. "A little was okay, but Leon was getting out of control."

Mr. B fed me like I was King Farouk, and like Leon, I was also good with the customers. It soon grew into a five-nights-a-week gig.

I'd realized back when I was a 20-year-old rookie that the nicest thing that happens every day is when someone asks for an autograph. And if you treat somebody well, he'll tell a thousand people.

A guy will come up and say, "I met you at a dinner 22 years ago at the Elks Club in Romulus." And even though you'd forgotten both him and the event, you say, "Oh yeah, what a great time that was." People are intimidated until you engage them, and you can't lose sight of the fact that you're a public figure.

I was doing a card show with Pete Rose around this time, and I heard a guy ask him what he was up to. "I do Pete Rose every day," Rose said frankly. It was the perfect answer from a public figure. I told Rose I was borrowing the line from that day forward.

I wrote a book about my time in prison and was in Detroit promoting it in early 1988. John McCullough, who was drunk off his ass, was interviewing me on WXYT-AM. It was pathetic, as if I was interviewing myself. The studio smelled like a Jim Beam test factory, and I kept laughing to myself, "If somebody lit a match, the damn building might blow up."

When the interview was over, I ran into station owner Chuck Fritz, who I'd known from my playing days. We talked for a few minutes when Chuck asked, "Hey, how would you like to host a show or two when somebody's on vacation or sick?"

I said, "Yeah, sure," but in a smart-ass kind of way. I thought he might be blowing smoke.

The very next week, Fritz called me at my hotel before I went to my gig at Mr. B's. "We've got a few days open next week from 4:00 to 7:00 in the afternoon. You interested?"

Chuck wanted to see if I could establish myself outside the realm of sports. It was a talk format, and that was fine with me. Sports talk is narrow, and our goal was to only touch on sports stories that spilled over into general news.

The nightclub job didn't begin until 8:00 at night, so I said, "Sure, whatcha payin'?"

Chuck offered $300 per show or $1,500 a week. I was in hog heaven. $1,500 a week plus $500 a night at Mr. B's was great money.

Before my first radio show, producer Robin Bailey told me that the first guest was the columnist and author Erma Bombeck. Bombeck had a new book out about when kids come back home to live. Bombeck would be joining us by phone from her home in Minnesota.

Robin told me that Bombeck was a real talker. "Ask her one question and she'll fill the whole eight-minute segment," she assured me. "This is the easiest interview you'll do." I had always been comfortable when I was interviewed, but it was unsettling having the shoe on the other foot. When the light went on, I could hardly remember my name, much less any intelligent questions.

I said to my new radio audience, "I'm proud to have on my very first show and first interview, one of the great comic writers of our day. She has a new book, *Back to the Nest*. Welcome, Erma Bombeck, and how are you?"

"Fine, thank you. How are you?"

"Great, Erma. So, how did you come to write this book?"

"My kids came home, and I wanted to share the experience." Then, dead air! Where were the talking machine, the humor, the chatter, and the jokes?

The Bombeck interview was the longest 16 minutes of my life. She was one step above comatose. We must have caught her off guard when she didn't think she had anything scheduled. I was totally flushed as I walked out of the studio to use bathroom. I said to Robin, "Whoever the hell is next, tell 'em they gotta talk."

The station received some nasty phone calls as I finished out the week. "We don't want this drug dealer on this station," they'd rail, or, "We're not listening anymore until you get rid of him."

A few weeks later, Fritz came to see me at the club. After I finished a set, he came over and said, "I'm here for a reason." He told me off the record that he had convinced McCullough to go in for rehab. Then he asked in a very straightforward manner, "How would you like to take over the show full time?"

I stayed composed so it wouldn't look like I wanted to jump through the ceiling. The concept of $1,500 a week guaranteed and the chance to develop something meaningful was a dream come true.

Chuck promised that if I took the slot from 25th in the market to the low teens, he'd double my salary, and in either case, he'd guarantee me a job for the next three years. His one condition: "Just don't get in the mortgage business or do anything stupid again. And if you have any problems at all, promise you'll come to me first."

"It's a three-hour drive from Fort Wayne," I told Chuck. "When I tell this to Sharon, she'll be here in an hour and a half!"

Rumors started to spread that Fritz had decided to bring back the ex-con McLain full time. As if on cue, my old nemesis at *The Detroit News*, Pete Waldmeir, the same Pete Waldmeir who filled in Bowie Kuhn on my exploits at the Shorthorn back in 1967, wrote one thing after another about what a "disgrace" I was, and "How could Chuck Fritz put a felon on the air?" Waldmeir had also wanted McCullough's job, and to tone him down, Chuck gave him some little fill-in duties here and there.

Talk radio amazed me. Normally, nothing I thought about mattered to anyone but myself. But when you go on the air, your opinions on almost any subject become lightning rods.

Once the audience started to warm to me, Chuck switched me to mornings, the number-one slot in radio. My life was now an open book, and I ate up the attention. I brought my family into the fray to create material. I'd talk of the doubts I had about a guy Kristin was dating, and the phone lines would light up with people saying, "You're right, the guy's a loser," or, "You better leave her alone, Denny, she's old enough to decide for herself."

I'd talk about Sharon's cooking, and about Denny Jr. being in the Air Force and participating in Desert Storm, and about my son Tim, the party animal, on his eight-year degree program at Western Michigan University.

I came home one afternoon and found Sharon in a giddy mood. She said, "I have good news and bad news for you, which do you want first?"

"Give me the good news first."

"Okay. You always wanted to be a grandfather, right?"

"Right, I do." But Kristin wasn't married and it made no sense. "Okay, what's the bad news?"

"Michelle is making you a grandfather."

"What the hell are you talking about?" I said in confusion and mounting fury. Michelle was 17, still in school, but had told Sharon she was pregnant and prepared to marry her boyfriend and have the baby.

It always amazed me how much more emotionally involved listeners got over family and personal issues than real-world political drama. I went on the air with Michelle's pregnancy and the dizzying concept of grandfatherhood, and the phones lit up with every imaginable story about the adventures and exploits of pregnant daughters. The two kids were at least getting married, and I reluctantly accepted it.

Kristin moved up from Tampa, and we had a beautiful home. Except for the steady pressure of needing good ratings, I felt bulletproof and back on top.

By mid-1991, about three years in, we had the highest ratings in the station's history. I had also started doing a TV show that helped fuel my new multimedia presence.

In 1990 Steve Antoniotti, the general manager of the local CBS affiliate, called to ask if I'd be interested in doing a pilot for a possible weekly half-hour show with his sports director, Eli Zaret. Eli had a reputation as the prick of Detroit broadcasting for his sarcastic and nasty commentaries. He was much more confrontational and opinionated than the typical white-bread talking head, and Steve said the two of us might catch lightning in a bottle.

Naturally, I said, "Why not? Let's give it a shot."

Antoniotti had also quietly predicted to his staff that one of two things would happen: it would either be the best show in town or they'd have the lead story when one of us killed the other.

It was around the All-Star break, and before we taped the pilot, Eli took me aside. He was the TV veteran who knew how to produce the material and had the responsibility of orchestrating all the elements.

"I don't know you very well," he began, "so I want to get a feel for how far you're willing to go. If I give you a hard time about, like, stranding Mickey Lolich at the airport at the '69 All-Star Game, are you going to be able to handle it?"

I stared at him for a second or two and said, "I've been to jail, and I'm not sure you're smart enough to know how to hurt my feelings. I'll tell you this, though—let's not lose sight of the fact that it's all about entertainment—pure entertainment."

"Good," Eli said smiling. "That's all I need to hear."

Television was a different animal, and it took me a few months to get comfortable with the *Eli and Denny Show*. We got very good at debating topics and were the first in Detroit to bring spirited sports talk to TV. We also involved viewers by accepting goofy sports challenges, and the show got great ratings.

◆   ◆   ◆

About two years into the *Eli and Denny Show* and almost four years into the radio show, our wonderful family life was shattered by Kristin's death.

To someone who hasn't been through it, you can't explain what it's like to lose a child. Whatever you imagine the words to mean, reality is much more unkind. Our parents taught Sharon and I to trust and accept that God always has a reason, and you never show weakness, no matter how severe the pain. You deal with it and move forward. But we could find no relief in accepting God's way. There was no escape from the grief. There were no consoling words, wisdom, or church doctrine to soothe the pain that went beyond what either of us could bear.

Radio and television already demanded a full-time commitment, but Kristin's death made me want to run even faster. I was in a fog, reaching for anything that could take my attention away from the disaster. But I couldn't distract myself from thinking about the horrific way she died and the role I played in it. I was desperate to stay busy and stay away from Sharon, the kids, and any other reminders.

There's a statistic that says the loss of a child causes divorce more than 50 percent of the time. I imagined I could hear my kids thinking, *Damn it, Dad, why did you have to meddle in Kristin's life, too?* I'd always meddled in my kid's lives, even when they were adults. I always thought I was right in doing it. But this particular intrusion into their lives had backfired so badly.

Not only was I guilty of forcing her to move to Michigan from Tampa, but I wasn't able to ease the pain everyone else was suffering. I was supposed to be the strong one, the "rock." Nothing penetrated my armor, but I felt like Kristin's death was killing me also.

You had to go through all the firsts, like her birthday and Christmas with the empty chair. Someone would recall an old childhood Krissie-ism, like, "Dad, did you know that the French speak French?" or, "Jerry Lewis gets older every year." She was always aware of what she was saying, just trying to entertain us. But the momentary lightness would quickly dissolve. Family dinners became more like family wakes.

I kept on traveling, looking for places to go. I was flying more than 50 hours a month in our plane, finding any excuse I could to avoid my family. I just wanted to be away from anything or anyone who reminded me of Kristin's death. I didn't have the tools to help my family or myself. And I didn't have the guts to ask anyone else for help. Had I been capable of rational thought after Kristin's tragedy, I would have tightened the circle around my family instead of wanting to avoid them and run away. And I would have insisted that we seek professional help to get us through an event that no one is ever prepared for.

If I could do it again, I'd let my family talk about her and cry out their feelings. Not talking about it with each other just made it worse for all of us. Instead of moving forward together, my choice was to run away and suffer in my own cesspool of grief and anger. For months after Kristin died, I thought about killing Leonard Martin, the truck driver whose negligence took her away.

When I'd get home at night, I'd shut the door to my office and scream at God, demanding an explanation. Over and over I'd ask Him, "Why her? Take me. Why her?" I'd scream, "You owe me, God, how could you do this? What did this beautiful young girl do to you?"

My anger was uncontrollable. I'd punch walls wanting to hurt God, and for next few years I determined that there was no God.

I still feel God owes me an explanation for what He allowed. I believe in God again, but to take a child, any child, is plain wrong. I have heard 10,000 explanations from priests, rabbis, clerics, and anyone else who thinks that they have an explanation. I can honestly say that no one ever gave me an ounce of comfort in trying to explain why God did what He did.

Sharon and I quickly became indifferent to each other, and our married life fell apart. Everything was an argument. I'd say, "Good morning." Sharon would say, "What do you care?" That's not the real Sharon. We were both angry, but I was also so incredibly angry and distraught that the family kept their distance from me. There came a point where Sharon could hardly look at me. We were in the same house but light-years apart. We couldn't even sit down and have a nice dinner anymore.

In the beginning, it was like Kristin's death wasn't the truth—as if it couldn't really be. When Sharon's sister Barbara arrived shortly after

Krissie died, she was coming up the stairs when Michelle said, "She's here." Sharon thought she meant Krissie was here. She ran to the top of the stairs crying, "Where is she?" She saw it was her sister and ran screaming into the bedroom. We were just in shock. It couldn't be Kristin, and it couldn't happen to us.

I only lost outward composure once that I recall. It happened in our bedroom the day of her death. After that, I didn't want to console or be consoled. We were downstairs a few days after she died, and Sharon wanted me to hold her. I found myself backing away. I didn't want to lose control, and I never did after that one time. Even when they were lowering her casket into the ground—the most heartbreaking moment imaginable—I didn't even break down then.

Sharon said much later that I acted like it only happened to me. My attitude had been, "I am so hurt, how am I going to go on?" Everyone else was there with the same hurt. But I was cold and uncaring, like my mother was, not helping anyone while my own pain made me feel like I was choking to death.

Robin, one of my radio producers, had given Sharon a book she said had helped one of her friends after a personal loss. It was by a guy named George Anderson, who supposedly could contact people in the afterlife and let the parents know if they were okay. Sharon had seen him on TV years before.

Sharon and Michelle both read the book and started badgering me to take them to see Anderson, who was somewhere in New Jersey. It seemed ridiculous, and I didn't want to hear anymore about it. But they kept on insisting, so I finally told Sharon to make the arrangements. It took us months to get an appointment, and we talked about it a lot before going to see a man claiming he would tell us what was going on in heaven.

When we were outside Anderson's office, Sharon was all gung ho and hyped up. I said, "I know what you're thinking, and you've got to remember he's not going to give you Krissie back. Are you going to be able to handle that?" She said, "Let's just see what happens."

You'd think that a guy who can talk to the dead would have a beautiful setup. But Anderson's waiting room was in the basement of a building, with simple furniture and no amenities. We'd already prepaid the $4,000 fee, so we just filled out some paperwork before being ushered in to see him.

It was a small office, barely big enough for the four people in it, and we sat in front of his desk and looked across at Anderson. We talked a few minutes about the little stuff, like where we were from and how the trip went. Anderson then seemed to mentally check out for a few seconds, as if he went somewhere else. When he focused on us again, he asked us to relate information about all of our deceased loved ones. He contacted my father first, and then several other aunts and uncles began entering my father's "room." Soon Krissie joined them, and Anderson told us she was still working with children and that she said she was fine. She told Anderson she loved us and missed us and was comfortable waiting for us to be together again, when it was time.

Anderson asked us a lot of questions and did an incredible job of coming up with names and events that he couldn't have possibly known.

All in all, Sharon was exhilarated and only showed disappointment when our time was up and the people waiting in the lobby took our place. It was disconcerting how, when that hour was up, it was up, no matter how deep Anderson was into our event. But Sharon truly believed contact had been made. I was still skeptical but realized the emotional value of the experience. It was the start of the getting-it-behind-us portion of the grief process, especially for Sharon. She had been desperate to find out from Anderson whether Krissie had suffered, and she felt incredibly relieved by the experience.

For the first time in months, there was a degree of happiness. We laughed a little on the way home, sharing Krissie stories, and we joked that knowing Krissie, she was up in heaven running the place.

In later listening to the recording he'd provided us, Sharon realized that we'd led Anderson to some of the names and events that he heard Kristin discussing. But he did seem to acquire a lot of information that we didn't give him. He was either a great magician or the real thing. We both choose to believe that he really did see our Kristin that day.

The irony of the trip was that we almost crashed our plane on the flight back. We normally parked our plane at the Howell Airport, but because of poor visibility and severe icing, we had to divert to Detroit's Metro Airport. As we started down the glide scope, our de-icing equipment couldn't handle the severe conditions, and I had only a small hole to see through as I landed. We skidded the first 500 yards on the runway until the wheels finally took hold of the runway.

Wouldn't that have been a story? Denny and Sharon McLain, after visiting with their deceased daughter, crashed and burned while landing at Detroit Metro.

It would have been some way to end a great day.

Chapter 27

Peet

In early 1993, about a year after Kristin's death, I was at a function somewhere in Michigan and wound up at a table with two guys named George and Roger Peet. They owned a company called Peet Packing, otherwise known as Farmer Peet's. It produced and distributed meat products and was based in Chesaning, Michigan, about 80 miles north of Detroit.

The Peets called me shortly thereafter about buying some commercial time on WXYT and also asked whether I would consider representing them around the state. Peet only had a small presence in Detroit but had been a major player in the meat business in the rest of Michigan.

I said I would. Working for Farmer Peet's looked like a good way to keep me out of the house, away from Sharon, and to further distract me from the constant sadness and guilt I felt over Kristin's death.

My duties were to read Farmer Peet's commercials on WXYT and to schmooze their clients. I'd drive around the state, have lunch with the clients, and then go to the local Rotary Club to tell baseball stories and sign autographs.

The relationship wasn't very old before I realized that the Peets were tired of the business and tired of each other. They had a third brother, Wally, who was such a lazy stiff and created so many problems at the plant that they paid him $50,000 a year just to stay away and fish in Florida.

The company was more than a century old, and this was the generation that wanted out. The father, George Peet Sr., wasn't even on speaking terms with George Jr. Peet Packing was deeply in debt and bleeding money, losing some $10 million the previous five or six years. There were major problems in all areas: too many employees, too many bad products, the equipment needed upgrading, and the Peets had been involved in a long, nasty war with their union.

From the beginning, the Peets made it clear to me that they hated their union. They claimed the union was crushing the company with overtime pay. But it was really the Peets's fault. They produced too many different products and too few good ones. Workers twiddled their thumbs for hours while production lines changed over.

The company had been for sale for four years, and the Peets had spent hundreds of thousands on search firms to find a buyer. A major company made them a lowball offer with plans to close the plant within a year. But the Peets didn't want to be pariahs in their small town and kept looking for a cleaner way out. In other words, the Peets didn't want to be the guys who shut down the plant and destroyed the town's economy. They needed someone to do that for them.

Peet Packing was in "default foreclosure" because of its failure to pay back a $1.4 million loan to First of America Bank. They had another loan of $1.5 million to the same bank, putting them nearly $3 million in default. Who in his right mind would buy this pile of shit?

I would, that's who. I was confident I could turn it all around.

Confidence is a dangerous word. There have been people confident that they could fly if they just jumped off a cliff and flapped their arms. But that's not confidence, it's insanity.

Peet Packing was such a lost cause that anyone thinking logically would presume I had an ulterior motive in buying it. Why would a guy who had rebuilt his life after going to prison do anything so ridiculously risky?

Peet

I was aware of the Peet brothers' desperation to get out, and I asked an accountant and casual friend named Roger Smigiel to look into the company with me. Smigiel had management experience running an engineering company and had saved that company by solving their union issues.

As we talked about taking over the company, Smigiel drew up what looked like the perfect business plan to both save the company and eventually make us very successful. The dysfunctional Peets had given up so long ago that some streamlining, creative thinking, and aggressive sales skills could make a profound difference.

Smigiel's plan called for paring about 100 to 125 of the approximately 300 employees and cutting the product line from an unwieldy 75 items down to the best 20 or so. He would move to Chesaning and run the day-to-day operations while I would continue to promote Farmer Peet's on my radio show and then go on the road and sell after my air shift.

I'd spent my whole adult life looking to match the excitement of winning 30 ballgames in a season. I'd struck out at much of what I tried in the '70s and '80s, but becoming a radio and TV star in Detroit helped convince me that I could now make a business work.

I was making about $400,000 a year and had a grandchild, with more on the way. I'd also provided Sharon with the stability she so deserved. She'd never demanded I be as big a star as her Hall of Fame father had been, but I still wanted to be.

With Farmer Peet's, I would find a new way to satisfy my heroic fantasies. Yes, I really and truly thought I could become a hero: when the great Denny McLain turned Peet around, he'd be hailed for his wisdom and foresight. The people in Chesaning would appreciate him for his courage and bravery in taking Peet Packing off the respirator and putting it back into the spotlight.

I would also draw my family closer and earn more of their admiration. Tim, Denny Jr., and my son-in-law, Mark, would work there. They didn't necessarily want to work there, but I'd make them do it. It would be perfect. I would leave the company to them and Sharon, and I would join Kristin in heaven.

Thirty years earlier, Charlie Dressen, sage that he was, told me that if I threw a changeup to Mickey Mantle, it would be at my own peril. But neither Charlie, rest his soul, nor Sharon, or anybody else could have gotten through to me on the Farmer Peet's deal. I became obsessive about winning the challenge of the meat game even though all I knew for sure about meat was that I still ate too much of it.

The Peet deal had more red flags than the United Nations. But when the bases were loaded and I had the ball in my hand, I never worried about bad things happening. I'd just find a way to strike the next guy out. I never doubted that I'd make Farmer Peet's into a great company again.

Smigiel and I went to lunch a few months after we bought the company, and I watched him pound down two or three drinks. I certainly misjudged his ability to run the company, and I didn't find out until deep in the deal that Roger was a drinker. Obviously, he had an impossible job to do, and if you start out with a drinking problem, things will definitely get ugly.

Eye-opener number two was a meeting held with First of America about the $1.4 million note. The Peets owed them the $1.4 million, and the bank also held the pension assets. So Smigiel said, "You've got a pension with almost $14 million in it. We're willing to make a long-term commitment to keep that pension money in this bank if you guys will loan us some additional money." That approach had failed for the Peets, and it wasn't going to fly with us, either.

The banker at First of America had been unreceptive from the moment we stepped in his office. You would have thought that Jeffrey Dahmer and Charles Manson were sitting there. I'd never seen a lender treat anybody that way.

Peet

The banker said, "No more loans, and we don't care what you do with the pension money. Move it to the moon if you want."

The $1.4 million note gave First of America "encumbered assets," which meant that it essentially owned everything with the name "Peet" on it. This particular banker had long ago grown tired of the Peets and their bullshit and wasn't ready for another song and dance from the new guys. He also had me sitting in front of him, a guy who'd gotten out of jail seven years earlier, and it was pretty obvious that he did not have a burning desire to deal with me. My standard ice-breaker of bringing an autographed ball wouldn't have worked any magic here.

Looking back, it's obvious that buying this company was insane. But this was my fatal flaw—twisting the truth to mean whatever served my mood of the moment. I'd gone to jail by conveniently ignoring the obvious, but this was a level of truth-avoidance new even to me. I was still convinced I was going to make the impossible work.

Actually, we did leave the First of America meeting with something. We got a commitment that they'd give us 90 days to pay off the $1.4 million before they started foreclosure proceedings. We figured that even if they did foreclose us, we could stall them by filing for Chapter 11 and use that time to get our sales up.

If we had the money to pay off the $1.4 million and get out of impending foreclosure, we could at least take over the company without a gun to our heads. But it was the tallest of orders to buy the company and start out behind the eight ball, needing to retool everything from the product line to the equipment to the culture of mistrust between the union and the Peets.

Even though the Peets had been at it for 100 years and failed, and we'd never produced a single hot dog, we forged ahead, undeterred. In January 1994 we borrowed $1.1 million from another friend of Smigiel's, Bill McNish, who happened to also own the insurance agency that wrote the Peets's business. The loan from McNish bought us 51 percent and controlling interest of the company from the Peets.

Roger and an accountant friend of his, Jeff Egan, who did projections based upon current sales, deduced that if we could sell an additional three to five million pounds in sales in the next 90 to 100 days, we could generate enough revenue to begin repaying McNish.

We needed to lay off some workers, and Smigiel told me how he'd get the union to play along with us. "Screw that union," he said. "I'll bust their charter and kick 'em out by the end of the summer." The day before we bought the company, we were wined and dined by the union. They knew they were doomed with the Peets, so we at least offered some hope.

Predictably, about a week later, we were the enemy. We held a meeting with the union leadership at the local Legion Hall, and the tone changed. They asked, "How are you going to do what the Peets couldn't do? How are you going to upgrade the equipment when the Peets couldn't do it? How are you going to sell five or 10 million more pounds of product when the Peets couldn't do it?"

These were the same guys who a week earlier kissed our asses and promised us a spirit of cooperation, knowing that the Peets were just months away from shutting down the place. It was such a negative meeting that I left before it was over. And it didn't take too many more moments like that to scare Roger to death. It turns out that he didn't have the balls to fight the union any more than the Peets had.

Like Roger Peet before him, Smigiel was so scared of the guys with the knives working on the ham that he wouldn't even go out in the plant. He probably thought they were gonna debone him, throw his carcass into the pork line, and turn him into sausage.

We took over Peet in January 1994, and my plan was to do my radio show until 9:30 AM and then spend the rest of the day selling. I figured

I'd be writing enough business to pay back McNish and also buy some of the new equipment we needed.

This too, was crazy. How could I do my radio show and resurrect a company in distress at the same time? I never allowed myself to add up the time it would take to wine and dine guys all over the Midwest while still taking care of my media responsibilities.

My rationale was that I didn't have to run the company, I only had to do sales. Smigiel was the one ordering meat, paying the bills, dealing with the workers, and putting gas in the trucks.

We still needed operating money, so Roger asked Egan to help him track some down. We needed a total of about $2.5 million to pay off First of America, make payroll, fuel the trucks, get the streamlining process started, and begin to pay back the $1.1 million we owed McNish.

Egan, who also had experience working with the Detroit police and fire fighters pension fund, told us he had an idea. "If you and Roger become the trustees of the pension fund, rather than First of America," Egan explained, "I can move the pension money from one bank to another. Then I can get you a loan. You can't use pension money as an asset to secure a loan. But a bank getting the opportunity to handle $14 million will then be disposed to loan you the money you need."

Egan looked like a valuable player. He was in the money business and he seemed capable and motivated to help us. And I knew nothing about pensions or pension law.

Lo and behold, Egan found help at his own bank, Michigan National Bank. "If you move the pension to Michigan National Bank," Egan announced, "I can get you a $2.5 million loan either from them or one of their subsidiaries."

Roger and I started jumping up and down because that was the answer to our prayers. I was sure I had put together the perfect team. I had two genius accountants and I was the world's best salesman. We agreed to move the pension from one bank to the other.

By mid-February, just over a month after buying the company, we got our $2.5 million. I had no idea that the $2.5 million came from the pension fund itself. Egan had transferred the $14 million Peet pension from First of America to Michigan National Bank. Then Egan had MNB wire $2.5 million to Egan's company, Vanguard Investments held at Comerica Bank. Vanguard is a name with great recognition value as a mutual fund company. There was also a company within Michigan National Bank that had "Vanguard" in its name. Egan called his own company Vanguard Investments to make people believe that the money had come from the Vanguard at Michigan National Bank (MNB) and not from Egan's newly created company.

Moving some of the pension money from MNB to Egan's accounts was an illegal act. You must be a bank, a financial institution, to hold pension money. The $14 million was moved properly from bank to bank, but Egan's slick moves with the subsequent paperwork to move a portion of it to his company had fooled both banks.

I never thought to ask about any of this because I assumed Smigiel was as straight as they come, and Egan had attended a seminary at one time to become a priest. What's not to trust about these guys and their dealings?

After giving us our $2.5 million out of the Peet pension fund, Egan's plan was to then get a legitimate loan for $3 to $5 million and pay back the pension fund. With Roger and I as the newly named pension fund trustees, and with the money being funneled into Vanguard Investments, Egan could then invest all the pension money and make more commissions off that.

What neither Roger nor I found out until the trial began was that Egan had actually taken $3,060,000 from the pension fund, kept

$560,000 for himself, and given us the remaining $2.5 million. It wasn't until after Egan had given us the $2.5 million and taken his commission that Smigiel realized it had all been pension money and not a bank loan.

All of the paperwork for transferring the $3.06 million from Comerica to Vanguard Investments, Egan's shell company, took place between Egan and Smigiel, and the court testimony attests to that. I'm not a details guy, and I trust too many people. At the time, I asked my lawyer, Joe Shannon, to make sure that all the documents were in order.

There were 35 pages of documents that Shannon prepared for Egan and Smigiel to complete the transfer of the pension fund from First of America to Comerica. Roger and Jeff edited them into final form and sent them back to Shannon. He approved them and returned them to Egan and Roger. The paperwork stated that Comerica would be the new pension trustee. But when it came down to the final day, Egan and Roger removed Comerica from the documents and made Roger and me the pension trustees. They changed just one sentence in 35 pages of documents. That was the one killer sentence, and a short one at that.

I believe that Roger had the same impression I did about the validity of what we were doing until Egan told Roger that he and I had to be named trustees for any of this to work. At that point, Roger just went along. We needed the money, and Egan had developed a trust level and believability.

Their belief, later proven correct, was that the two banks would never take the time to read 15 pages of small print and notice that Comerica was removed as pension trustee. At that point, Shannon still thought that Comerica was the pension trustee and that we were getting a loan from Comerica based on having allowed them to hold the $14 million in pension monies.

Egan said that as he wired money between banks he had to have our signatures on all documents. Fair enough. A week or so before all the money started getting moved around, I met Roger and Egan at the Flint airport and signed six blank sheets of paper under the wing of our airplane. I was rarely at the plant, and it was a matter of convenience. In the entire time that we were a part of the ownership at Peet, I was in the plant fewer than 10 times. By signing the blank sheets in advance of when he would need them, Egan would have my signature on all the necessary transfer papers.

I was aware that there were strict protections involved with pension monies and had told both Egan and Roger that I would never do anything again to go back to jail. I made the statement several times to both of them and to our attorneys, "I can't do anything illegal that will send me back to jail."

There was a conversation with Joe Shannon present that stated what the pension laws were in early January 1994. At that meeting I said any number of times that I would never do anything to go back to jail. I kept asking Shannon to make sure that nothing could occur that wasn't legal.

Whatever we did, my intentions were not to illegally borrow from the pension plan. My God, I was naïve, inexperienced, and should never have taken on this project. But taking money illegally was not in my game plan whatsoever.

We paid off First of America the $1.4 million and then took the other million and paid bills. Yes, Roger bought a Harley-Davidson motorcycle and Roger also bought a country club membership through the company, like company presidents are known to do. We also put $10,000 down on a condo in Puerto Rico, but we were doing business in Puerto Rico. In fact, the guy who we were selling meat to in Puerto Rico extorted us to purchase the condo. He said that if we bought his daughter's condo for list price, he'd guarantee us business for the long-term.

We were wining and dining customers all the time. But when the shit hit the fan, the government focused on the toys. Roger could have bought a bike on his own. But when the government got involved, the things we did to create sales and market the product, like the condo and the country club membership, all appeared to be illegal.

I actually did sell enough meat to substantially increase production. I sold more than five million pounds of new orders before the summer of 1994. But we couldn't produce it because we hadn't been able to afford equipment upgrades or get the union to agree to cut the payroll, eliminate overtime, and reduce other perks, like three breaks a day that would often stretch to 30 minutes each. The down time in changing over the product lines also made Peet Packing enormously inefficient, and we couldn't produce the orders I had written.

At some point in the spring of 1994 I got a call from the president of the union, who asked me, "When was the last time you saw a report on the pension?"

"I just got here in January," I said. "How would I know?"

I called Roger and he said, "Don't worry about them, Egan will get 'em any documents they need." It was then that Roger explained that the $2.5 million had been pension money, not a bank loan, but that it wasn't a problem.

After the union spoke up, I was furious and demanded an explanation from Egan. Egan assured me. "This'll be cleaned up right away," he said, "and then we can go borrow what we need. The fact that we'd initially used pension money won't make a difference."

At this point, after the union chief brought it to my attention and Egan explained what had happened, I should have gone right back to the union and right to the appropriate government agencies and discussed how to fix it.

After the union approached me and reported it to the authorities, federal agents came to me and said, "This problem can probably go away if you'll come forth and tell the government everything."

I called another of my attorneys, David Dumouchelle, who said, "Tell those guys to go to hell." That was huge mistake. At that point I still didn't know the whole story. I didn't learn the last 30 percent of it until the trial. The government needed somebody to put the pieces together, and Dumouchelle told me to tell them to get out of my office.

I would never have approved using the pension fund if I was told it was illegal. But when the trial took place, there was the fatal document—government exhibit 27—the transfer of $3,060,000 from Comerica to Vanguard, and it had my signature on it. Exhibit 27 had begun as one of the blank documents I'd signed by the plane in Flint.

Then they indicted all three of us.

Egan testified that he got First of America to move the pension money to Michigan National Bank. Then Egan prepared the paperwork necessary to move it to Vanguard Investments, his company with its assets at Michigan National. MNB was then bought by Comerica, and Comerica is listed on the $3,060,000 transfer.

When Egan began his testimony, he mentioned that I had been adamant about not doing anything illegal because I was already a convicted felon. The judge should have called a mistrial right there. My past legal problems were never to be mentioned in court to prejudice the jury.

The following is taken from court records and is Egan's testimony regarding his informing me of how the money had been illegally moved. The attorney asking the questions is Egan's own attorney, Stephen Robinson:

Q: Did Mr. McLain express some concern about whether this could send somebody to jail?
A: Yes, he did. He said, "Could we go to jail for this?"
Q: And how did you respond?
A: I responded, "No."

Q: And why did you say that?

A: Because I didn't believe that he could go to jail for doing it.

Q: Despite the fact that you knew it was against the law?

A: Yes.

Q: Did you specifically discuss with Mr. McLain and/or Mr. Smigiel that this was supposed to be a short-term loan?

A: Yes. And actually, when we left that meeting, I said, "Do you know what the most important thing is over the next 90 days?" And they said the answer to that question was, "To get the money paid back."

Q: Did you discuss what would happen if people found out what had occurred?

A: Yes, I did.

Q: Explain that.

A: It was in the context of, you know, "Will we go to jail?" And my answer was that the answer is "no," and that we may be on the front page of the papers and it will look terrible, but we wouldn't go to jail.

Q: Did you, yourself seek any advice from an attorney about the ramifications of what you were proposing?

A: I did not.

Q: Why not?

A: Because I knew that the answer would be, "Don't do it. It's illegal. It's not kosher."

Q: Why did you pick the name Vanguard Investments, Incorporated?

A: The reason I picked that name was it would help to keep the transaction discreet. It was well-recognized name and wouldn't stick out.

The following is cross examination of Egan by Thomas Cranmer, Smigiel's attorney:

> Q: Now, when you mentioned that this was in a gray area or illegal, Denny had an interesting response, didn't he?
>
> A: Yes.
>
> Q: Denny essentially asked you if this was a plan that might cause him to end up in jail, right?
>
> A: That is correct.
>
> Q: He asked you that, didn't he?
>
> A: That's correct.
>
> Q: And Denny told you that he'd been to jail before, right?
>
> A: Correct.
>
> Q: And he had no intention of going back to jail, right?
>
> A: Correct.
>
> Q: Did he sound serious to you, Mr. Egan, when he asked you that question?
>
> A: Yes.
>
> Q: He didn't seem to be joking, did he?
>
> A: No.
>
> Q: And you told him it wasn't anything he could go to jail for, right?
>
> A: That was my belief.
>
> Q: You knew, didn't you, Mr. Egan, that if you told Denny and Roger this was something they could go to jail for, the deal was done and over, right?
>
> A: Sure.
>
> Q: You wouldn't be going ahead, right? No commissions for you, right?
>
> A: Not necessarily.

Q: The mortgage loan was supposed to be for $2.5 million?

A: That's correct.

Q: But it ends up that the amount that's transferred is over $3 million, right?

A: That's correct.

Q: Did Denny and Roger share the commissions that you got from your investments of these monies?

A: No. It's illegal to share securities commissions.

Q: Okay. So, therefore, they wouldn't do it and you wouldn't do it, right? It's illegal for them to share in your commissions?

A: Correct.

Q: You never told Denny McLain or Roger Smigiel that it was a crime for them—for the three of you—to do what you were doing, did you?

A: No. If I knew it was a crime, I wouldn't have done it.

Q: And you never told them that, did you?

A: No. We all assumed it wasn't a crime.

At the trial, we clearly saw government exhibit 27, the document signed by Roger and I that moved the money to Vanguard Investments. I knew, however, that I hadn't signed it in its finished form. It had been one of the blank documents I signed at the airport.

At the trial, Egan testified in regard to government exhibit 27. Again, the "Q" is his lawyer, Stephen Robinson. The "A" is Egan:

Q: Did you have a role in preparing this document?

A: Yes. This document was prepared by our office. It was typed up at my request.

Q: Is it signed?

A: Yes, it is signed.

Q: By who?

A: By Roger Smigiel and Dennis D. McLain.

Q: Were you present when it was signed?

A: Yes, I was.

Q: Where was it signed?

A: It was signed at the office at Cambridge. [Egan's office]

Q: By Mr. McLain and Mr. Smigiel?

A: Yes.

Q: It was all filled in before they signed?

A: That's correct.

Q: Now the date on that is February 15, is it not?

Q: Do you know what was done with exhibit 27 after it was signed?

A: Yes. I personally hand-delivered it to the trust department at Michigan National Bank.

Egan was lying. I was not there on February 15, the date he claimed I signed that paperwork. But Egan, in exchange for his testimony, pled guilty to a felony charge and was spared a jail term. I was actually on the radio doing my show on the morning that Egan stated in federal court that I was in his office signing a phony document.

I believe that until the last minute Smigiel had assumed that the loan was coming from the bank and not the pension plan. But when Egan told him that in order to get it done, Roger and I had to become trustees, Roger went along.

As it turned out, there were many reasons why the pension money should have never made it to us. First of America never read the fine print, nor did Michigan National. They have legal departments that are assigned to read documents to make sure that the bank is held harmless. They failed miserably to protect both the bank and, ultimately, me, their client as owner of Peet. I have come to realize that most people and institutions are like me: they don't read all the fine print. Had either bank read Egan's falsification of Joe Shannon's documents that made Roger and me the trustees, the money never would have moved from bank to bank.

Egan now had control of $14 million and had his first commission check of $560,000 in his pocket. He spent it on stocks for his personal portfolio that he later had to pay back. The two banks were also put on the hook for the bulk of the money, having also been duped by Egan.

If I had testified, I might have gotten off. But Dumouchelle was against it because he felt that Egan's lawyers would drag out my past convictions and skewer me on that. We instead counted on my co-defendant, Smigiel, to spell out the involvement of Egan, the government's star witness, and effectively take me out of the deal. But after I declined to testify, Cranmer decided that Smigiel would get nailed, and Roger never took the stand, either.

I was furious. Egan had never been rebutted by either of us. But it was too late.

The jury was looking for me to say something, and I had chosen not to speak. Roger and I were convicted of "masterminding" the pension fund transfer. The conviction ordered that the pension money be paid back but didn't specify by whom and how much.

◆　　　　◆　　　　◆

About a year later I was preparing for the civil trial that would determine who had to pay back what. First of America and Comerica were on the hook for failing to properly read Egan's doctored paperwork and allowing pension money to be transferred illegally. Roger and I were on the hook for using the money to pay back the $1.4 million First of America loan, to pay company bills, and to buy the toys—the Harley, etc.

Egan had fooled two banks, which later had to pay restitution to the pension fund. Meanwhile, Peet Packing had to be shut down, although it was inevitable that it would have happened with or without us. But we were the idiots who allowed ourselves to be the evil face on it.

As I pored over documents for the civil trial, I was sitting in a one-man jail cell in Valhalla, New York. The cell had a tin sink, a tin toilet with no seat on it, and a bed with a hard, flat pillow. Killers, rapists, and child molesters were all around me.

I was looking at government exhibit 27 when a lightning bolt struck. My heart stopped as I looked at the top of the document and saw that it had been faxed at "09:00 AM on February 15, 1994." I said, "Holy f*ckin' shit." There were two versions of the document—the original and the one that had been faxed and had time of day written on it.

I was on the air at WXYT at 9:00 AM that day. I couldn't have been at his offices signing the document. I called my lawyers, and we immediately got in touch with Pat Sheehan, my former producer. In a matter of days, he produced the old guest logs and affirmed that I had indeed done a show that morning. Sheehan's logs listed the big stories that week. The Olympics were beginning in Nagano, and Nancy Kerrigan and Tonya Harding were practicing at the same rink under intense scrutiny a month after Harding had had her thugs attack Kerrigan.

We had blown it at the trial, never having been shown the document that had the fax time on it. Egan had faxed one and hand-delivered the other.

Egan testified that I knew every step of the scheme. But he also testified that the deal didn't fall into place until that very morning and that Smigiel and I were there and we signed it together. Smigiel wasn't even there. Had we brought that to light during the trial, Egan's credibility would have been shattered.

It had gotten by all of us. I looked at the original document when it was introduced and knew something was wrong with it, but I couldn't get my thoughts straight at that moment. Had I seen the faxed copy with the 9:00 AM time on it, I might have made the connection that I couldn't have been there.

God forbid you should ever go to federal court—you won't even remember your name. You think a 3–2 pitch in the bottom of the ninth is pressure? You think landing an airplane in bad weather is pressure? Let me tell you what pressure is—pressure is sitting in the middle of a courtroom with 12 people who you don't share a lifestyle with, looking at you and thinking, *That scumbag—how could he do that?*

You can feel it. And every time somebody asks a question, your mind starts to tumble: *Where was I? What did I do? What did I say?* You've seen so many documents with the government's name on it that you start to wonder, *Was I really there that day?* And don't forget: that indictment says, "United States of America against Denny McLain." It's overwhelming.

Egan told the truth 98 percent of the time. But he lied about my prior knowledge of where the money was coming from, and he lied about my presence when exhibit 27 was signed. We all missed it, and the government withheld the faxed copy of exhibit 27 until the civil suit began more than a year later. When we had the chance, why didn't we ask when the document was sent or faxed during the trial? I don't know. Everybody was asleep. But it clearly showed that Jeff Egan was alone in that office and lied through his teeth.

The prosecutor purposely stayed away from the faxed document during the trial because it would've clearly shown Egan to be a government liar and the prosecutor as his accomplice in perjury. If he had asked Egan about the faxed notation at 9:00 AM and where McLain was at that time, Egan would have had to lie. It was impossible for me to be in two places at the same time, wasn't it?

The prosecutor also has a duty to disclose evidence favorable to the defense and the court, and he chose not to do that.

When the realization struck me amid the confinement, danger, and squalor of Valhalla, I had no money and had to use lawyer acquaintances I'd met in prison. We filed an appeal under what is called rule 33. Rule 33 is designed to let new evidence discovered after a trial be used as grounds for a retrial. The trial judge was United States District Judge Patrick J. Duggan.

Here is what Duggan answered on March 17, 2000:

> Defendant argues for a new trial and requests this Court to set aside the jury verdict because of "newly discovered evidence and in the interests of justice and the due process of law."
>
> In order to warrant a new trial based upon newly discovered evidence, defendant must establish the following four elements: "1) the new evidence was discovered after the trial; 2) the evidence could not have been discovered earlier with due diligence; 3) the evidence is material and not merely cumulative or impeaching; and 4) the evidence would likely produce an acquittal."
>
> Defendant's claim of "newly discovered evidence" centers on an exhibit that was introduced by the government trial (exhibit 27). The exhibit was defendant McLain's and defendant Smigiel's written direction to Michigan National Bank to transfer more than $3 million from the Peet Packing Retirement Income Plan to an account held by Vanguard Investments at Comerica Bank. Defendant claims that the exhibit denotes that it was faxed from defendant Jeffrey Egan's business, Cambridge Financial, at 9:00 AM on February 15, 1994. Defendant claims that he was "on the air" at WXYT radio in Detroit from 6:00 AM to 9:00 AM that day, and therefore defendant Egan is somehow a perjurer.

The fact that the exhibit upon which defendant hinges his "newly discovered evidence" claim was as an exhibit that was introduced at trial is fatal to his claim. Because the exhibit was introduced at trial, it is impossible for defendant to meet even prong one of the test for a new trial, to wit: the new evidence was discovered after the trial. Moreover, defendant's knowledge of the exhibit precludes him from meeting prong two's requirement that the evidence could not have been discovered earlier in the exercise of due diligence.

The Court finds defendant's reply to the government's argument unavailing. In this Court's opinion, defendant should have known by the time of trial, not 17 months after the jury rendered its verdict, whether or not he was "on the air" at WXYT on February 15, 1994.

Accordingly,

It is ordered that the defendant Dennis McLain's "motion for new trial—Rule 33" is DENIED.

Patrick J. Duggan
United States District Judge

We blew it, even though I disagree with Judge Duggan. Had the facts of my not being present been brought forth, I could have never been convicted. Why shouldn't I be allowed to present newly discovered evidence and facts proving I wasn't there when a critical document with my signature on it was created? Years later, DNA evidence would be examined in judgments around the country, and there are hundreds of guys who got out of Illinois prisons when facts were presented long after trial. Don't all cases deserve that kind of total justice?

Dumouchelle, of the highly reputable Butzel Long law firm, later wrote in an affidavit that the U.S. attorney on the case wouldn't allow us to review all of the documents in their possession. That prohibition, said Dumouchelle, "of not permitting McLain access to the entire case file was totally unfair."

All in all, although I hadn't initially known that the loan had been pension money, I also didn't come forth later, as I should have, to blow the whistle on it when I had the chance. An FBI agent said after the conviction that I didn't have to get indicted. He told me that all I had to do was tell the prosecutor I was sorry, wasn't aware at the time that it was pension money and not a loan, and pay back the money. Instead, on the advice of Dumouchelle, I'd basically told the Feds to take their best shot and go from there.

They did, and they won.

I was the same stupid masochist who stood on the front lawn at sundown, daring my dad to whip me if I was a minute late. I was the same stupid masochist who trusted Jiggs Gazell with my money at the Shorthorn. I was the same stupid masochist who called Tigers fans the "worst in the league," daring them to lash back at me. And I was the same stupid masochist who went to jail in 1985 for loaning my plane for cocaine deals and looking the other way, daring the government to nail me.

As I sat in jail for the next six years, I had plenty to think about and suffer over. One conclusion I had no trouble reaching is that I allow lunatics to find me. It's like alcoholics. Alcoholics find each other. For some reason, every lunatic with a deal finds me and I open my arms to him.

Jeff Egan was a former theology student with an MBA in accounting and a pension expert who was sitting on several pension boards around the country. Imagine that being the guy who got you. Roger Smigiel was a former IRS enforcement agent in the criminal division. You've also got one of largest law firms in Michigan handling your matters. How can it go so wrong? How can it get so bad? How?

Chapter 28

What Was I Thinking?

I made a million mistakes with Farmer Peet. No question, both my actions and subsequent lack of action when I should have taken it caused unbelievable damage. People lost jobs, and we couldn't deliver what we promised. The two banks that allowed the pension money to be illegally transferred paid the bulk of it back. The fact is, not one Peet retiree has ever missed a check. Still, people suffered because of our inability to get the company where we wanted to get it.

I was guilty of the same twisted thinking that allowed me to believe I could make it back to the All-Star Game in 1969. Sometimes, the more impossible the odds, the more convinced I became that I'd find a way.

I was determined to make Peet a rousing success and use it as a platform to bring my family together after Kristin's death. I wanted my sons and son-in-law to work there and carry on my legacy. Instead, Peet almost caused me to lose my family altogether rather than become a rallying point for it.

Life is a paradox in so many ways. My father's death meant that he couldn't beat me with the leather strap anymore. But it didn't prevent me from finding other ways to flog myself.

As the grocer who says, "I gotta sell more Pepsi," I think attorneys take cases with the same thought process. The lawyer says, "I gotta have another case." That's just business.

Another reason I didn't go downtown to talk to the FBI to straighten out the Peet mess when I had the chance was because I'd been through the legal system and had built up a tremendous grudge against the federal government. You can't trust the federal government, especially the prosecutor's office. Ex-prosecutors have frankly admitted that, above all else, it's the conviction they're after, not necessarily what's truthful and just.

A conviction should be based upon guilt and shouldn't be based upon playing a numbers game. Here's the best example from my case: the prosecutor, Stephen Robinson, knew my exact whereabouts hour by hour. Shouldn't he have said, "By the way guys, Denny wasn't there on February 15, 1994, when Jeff Egan drew up the loan documents"?

There's an element in trials called "fundamental fair justice," where both sides exchange what evidence they have. Robinson knew that I wasn't in Jeff Egan's offices. In all of our appeals and the rule 33 explanations, Robinson never denied the fact that I wasn't there on February 15. Never. But he didn't want to call the government's star witness a liar and kill his case. He knew I wasn't there, but he never told my drug-infested attorney.

That's right. My attorney, David Dumouchelle, was on pain pills for a bad back all through the trial. One day the bailiff came over and said, "Is he alright?" I said, "He's old and needs some rest." The bailiff said, "He's younger than you!"

The slickest thing Robinson did, and I have to applaud him for it, is that in every bit of testimony Egan made, he had Egan say, "they said"; "they got together"; "they told me"; "they did this with me"; "they called me." I had not been meeting with Egan and Smigiel on a daily basis. I probably saw Jeff Egan twice in my life before we bought the company. But they structured his testimony to make it sound like it was always Roger, Jeff, and me together, whether I had anything to do with what transpired or not.

What Was I Thinking?

Prosecutors purposely mislead, and a judge rarely chastises prosecutors. The judge will just tell the jury to "disregard what you just heard." Do you really think a jury is going to disregard something like that?

It's like when Egan said, "McLain was concerned about his other felony convictions." Robinson knew he wasn't supposed to say that I was a felon, but he still led Egan along the path with a series of questions that allowed him to get that shot in.

We are a win-at-all-costs society. We all talk a good game about trying to lead ethical and honorable lives, but when it comes to winning, people will do almost anything. That's partly why sports are so popular. In my day, pitchers threw spitballs. Later, they took steroids. Even in college sports, coaches will start false rumors to gain an edge. In 2004 Michigan football coach Lloyd Carr had to publicly announce he wasn't quitting so that other coaches couldn't use that rumor to undermine his recruiting efforts.

I was no different. There was no better guy in the world than the Orioles Boog Powell. But it seemed like he was 200 for 201 against me. In 1968 he hit a viscous line drive at my crotch that I luckily turned into a triple play. After that, I finally said to myself, "Boog Powell isn't going to beat me anymore. I'm gonna hurt him." The next time I faced him, I hit him in the hand with a fastball that "got away" inside. I'd had enough. I got pissed off and broke his hand. That's winning at all costs.

Did you know that we have well over a million people in our jails? There are another 8 million in some form of custody—incarceration, probation, parole, the tether—that's 9 million people, and that doesn't include those who are off probation and parole but who remain moving targets.

Americans still argue that our legal system is the best, and despite all the warts, it is.

Chapter 29

Back to the Slammer

I was convicted in December 1996 for my part in the Peet mess. I figured I had about six months to tie up loose ends and make some money before I was sentenced and sent away. Fortunately, my brother-in-law, Lou Boudreau Jr., had come to me in late '93 with a strange idea.

Louie had picked up a prepaid calling card and was convinced that the concept was going to spark a boom. I didn't get it. I said, "Lou, who in his right mind would prepay for long distance?" Sure enough, a few months later we started seeing prepaid cards all over the place and decided to jump in. We started a company that supplied wholesale long distance for smaller carriers and also sold prepaid phone cards.

To sell long distance effectively you need a switch, which is a large piece of equipment that can handle hundreds of thousands of calls at the same time. Every call made in America has to go through a switch. We bought one, produced our own prepaid calling cards, and leased the switch to other companies in the prepaid business.

Business always produces problems, but our biggest problem wasn't with our customers, it was with one of our suppliers, MCI-Worldcom. MCI was over-billing companies up to 30 percent per month. When you'd argue with them about it, they'd say, "Okay, what do you want to settle for?"

MCI's strategy was to embellish their receivables in order to boost the supposed value of their company. At one point they claimed to have $22 billion in receivables, three times the real number. CEO Bernie Ebbers and his crew destroyed dozens of businesses and cost investors billions of dollars with fraudulent transactions and strong-arm tactics. Ebbers was finally convicted in 2005. Good riddance, Bernie, you no-good thief.

The FBI had come to me for information to support their case against MCI-Worldcom but soon determined that a guy on his way to jail wasn't the right kind of witness to testify on their behalf. As I laid out the nature of the MCI fraud to the Feds, I sensed that they wanted me to lead them even beyond Ebbers to someone else, but they never revealed who that was.

◆   ◆   ◆

In June 1997 I was sentenced to eight years, and in early July reported to McKean Correctional in Bradford, Pennsylvania, about 80 miles east of Erie, near the New York border. The day I reported, Sharon filed for divorce. I couldn't believe it. I was livid and called her. She said, "I've had enough. I can't take any more." It shook me up so bad I wanted to run out of prison and sprint all the way to Detroit to see her. I understood why she would do it, but it was still a crushing blow. She had talked it over with the kids, and they supported her decision.

I ranted and raved, trying to get her to change her mind, and even wrote to her attorney to have him convince her. But it didn't work. After ignoring me for a few weeks until I calmed down, we started talking again. I desperately needed her support, and, saint that she is, she told me she'd never fully abandon me.

McKean was in the hills near the Allegheny National Recreation Area, and I never expected it to be nearly as knock-out gorgeous as it was. There were two facilities at McKean. I was at the camp with mostly white-collar criminals. Across the street sat a huge federal correctional institution (FCI), a so-called "big house." The FCI held 1,200 level three and four inmates—violent people doing serious time or life. It was a night-and-day difference between the two places.

The FCI had sophisticated security, with barbed wire, spotlights, and guards with high-powered weapons patrolling the periphery in trucks 24 hours a day. No one, including family members of the inmates, could enter the FCI without detailed ID and a thorough screening.

Although most of the prisoners at the camp were white-collar criminals like me, there were also drug dealers who cooperated with authorities. They don't put rats in the FCI because rats get killed in hard-core prisons, and that causes problems for everybody.

The camp had no guards, fences, doors, bars, or locks. In fact, they even told us, "Leave if you want, but it'll cost you at least another five years after we catch you." That's not to say it was a country club because it was still jail and we were confined in uncomfortably close quarters.

There were 110 cubicles measuring seven feet by eight and a half feet that were open at the front with a five foot wall that separated each cubicle. They were designed for one person, but the number of inmates fluctuated between 180 and 230, so we had to double up. When you and your roommate, or "bunkie," were in the cubicle at once, it was ridiculously tight. One guy had to be sitting on the chair near the entrance or lying on the bed.

Besides the bunk bed, the living space of 60 square feet also included two lockers and a desk. You weren't allowed to keep anything in the cubicle unless it fit in your locker. I'd make deals with guys to stash Diet Pepsi in their lockers in exchange for cans of tuna and pasta from the commissary.

There were 40 guys on each floor, or "pod," who shared three phones and one bathroom that had only two toilets, three showers, and four sinks. Even when guys did clean up after themselves, 40 men using just two toilets is a sanitation nightmare. Most inmates respected the unwritten rules of cleanliness, but when someone didn't, he was taken aside and given a message. The message generally was, "We're not getting sick because of you. If you continue to act like a slob, you won't be here."

If the inmate continued to show disrespect, he'd get a bucket of piss thrown on his bed, or his bed might mysteriously catch fire one night. Prisons have a way of taking care of those who cause problems. And those who cause problems usually wind up in the isolation unit.

You can tolerate a lot if things are somewhat sanitary, and for the most part, it was. You were given cleaning materials every day for the cubicle, and if you let things slide, the guards could deny your commissary privileges or even send you to isolation. It wasn't that they cared about us, but filth leads to illness, disease, and additional medical expenses.

Thievery was also a problem that usually met with swift and decisive justice. When I first arrived, there was an epidemic of stolen sneakers that were showing up on different feet in other pods. When news reached the camp administrator about this, he held a pod meeting to say, "When you find the thief who is reselling the sneakers, feel free to throw a blanket party."

Three weeks later they found the kid who was stealing sneakers. He was accosted in the hallway, had a blanket thrown over him, was wrestled to the floor, and was beaten unconscious. When EMS got there, he was still out cold and had two pair of his own sneakers tied around his neck.

The only way to avoid conflict in prison is to never overreact to anything or anybody. From the minute I arrived at McKean, I constantly reminded myself to stay calm, follow the rules, and to not make life one iota more difficult for my keepers. Those who don't follow that code wind up in a lot of pain as well as the hell of isolation.

In one notorious incident, a kid from Detroit had finished an afternoon visit with his girlfriend. When she left, he had her drive by the woods at the back of the camp at a determined time to meet her there. She had to make a few loops around the camp before he emerged from the woods, jumped in the car, and sped off to a nearby Howard Johnson hotel. The plan was to spend a few hours there and then sneak back before the afternoon body count. Unfortunately for the amorous pair, someone had noticed her circling the camp and reported it to the security post. By the time she picked up her boyfriend, an unmarked car was following her.

When the couple arrived at HoJo's, the local police were informed of their whereabouts and soon arrived, en masse. With guns drawn, they broke down the door, caught them right in the act, and hauled him off to the county jail on escape charges. He had just nine months left on his sentence. Even worse than the extra five years tacked on was that the escape had embarrassed the warden and they stuck him in the maximum security FCI across the street to do his time.

Typical of prison settings, you could get your hands on anything, including drugs and booze. With no fences surrounding the camp, banned materials had easier routes inside. Visitors would toss stuff in the woods when they left, and guys would go out later and sneak it back to the pod.

All things considered, McKean was about the best a prisoner could hope for—a veritable poster child for the Bureau of Prisons. The camp administrator demanded that it would stand as the shiniest place anybody had ever seen. Wardens and administrators want promotions, and they kissed more ass to get ahead than the inmates did.

The administrators supervise a prison. It's the inmates who do the work of running and maintaining it. We were mechanics, cooks—you name it. We worked five days a week and got holidays off. I spent my days as an orderly sweeping floors and later became a camp driver. I'd drive inmates and prison personnel all over the compound in a variety of vehicles, depending on the assignment. Prisoners in the camp never went inside the FCI across the street, but we'd drop people off at the gate.

We worked with a paging system. When somebody needed a ride, they'd get on the PA and say, "Camp driver to the FCI," or to "camp administration" or "to the food service area." I'd start my day at 5:00 AM and be done at 3:30 PM. Most of my driving involved taking guys to and from work. By mid-morning I'd be able to sit and listen to the radio. I'd tune into Rush Limbaugh and Jim Rome while waiting for assignments, and I'd sometimes catch a nap while those two assholes prattled on in the background.

Aside from working, I'd spend as many hours as I could combing through transcripts of my trial, looking for errors to help build a good appeal. I also hooked up with a great group of guys who ran the poker, pinochle, and bridge games because that's where the money is in the slammer. I played whenever I could and won more than my share of commissary loot: pop, tuna, cookies, and Ho Hos. Man, I loved Ho Hos—even better than Twinkies, my favorite snack in the big leagues.

I'd been at McKean for four months when my Detroit attorney, Chris Andreoff, called to say that the U.S. Attorney's office in New York informed him that the FBI might bring me in to testify in a case they were preparing. They had some questions about the prepaid card business and wanted to talk about some customers I had dealt with in New York.

I knew I'd done some business with bad guys, but they'd all paid up front to use our switch, and we'd never had any problems with anybody. In November 1997 the warden at McKean told me I'd soon be leaving for an undisclosed location in New York.

Since I'd reported to McKean on my own, I naïvely asked the camp administrator if I'd also be responsible for getting myself to New York. He laughed and said, "No, we'll be taking you."

The next day I was stripped-searched, given a brown khaki uniform, put in leg irons and wrist chains, and led to a bus with 35 others in the same condition. We were headed to the federal penitentiary in Lewisburg, Pennsylvania, for reassignment. Lewisburg was about 150 miles away and in the center of the state, about 20 miles south of Williamsport, where they hold the Little League World Series. Lewisburg was a notoriously horrible place where Jimmy Hoffa and Al Capone had spent some time.

Our lunch for the three-hour bus ride was a sandwich consisting of a single piece of baloney and a slice of cheese that looked like it might have been part of an experiment a few hours earlier. The condiment was a packet of mustard—but you're handcuffed, and it's a Houdini move to get the goddamn mustard on the meat.

After being stripped-searched again upon our arrival in Lewisburg, I was held in a seven foot by nine foot cell. Unlike the free movement allowed at McKean, Lewisburg was a total lockdown—you got to leave the cell every other day for a shower, and that was it. Otherwise, you lived, slept, ate, and shit in the cell. Everything, from the strip search and leg irons to the total lockdown, is part of a process designed to degrade and humiliate you—and it definitely does that.

The degradation and confinement of the first day at Lewisburg was so overwhelming that by 8:00 I wanted to shut the world out and sleep. My bunkie was a guy named Lanny, and I asked him if it was all right if I turned the light off.

Lanny got a panicked look and said, "If you turn the light off, 9 million cockroaches will run all over us." I took his word for it and slept with the light on. Larry was moved out the next day, and that night I turned off the light to see if he was exaggerating. Within minutes, I felt things crawling in my ears and mouth. I jumped out of bed trying to shake them off me and turned the light on. These were industrial-sized cockroaches, far and away the biggest I'd ever seen. From that point on, I slept with the light on, my socks on, and toilet paper stuffed in my ears, never again offering darkness to the rats and cockroaches that lay in wait.

There is nothing that can make you as despondent as being in a dirty, cockroach-infested jail cell with a pervasive stench and having no contact with the outside world. In Lewisburg, no one outside the Bureau of Prisons knew where I was.

The cell doors were solid except for two slots they could open from the outside. One was about one foot wide and four inches high that they would open to slide you your food. The slot above it, about eye level, allowed the guard to look in to make sure that you hadn't escaped, committed suicide, or killed your bunkie. When you had to shit, you'd slide a card over the slot that told the guard you were in the process.

When the other guy used the toilet, you had nowhere to go. The cell is only nine feet long, and they fed you three starchy meals a day. I didn't eat much because I didn't want to shit in front of anybody else. The lack of privacy in a place like that is almost beyond comprehension. And your bunkie passing gas in a confined setting is almost beyond revulsion. After Lanny left, I had another bunkie at Lewisburg who couldn't handle the food and almost farted me into a state of suffocation. I begged him to stop, but he couldn't control himself.

I felt I was on the brink of insanity at Lewisburg. You're helpless, and the Bureau of Prisons can do anything they want to you. They can beat you and say you fell in the shower. You've got to say, "Yes, sir," "no, sir," "okay, thank you, sir," all day long. Your destiny is in the hands of a guy making $30,000 a year in charge of 50 inmates desperate to escape a hell-hole. He tells you what you're going to do and when you're going to do it.

After a few days at Lewisburg I started imagining that they weren't really going to transfer me and I'd never get out. I was ready to end it all like I had been at the county jail in Bradenton the night of my conviction in 1985. I looked for ways to kill myself, but it was obvious that nothing would work. I could try hanging myself from a pipe, but the pipe would never hold me.

On my eighth day at Lewisburg I got the welcome news that I'd be taking the bus out the next morning. It was the same routine again:

strip search, wrist and leg irons, and a baloney sandwich on the ride to Stewart Air Force Base in New York. The sandwich, by the way, even with the "experimental" cheese was 100 percent better than the food at Lewisburg. At least the bag lunch was safe. I'd seen enough of what goes on in prison kitchens back in the Big A, and I thought about it with every bite I took there.

Stewart was a depot where buses and planes arrived from county and federal prisons all over the Northeast. The Bureau of Prisons Air Fleet based there was affectionately called "Con Air," and fortunately, both Lewisburg and where I was now going were close enough that I could avoid Con Air. Just walking up the stairs to the plane with cuffs and leg irons was more work than I could imagine.

When the doors of the bus opened at Stewart, it was a scene right out of the movies, with a dozen marshals holding guns on the 35 of us in cuffs and irons. As other busses also unloaded, a chief marshal yelled out names and orders while other marshals checked paperwork and mug shots to make sure we were sent to the right place.

One inmate who had been on our bus had been told to board the plane. He said, "I'm not on that plane, I have a court date in Manhattan tomorrow—you f*cked it up."

The marshal yelled, "Oh really? You wanna see what f*cked up means? Get on the f*ckin' plane." They forced him up the back stairs of the 727. Whether or not the marshal had the right order wasn't the issue. It was about power and being in charge.

Two marshals approached me and another inmate and told us to get in their van. I'm thinking, *What a break—I'm away from Lewisburg and out of the bus.* I asked one of the marshals where we were going, and he said, "You'll know when you get there."

On the ride I was told that each Con Air flight had at least 15 U.S. Marshals, two of whom were armed with Uzis sitting in enclosed cages at the front of the plane. The opening announcement on each flight was, "Stay in your seats. If you need to use the bathroom, call the marshal and he'll take you. If you get up without asking, we'll shoot you."

The demonstration of firepower at Stewart was staggering. Aside from the marshals who "greeted" us with machine guns, dozens of other heavily armed guards ringed the entire area, ready to shoot. Most of them looked so young I thought, "Wouldn't it be better if the older guys had the guns instead of the kids?"

It wasn't as if you could escape. Anyone who tried to run with cuffs and leg irons would get 100 pounds of lead in him before taking a second step. I was not only in the midst of violent criminals, but if I accidentally tripped, it was possible that a hyped up gunman could fill me full of holes.

The van took me and the other prisoner to the Westchester County Jail in Valhalla, New York. The van had iron bars between the two of us, and more iron bars between us and the marshals in the front seat. Inside the van they removed the irons, strip-searched us again, and put us in orange jumpsuits. At McKean we wore green, at Lewisburg it was brown khaki, and here it was orange. It was the first time I'd had the handcuffs off all day.

For the moment at least, it didn't seem all that bad.

Chapter 30

Valhalla

As they fingerprinted us and took mug shots after arriving at Valhalla, I endured the standard humiliation of guards asking me, "Are you that Denny McLain? Did you really dish up that homer to Mickey Mantle? How did you wind up in this place?" Some suggested that if I needed anything, they'd see to it that I got it. I was taken to a one-man cell. It was the basic seven foot by nine foot with a pillow, blanket, rubber mat for a mattress, and a steel toilet with no seat.

The next morning I signed a few dozen mug shots and baseballs for every cop in the place. I couldn't refuse, could I? And I also couldn't tell the warden I was being harassed or the guards would have made my time there even more miserable than it was bound to be. To this day, I keep waiting to see my autographed mug shots show up on eBay, but none have yet.

The degradation that hit me so hard at Lewisburg was sustained at Westchester, but at least I wasn't locked down all day. It was a far cry from the Spartan filth and bleakness in Lewisburg. I was in an air-conditioned, fairly clean pod of 40 one-man cells with three pay phones and a commissary. There was a common area that had a TV on each side, and both TVs were on so loud you could hear them in Chicago.

My cell was right next door to the two showers that ran all day and served as a home base for sex and perversion. Some guys would lather up in the shower and shave their entire bodies. If a female guard were on duty, some guys would stand behind the half wall and look at her while they pleasured themselves. And there was usually a fair amount of "pleasure" on the shower floor. You really had to tread carefully, and you never, ever touched the walls.

One guy in the pod knew how to manipulate a newspaper into feeling like a woman's vagina. Inmates would trade a can of tuna or soda for one and take it to bed with them.

Prostitution flourished in the pod and in the law library. Visiting other pods wasn't allowed, but meetings could take place in the law library. The prisoner-prostitute would peddle his services, with his pimp serving as lookout. Blow jobs and anal sex were for sale for contraband goods or commissary items. The whore's gang, or his biggest customers, protected him. Anyone who failed to pay because a relative forgot to send commissary money risked getting beaten within an inch of his life. Guys would lock themselves in their cells for days until their money got there so as to avoid beatings.

When I arrived at Valhalla, everybody in my family was angry with me, and I was rarely sent any money. Without money for the commissary, you had no choice but to eat the vile slop they served in the cafeteria. Prisoners depend on outsiders for assistance, and when the money doesn't arrive, it's a bad day. Mail came five days a week, but most inmates never got any mail. I was still getting autograph requests and lots of legal stuff, but never the kind of mail that I yearned for—mail that said that my wife and family loved me. I felt cast aside, abandoned, and undeserving of their support because of what I'd put them through.

316

Valhalla

The toughest guy in the pod controlled one of the two TVs. The Latin Kings gang controlled the other, and you didn't go near it unless you were one of them. They were, far and away, the most feared group in the jail. There were lots of them, and when you had trouble with one, you had to fight them all. Guys who crossed the Latin Kings suffered some merciless beatings. I avoided interaction and confrontation with the Latin Kings at all costs.

There was a microwave and a hot water tap for coffee and tea. Smoking wasn't allowed, but guys hid in corners and the pod still managed to smell like the Marlboro testing grounds. You could leave the cell from 7:00 AM until 9:00 PM to watch TV, write letters, or play cards. Your brain rots when all you do is play cards and watch TV, and there was a lot of cerebral rotting going on in Westchester.

There was an enclosed basketball court outside, which I referred to as the "Arena of the Gladiators." Basketball was played with a degree of anger and passion I'd never seen before. From the basketball court, you could see the jets landing at Westchester County Airport. I'd watch them come and go and reflect on the number of times I'd flown my own plane into that airport. It was hard not to dwell on the depressing fact that I was in prison eating shit out of a bowl while jets were landing a mile away. Where's the waiting limo to take you home when you need it?

Back on the pod, an unarmed corrections officer would sit at his desk with a panic button on his belt and observe the 40 guys under his watch. He can't have a gun and risk being taken by surprise, so a swat team stays on duty in a nearby room, exercising and eating while waiting for the next event. If the officer hits the button, the swat team storms the floor dressed in Darth Vader gear.

The swat team guys looked like they were straight out of *Conan the Barbarian*—pumped up, heavily armed steroid freaks chomping at the bit for action.

The first time the swat team raided the pod 15 of them burst in, screaming, "Hut, hut, hut," and it was one of the scariest things I'd ever witnessed. The most disciplined army in the world didn't march any better than these guys. When they were heard coming down the hallway, inmates scrambled back to their cells for safety. If you weren't in your cubicle when they stormed in, you were a candidate for a beating. The theory is that by not getting to your cell quickly enough, you had deliberately disobeyed a direct order from a guard. Allegedly, this put them at risk. But how can they be at risk when they're the ones with the combat training, body armor, mace, clubs, and guns?

One day a black guy and a Hispanic guy got into a fight over the TV. The black guy was getting the worst of it and tried to break free. But the Latino was all over him, punching, kicking, and delivering a savage beating. Typically, the guys on the pod gathered around to cheer the action. The pod cop hit the panic button, and as the swat team charged down the hall and the inmates moved to their cells, the Latino pulled a Mike Tyson and bit off the black guy's ear.

As blood spewed everywhere, the black guy rolled into a fetal position, both hands covering where his ear used to be as the pummeling continued. A few Latinos who hadn't run for their cells were also kicking him as the Darth Vaders arrived, swinging clubs, spraying mace, and screaming at the inmates to get into their cells.

The Latino who started the fight was so caught up in his fury that he also tried to fight off the SWAT team—an idiotic proposition if ever there was one. He was maced and pounded into submission with billy clubs. While the SWAT team waited for the paramedics to arrive, the two men moaned and writhed in pain on the floor.

The paramedics put the ear in a plastic bag, administered some treatment, and carried them both out on stretchers. Both were thrown in isolation and we never saw either one again.

Valhalla

Fights happened daily in Valhalla. The place made you feel like an animal trying to survive. You were afraid to take showers because, if someone didn't like you for whatever reason, he might steal something from your cell or plant something that could get you in a ton of trouble.

They followed protocol after every SWAT team incident. After quiet is restored, they pull inmates out of their cells, one by one. Each is stripped, cuffed behind the back, and ordered to stand outside his cell while the swat team tears through his belongings, looking for drugs, weapons, shanks, and clubs. Each is then thrown back in the cell with the cuffs still on. They then have him back up to the slot in the door to get uncuffed.

It's a tricky position to get into as the final act in yet another degrading situation. You must endure this treatment whether or not you were involved in the initial incident. I found it incredibly intimidating that the same Darth Vader who may have asked me for an autograph was now the guy threatening me bodily harm.

On one occasion, an inmate farted in the face of a Darth Vader as he looked in the slot to uncuff him. They beat him, took him to isolation, and he was never again seen on the pod.

During another Darth Vader incursion, I was pulled out of my cell, handcuffed behind my back, and, when the cop pushed my face up to the wall, he said, "I promised a charity that you would sign a couple of balls. I'll bring 'em to you tomorrow." What do I say, "Go f*ck yourself"? I said, "Yes, sir, sure will. Now get me the hell out of these cuffs."

The isolation unit is beyond bleak. There are no blankets or toilets, and the prisoner has to pass his waste into a bucket that's removed just once a day. Sounds like a pretty aromatic way to do time in Westchester, doesn't it?

As with each prison setting, I was consumed with just trying to fit in at Valhalla. You try not to say anything, do anything, or react to anything. If you do, you risk pissing off the cops or inmates. You have to act like you're on Prozac, controlling all your emotions.

Intimidation among the prison population was a fact of life at Westchester. The inmate who's there for the first time will be extorted for money, food, and sex. If he's a white-collar guy who's never been in jail before, he's scared to death the instant he arrives. He desperately does whatever he thinks he needs to do to avoid getting beaten or sexually assaulted. The extortionist will put his arm around him and say, "Just make sure you buy me a case of Pepsi and Ho Hos every week and no one will f*ck with you."

If it gets to the point where he can't effectively defend himself, he can request protective custody, a step up from the toiletless isolation unit. For some, the boredom and bleakness of protective custody is better than the fear and paranoia of the group setting.

The camp at McKean was tame in comparison to the county jail, but when a mark walked in, he could also fall prey to the guy who says, "I'll take care of you, and here's the list of the stuff I need from the commissary."

On my second day at Valhalla, the marshals put me in cuffs and drove me to the U.S. Attorney's office 15 minutes away. I was ushered into a conference room where they took off my cuffs and introduced me to a secret service agent, two U.S. attorneys, a cop from the organized crime task force, an FBI agent, and my court-appointed attorney, Dominic Porco.

I couldn't afford my own attorney, and Porco was a typically overworked and underpaid state and federal lawyer. But he was a delightful guy and knowledgeable about federal criminal law. They let Porco and I talk in a side room, where he asked me, "What do they want with you?"

I said, "Dominic, I don't know beyond asking me about prepaid calling cards." I told him I didn't know what aspect they were curious about because we had paid our withholding taxes and had played it straight.

We went back to the conference room where the others were waiting, and the first thing the secret service guy said was, "Would you like something to eat?"

I figured I'd lighten the mood, so I looked at him and said, "I'm glad you asked. I've been locked up since July—I could really go for Kentucky Fried Chicken."

He stood up and said, "You want potato salad and coleslaw with it?"

"I sure do," I said, rubbing my hands with mock glee. I figured they were pulling my leg and that the standard institutional baloney sandwich would eventually find its way to the room.

It was then that the female prosecutor, Carol Sipperly, took charge. "Good," she said. "Now that we've got the menu out of the way, tell us everything you ever did with John Gotti Jr. And after you tell us everything we need to know about your dealings with John Gotti Jr., I'll get you home faster than you can believe." She continued to look me in the eye and then said evenly through clenched teeth: "You give me John Gotti Jr., and I'll make an application to the courts tomorrow that will get you home. That's home. H-O-M-E."

She sat back to listen. The room was real quiet now. As you can imagine, the word "home" is incredibly powerful to people in my position. But so is the word "Gotti," and I broke the silence by saying, "If John Gotti Jr. walked into this room right now, I wouldn't know it. For all I know one of you might be him. I've never met him, and I've never even talked to him."

Sipperly and a secret service guy looked at me with such disdain that I thought I was about to get beaten up. Sipperly leaned toward me, hands on the table, and while slowly shaking her head for dramatic impact said, "Read my lips—we've got pictures of you two together and we've got tapes of you two together. Don't feed us that garbage, damnit!"

I was dumbfounded. Had I been with Gotti Jr.? Did he come to me as somebody else?

Besides that, I was still in the moment, thinking, *Now I'm not even gonna get the chicken.* I was starving for real food.

Porco broke the tension. "Time out, everybody. Can Mr. McLain and I talk alone again for a minute?" This time it was the others who got up and left the room. After the door shut, Dominic said, "Denny, I never believe much of what they say, but is it possible they have pictures and tapes of you and Gotti Jr.?"

I needed to make this point clear. "Dominic, I have no f*cking idea. If I've ever met the guy, he came to me under another name. If I've ever talked to him on the phone, he was identifying himself as somebody else."

"I believe you," Dominic said in an unconvincing manner. "But you do understand, right? They're trying to make you a deal. They're trying to send you home. They want Gotti Jr. so bad that they don't even care if it's the truth."

I told him I understood. Then Dominic said, "Fine. Tell them the truth. But if they have these pictures and tapes, you do understand that you'll do another 20 years."

"I assure you," I said firmly so as to leave no doubt, "I have never met these people."

Dominic opened the door and motioned them to return. As they filed in, I noticed that the secret service guy, Nino, had the KFC with him. I whispered, "Dom, do you think they'll let me have the chicken?"

Nino placed the KFC bag, in its regal splendor, in front of me on the table and said, "Here's your lunch. Now, have you guys reconsidered?"

Dominic carefully explained that I had already told them what I knew—that I had never met or talked to Gotti Jr. "If you have him on tape," he explained, "then Gotti came to him under a different name."

Nino said, "That's bullshit." So Dominic suggested that Nino take me into the other room if he wanted to pursue this any further.

Nino got a look of resignation on his face and said, "C'mon, pick up your meal. Let's go." I hadn't opened the bag yet and I still wasn't sure he was going to let me eat it until I told him what he wanted to hear. The smell coming from the bag was making me salivate. I felt like one of Pavlov's dogs as Nino and I walked down the hall to the other conference room.

I sat down and was about to attack the chicken for the second time when Nino said, "I've got pictures and tapes."

Now I was getting pissed. I held off sticking a drumstick in my mouth and instead pointed it right at him. "If you've got pictures and tapes then you need to bring them out here and let me identify who the hell I was talking to. But I can't imagine that you have any. I'm tellin' ya, if the cocksucker walks in here right now, I don't know him."

Nino told me that Gotti Jr. was also in the phone card business and revealed that my son-in-law, Mark Lauzon, had met with "Anthony something or other" who worked for Gotti Jr. I told him I didn't know who Anthony was and guaranteed him that if Mark had met with Anthony, he didn't know he was in the mob. I didn't know everybody Mark talked to because we routinely talked to 25 people a day. I told Nino, "If Anthony was one of the guys distributing cards for Gotti Jr., show me the tapes, and I'll tell you who I thought it was."

There was a silence as Nino leaned back, thinking it all over. I used that opportunity to say in my most sincere voice, "Nino, I want to go home. I'll do anything for that. I'll tell you what—you tell me what to say. If you want him so bad, write it down. Then we'll go to a grand jury. I'm a professional entertainer. I'll do what it takes. That's how bad I want to go home."

Nino seemed to perk up to that. He said, "In a couple of days we'll meet here again and I'll lay out the road map for you and tell you exactly what you did."

I dove into the KFC. As I savored it, I thought, *This is wild—I can't wait to learn what it was that I did with a guy who I never met or talked to in my life.*

As I was wiping my hands from the best meal I'd had in five months, Nino started to go into what it would mean to testify against the Gambino family and what type of protection I would need. He said that if Giotti Jr. even thought I might testify against him, I'd need the Secret Service to watch me 24 hours a day and that I'd later need the witness protection program.

I was angry. "Witness protection program? Are you serious? Where the hell is Denny McLain gonna live? You gonna send me to Greece? Where could I go in this country to be Sam Schwartz? F*ck that. The first time somebody calls me for a card show, I'm going. I might be Sam Schwartz on Friday, but on Saturday I'm picking up a check at the card show as Denny F*ckin' McLain."

As it turned out, they never had any pictures or tapes with Gotti Jr. and me. It was all bullshit. Nino believed my story and told me so. He also said, "If you continue to cooperate, it won't cost you any additional jail time."

I said, "More jail time? I haven't done anything."

Nino laughed. "Do you really think you have to do something for us to indict you?"

"Then what do you want?"

"I want you to go back and tell everybody in the other room how this prepaid phone card thing works. We want to know how they manage to keep on scamming these phone companies. We wanna know how they get the money and where it goes."

We went back to see the others, and I explained it as best I could. The Mafia was apparently the biggest player in the phone card business. Their method was to identify themselves as a business to AT&T, MCI, and the other big carriers, and put up $2 or $3 million in cash to buy a few million minutes of airtime. Then the carrier would give them a credit line of $8 to $10 million based on certain stipulations and terms. They would quickly run through the minutes they'd bought, and then within a matter of a few more weeks would owe another $8 million. Rather than pay, they'd move on to the next carrier and get the same deal. They did it over and over again, and the carriers weren't sophisticated enough to cut them off.

Once the mob had run up the tab they weren't going to pay, they'd then put out many more prepaid cards than the switching system could handle. Customers would encounter endless busy signals before the carrier would finally shut it down.

Even when you beat a phone company for $8 million, they still weren't hurting. The $2 million you initially put down covered everything. The phone companies are just rolling the dice anyway. The traffic costs them half a cent per minute, and they're charging the shit out of you at three or four cents. The mob rolled over one company after another.

After I gave them what I knew about the phone card business, and even though they were pretty sure I didn't know Gotti Jr., Nino still wanted to pursue the concept of me turning over on him. Nino even went to Detroit and met with Sharon and Michelle to talk about the witness protection program and scared the daylights out of both of them.

Each time I was taken outside to meet with Nino, I went back with a sense of terror. I was a dead man if it ever got out that they were talking to me about trying to get Gotti Jr. Members of Gotti's crew were in there somewhere, and I was an easy prey.

I liked Nino. He was 28, single, handsome, brash, wore a badge, and carried a gun. The day I met him he told me that for working with him on the Gotti Jr. affair he would get me what I needed at Valhalla. I said, "Great, I really need a Walkman with a headset because they didn't let me bring my stuff from McKean."

On our way back to the jail, Nino had the marshals pull into a Kmart, and he ran in and bought me a hundred dollar unit with an extension cord. When we got back to the county jail, he also gave me $60 to put into my commissary account and regularly put $30 a week into it for me. When you're in confinement and not getting cash from home, $30 a week seems like a lot of money.

I was pleasantly surprised at the quality of the law library at Valhalla. They also had typewriters we could use. It got me away from the violence, sex, and mind-numbing activities in the pod. I made commissary money writing letters for the illiterate guys and doing research and filing briefs for guys in divorces.

The law library was open from 9:00 AM until 9:00 PM each day, and I spent so much time in it that the warden appointed me "law clerk" for the entire facility. He gave me a little office with access to the Internet where I could do research for him and be left alone for most of the day.

I still wasn't sure what the government wanted from me, but with a Walkman and a way to earn money for Diet Pepsi, I resigned myself to making the best of it at Valhalla.

Chapter 31

Gotti

I'd been at Valhalla for a few months when the grand jury came down with an indictment against John Gotti Jr., the boss of the Gambino crime family. His father and previous Gambino boss, the Dapper Don, John Gotti Sr., was already locked up for life on convictions for murder, extortion, racketeering, jury tampering, and conspiracy to commit all those crimes. Sammy the "Snitch" Gravano had done in the Dapper Don.

On January 21, 1998, the Feds, NYPD, FBI, the sheriff's department, and the Secret Service made a sweep of the Gotti crew. The cops started knocking on doors at 5:30 in the morning, rounding up anybody they even thought might be one of Gotti Jr.'s coconspirators.

Helicopters and a SWAT team descended on Gotti Jr.'s Long Island estate. His wife and kids quaked in fear as the choppers and dozens of armed men surrounded the estate before Mrs. Gotti had the opportunity to tell them he'd left an hour earlier to work out. Great surveillance, huh? Gotti Jr. turned himself in later in the day, sparing the government any further embarrassment.

The helicopters and SWAT teams are part of the "show" as authorities invite the media to cover the crackdown in action and play it up as a giant win for the good guys. They hauled the 20-plus member Gotti crew to a Yonkers armory for booking, with reporters and cameras on hand to capture it all.

The story of the roundup was splashed all over the tabloids and TV, and what happened soon became legend at Valhalla. The armory apparently looked like an Italian gentlemen's club for the booking process—cops mingling with arrested Italians in three-piece suits, pajamas, and jogging suits, sharing coffee, bagels, and donuts. It was made to sound like a mob "sit down," except for the fact that is was between the Feds and the Gotti crew. The only thing missing was Dean Martin singing "That's Amore."

When I watched the story on TV that night, I was struck by how fascinated New Yorkers are with organized crime and mob history. Part of New York's thirst for entertainment is to eat up Hollywood-esque stories of mob intimidation, which then turns ruthless murders like Gotti Sr. into celebrities. Gotti Sr., with his $5,000 suits and love for the spotlight, remained a larger-than-life figure even as he rotted away the remainder of his life in jail.

The day after Gotti Jr.'s crew was rounded up, they brought me to the federal courthouse in handcuffs and shackles. I thought I was going to be interviewed again. But when I arrived, a cop brought me to a separate holding cell and said, "Relax, read a book, there's a lotta guys they're gonna see first, so they won't get to you for a while."

I asked, "Get to me for what?"

"You've been indicted with your pal Gotti this morning," was the matter-of-fact reply. "Didn't you know that?"

"What?" I yelled. "Indicted for what? I don't even know goddamn Gotti."

The marshal chuckled, "Yeah, and I'm Wyatt Earp—you can tell that one to a jury."

A while later, Dominic Porco visited me in the holding tank, and I jumped all over him. "What happened?" I screamed. "I thought I was helping them with Gotti."

328

"I know," Dominic soberly replied. "I just found out. I got a call from Gotti's attorney this morning. He said he needed to talk to me about you and Jr. I told him the same thing we told everybody else—that you never met the kid and had nothing to do with him."

I asked Dominic if he had bawled out that bitch of a U.S. attorney, Carol Sipperly.

"Yeah, I did, and you're not gonna believe this. She says she indicted you for your own protection."

"My own protection! What the hell does that mean?"

"She says it would have been hard protecting you here in the county jail if you weren't indicted," Dominic explained. "By indicting you, Gotti will think you weren't just brought here to testify against him. But the real reason she did it was to make sure you'll still be motivated to help her."

I was furious and scared all over again. I shouted at Porco, "Those f*cking U.S. attorneys indict a guy they know had nothing to do with Gotti, and they want me to help them, too? They'll f*ckin' get me killed. Where was the promise to let me go home if I helped?"

That was another bad dream. I'd been led to believe that because I cooperated in telling them how the prepaid phone card system worked, they would just let me go back to McKean, finish my time, and put into the court a sentence reduction because I'd been so helpful.

I waited in the holding cell for eight hours as they brought in three or four of Gotti Jr.'s guys at a time to read their charges and tell them whether they'd make bail. I was in the last group, and the judge read an indictment charging me with conspiring with Gotti to steal from MCI. When he was done reading it, Porco whispered to me, "Don't worry about it, we'll get it untangled."

I wanted to believe him, but I'd heard "don't worry about it" from every attorney I'd ever hired. What always happens is, they get a check, and I wind up going to jail.

The indictment against Gotti was 80 pages long, and there were exactly 60 counts against him. Name a crime and it was in there somewhere: loan sharking, money laundering, obstruction of justice, illegal gambling, mail fraud, wire fraud, taking down labor unions, beatings, extortion, and attempted murder.

I was the last guy named on the indictment and one of only two non-Italians. It looked like it was right out of an episode of *The Sopranos*, complete with classic Mafia aliases and nicknames so as to avoid any possible misidentification.

UNITED STATES OF AMERICA, Appellant,

v.

JOHN A. GOTTI, also known as John Jr., also known as Junior; MARIO ANTONICELLI, also known as Little Mario; GREGORY DEPALMA, also known as Greg, also known as Ron; VINCENT ZOLLO, also known as Vinny; Defendants-Appellees;

LOUIS RICCO, also known as Louie Bracciole, also known as Louie Brash; CRAIG DEPALMA; MICHAEL SERGIO, also known as Mikey Hop, also known as Hop; STEPHEN SERGIO, also known as Sigmund the Sea Monster; DOMINICK LOIACONO, also known as the Butcher; LEONARD MINUTO SR., also known as Cliff, also known as the Turtle; STEVEN FORTUNATO, also known as Guappo; PETER FORCHETTI, also known as Fat Pete, also known as Jonesie; ANTHONY PLOMITALLO, also known as Anthony the Carpenter; WILLIAM R. MARSHALL, also known as Willie; ROBERT SANSEVERINO, also known as Bobby Sans; CHRISTIAN BINNIE, also known as Chris; JOHN

Gotti

FORCELLI, also known as Bart; MARCO BARROS; MICHAEL ZAMBOUROS, also known as Michael Z.; SALVATORE LOCASCIO, also known as Tore; ANGELO PRISCO; JOHN SIALIANO, also known as Goombah Johnnie; DENNIS MCLAIN, also known as Denny, Defendants.

They were accusing Gotti and me of stealing $50 million from MCI, the same MCI of CEO Bernie Ebbers, who was later convicted for defrauding investors and customers like me for about $20 billion. I don't even have enough cash in my commissary account to buy a snack, and I'm sitting there being told that I, along with John Gotti Jr., a partner I'd never met, stole $50 million from Ebbers. As a famous sports agent once said in a movie, "Show me the f*ckin' money!"

Gotti Jr.'s legend began on December 16, 1985, when Gotti Sr. arranged a dinner meeting with his Gambino boss, Paul Castellano, at Sparks Steakhouse on 46th Street. Gotti Sr. had felt since 1976 that a dying Carlo Gambino should have named him his successor as boss instead of Castellano. In early December 1985, Castellano had lost a major source of protection within the family when his top underboss, Aniello Dellacroce, died of lung cancer.

As Castellano stepped out of his stretch Lincoln limousine he and his unarmed bodyguard were gunned down by three men who then fled to a waiting car parked nearby on 2nd Avenue. It was no mystery that Gotti had called the hit. In fact, Gotti and his hit man du jour, Sammy "the Bull" Gravano, watched the hit take place from a car across the street. Needless to say, despite the fact that it was rush hour, no witnesses ever stepped forward.

The elimination of Castellano made Gotti the new head of the Gambino family, and it had played out in all its gory glory right there on the streets of New York. Gotti was originally labeled the "Dapper Don," but as embarrassed law enforcement agencies repeatedly failed to make charges stick, he also came to be known as the "Teflon Don."

Gotti flaunted a flamboyant public lifestyle and left a trail of dead bodies all across New York City. A special "Gambino Squad" was created to take him down. As the agency's obsession to get him grew, the media and public became increasingly awed by Gotti's blend of style and ruthlessness. Gotti would come to court and step out of a limo in $5,000 Italian suits, smile broadly for cameras. and hold open courthouse doors for ladies.

He was finally done in by his own braggadocio when his home base, the Ravenite Social Club, on Mulberry Street in Little Italy, was successfully bugged. The wire taps of Gotti giving orders like, "I want him dead," made for incredible courtroom theater. Sammy the Bull had turned over on him, and the Bull's testimony about the dozens of guys he'd whacked at Gotti's behest was chilling. Gotti's only angle of defense had been to call Gravano a liar and subhuman. But how much more human was the guy who told him who and when to kill?

The trial of Gotti Sr. gripped New York in 1992. After five months, during which time he was also accused of trying to bribe the jury, the "Teflon Don" was convicted in Brooklyn's federal district court and sentenced to life in prison without the possibility of parole.

When the verdict came down, an angry Gotti stood, pointed toward the prosecution table, and called out to reporters, "The 1919 White Sox," to emphasize that the prosecutors had fixed the case.

Then, almost by default because a few other potential successors to his father pleaded guilty to charges of racketeering, John Gotti Jr. took over the reins of the Gambino family.

Gotti

◆   ◆   ◆

After a day that lasted more than 12 hours, they loaded those of us who didn't get bail in two vans to go back to Valhalla. I was in shock from this unexpected link to an infamous mobster and had no desire to talk to anybody. I was feeling like a misfit in this group of characters, when one of my alleged coconspirators in the van with me asked who I was.

I simply said, "Denny McLain," hoping he'd leave me alone.

No such luck. The guy said, "Hey, I'm Mikey Hop. Are you Denny McLain the baseball pitcher?"

"Yeah, one and the same."

He smiled, nodding as it sank into his thick head. "So, what the f*ck are you doing here?"

"You tell me," I said as politely as possible under the circumstances, "I don't know any of you, and I'm indicted with you and Gotti Jr."

Hop stared at me for a few seconds, his wheels slowly turning, and then blurted out, "So tell me, how was it pitching in Yankee Stadium against Mantle, Pepitone, Berra, and them guys?"

I couldn't believe it. "You're kiddin' right?" I asked incredulously. "We just got indicted, and we're gonna talk baseball?" Then I thought better of making any more enemies and said, "It was great, a lot more fun than this shit."

The guys in the van all laughed. With my future all the more uncertain, at least I was providing some comic relief for the wise guys.

They brought all of us into the holding area at the county jail so they could take off our shackles and reprocess us. A young guy who looked about 35, who had obviously come over in the other van, approached me from the end of the bench and asked, "Denny McLain?"

"Yes, sir."

"I'm John Gotti Jr., how are ya?"

333

I could have fallen over. Within seconds I was sweating through my jump suit. As my throat constricted and I was gasping for air, he said, "I apologize. I don't know why they would put you in an indictment with me. Have we ever talked? Have we ever met? Have we ever done business with each other?"

I said, "No, unless you called me under another name."

"Making up names isn't my style. I'm sorry you wound up in this."

For the moment, at least, Gotti Jr. came off as a prince of a guy. I was escorted back to the pod. Within 15 minutes in came Gotti, and they plunked him in the cell right across from me. It was obvious that Sipperly wanted me to keep an eye on Gotti's activities and become her snitch.

Gotti Jr. came over the next morning and we talked for more than an hour, trying to figure out the common denominator between us. He told me he had nothing to do with illegal prepaid cards and that the one company he had in the phone business didn't do the turnover thing I'd described to the prosecutors. He threw out some names to try to make the connection, but there wasn't one that I recognized.

I told him that one of the allegations we'd heard was that there were tape recordings between us. But the best we could figure was that a distributor who sold cards for us had told Gotti that "McLain was a player and he'll work with you; he'll get you a line of credit, get you your cards, and he's a good motherf*cker."

I told him that my guess was that the Feds then assumed that he and I had gotten into bed together in the card business.

As for playing the part of Sipperly's snitch, whenever Nino talked to me his first question was, "Who's talking with Gotti, and who's visiting him in the library?" I would matter of factly say, "All he does all day is read transcripts and play cards."

I was stuck in that shit hole of a county jail because all 23 defendants had to show up for every hearing, even the guys who were out on bail.

Gotti

There were a series of hearings in the Gotti Jr. case, and each time it was the same 23 guys, plus 30 or 40 attorneys and tons of media.

A few weeks into the process, Gotti Jr. told me that I needed to attend an attorney's meeting he'd scheduled in the visitors room. Of course I went. Whatever Gotti asked anybody to do had to be done. But when I arrived, I looked for Porco and noticed he wasn't there. I asked another attorney in the room, "Where's Porco?"

The guy said, "He's not necessary for this meeting. We just wanted to find out from you what you planned on saying and why you're in this case."

I felt alone in the storm and scared shitless again. I told them the truth, which was also what they wanted to hear—that I had never met Gotti Jr. and had nothing to say to anybody. That seemed to satisfy everybody and, two days later, I noticed that my commissary balance had increased from almost nothing to more than $500. Hell, for $500 in commissary dough, there was a lot I'd do, short of testifying against Gotti Jr. Now, thanks to Jr.'s largesse, I was living it up in the county slammer.

A few days later Porco came by and told me, "I've got good news— all you gotta do is plead guilty, and they'll let you go."

It was another twist in the drama that I couldn't fathom. Dominic explained that prosecutors don't like to retract an indictment because it's an admission of a mistake. They don't admit mistakes if they can avoid it. The prosecutors knew they had a bad case with Gotti Jr. and me and wanted me out of it. If the jury came to recognize that I didn't belong in this outrageousness, they might be swayed to think that the rest of it might be phony. My end of the bargain was to simply admit guilt and be let go.

I couldn't do it—there wasn't an ounce of truth to the allegation in the indictment and they knew it. If I copped a plea, it would suggest to a jury that Gotti Jr. and I did do something illegal with prepaid cards. I'd made foolish gambles fighting prosecutors in the past, but they had nothing on Gotti Jr. and me, and that was that.

Meanwhile, Gotti Jr. quickly became the most influential person in the pod, and watching him exert his influence at Valhalla was eye-opening. Besides being a crime family capo, he was also a bodybuilder. He was intimidating in every imaginable physical and psychological way, even though he was quiet and almost scholarly in appearance—180 degrees removed from the mean-looking and flamboyant character his father was.

Three or four times a week he would commandeer the law library to have "sit downs" with codefendants from other pods to make sure they all remembered their roles when it came to testifying. He also played the part of peacekeeper on the pod and demanded that his guys didn't act out with any aggression or anger. Cops don't like turmoil, and when trouble starts, everybody gets locked down.

I desperately needed to stay on Gotti Jr.'s good side, and I went out of my way to be his buddy. I kissed up to him like everybody else did. After all, he was a Gotti, and like his charismatic dad, he was both feared and adored. There wasn't a guy on the pod who wouldn't do anything he asked. Keep in mind that these were criminals and many wanted to become part of his crew. Gotti Jr. had the power to say, "I got a place for you in my organization when you get out."

His omnipotence was such that if he told somebody to kill Denny McLain, you wouldn't be reading this. I was the only non-Italian to even get near his inner circle. I wasn't happy that my name was on the indictment but, seeing that it was, I wanted him to like and trust me.

Gotti Jr. and I finally determined that the common denominator—the guy who had mentioned my name in the tapped phone conversation—was a fraud named Mike Zambouros, who was also named in the indictment. We found out that Zambouros had been under investigation for SEC violations with public companies. He wasn't part of Gotti's crew but had tried to sell prepaid cards to Gotti's guys. Gotti Jr.

seemed comfortable that we had no history, and that meant I had no motivation to turn on him.

Since I was the law clerk and had the cottage industry of typing for people, I started doing some research and typing personal letters for Junior. When he met with his crew, he'd order everyone else out of the library except me. I'd type for him while the meeting was going on, researching wiretap law and the like.

Sucking up to Gotti Jr. also got me in on the graft he created. Two or three times a week, cops would bring food to the pod after lock-down at 10:00 PM. They'd take it to our cells or let us gather in a corner and chow on KFC, McDonald's, deli food, or pasta. There wasn't a lot to like in jail, but eating real food on the sly with the Gotti crew was exhilarating. It's amazing how we learn to adapt to our environments and revel in the little things. The guards had to be getting paid for the clandestine food runs, and the cash probably came from the outside.

Gotti Jr. hated the black and Latino inmates, who he stereotyped as morons. Ironically, a much talked about TV movie on Gotti Sr. was shown in early 1998, and everybody in the pod was excited to watch it. The promos for it played all week, showing Gotti Sr. in the worst possible light, and I wondered how Junior would react. When the show was about to come on, a few black guys started calling out, "Hey, Gotti, c'mon over here. It's the movie on your dad."

Both TVs were tuned in to the special, and out of 40 guys, 38 watched—everybody but Junior and me. He retreated to his cell with the door shut, and I spent an hour on the phone. The movie succeeded in making his dad out to be a giant asshole. Gotti Sr. was an asshole, but it was still his dad, and I was embarrassed for Junior.

I started feeling safe enough around Gotti to kid with him. One day when his buddies were bitching about guys they had it out for, I said to

Junior, "If your dad ever gets out, I've got some people I'd like him to see for me." Junior laughed. Thank God he liked my sense of humor. Hell, he was barely 30, young enough to be my son.

Two guys on the indictment were a father-and-son team—Michael and Stephen Sergio. Sergio Sr. went by the nickname "Mikey Hop." Son Stephen, according to the indictment, was known as "Sigmund the Sea Monster."

Oddly, Stephen had never even heard of that nickname, and that's because the prosecutor, Carol Sipperly, had made it up. Government prosecutors like using nicknames because they make for a more entertaining story. Imagine that, federal servants juggling the truth to garner favor with the media. You'd think they'd be above story fabrication and lying, wouldn't you?

Junior told me that neither of the Sergios had been in his crew but were examples of lower-level crooks who liked to drop the Gotti name to increase their powers of intimidation. Both Sergios incessantly sucked up to Junior at Valhalla. If he needed a glass of water or a pen and paper, they would scurry for it. I tried my George Susce–Ted Williams line with Junior, saying that if he ever stopped short, Mikey Hop's nose would get stuck up his asshole. The kid laughed. Thank God again!

Stephen, the younger Sergio, also employed my services as a typist. He desperately wanted to write a book about his exploits as a wise guy and repeatedly called Bo Dietl, the former New York cop who serves on the cast of the Don Imus radio show, to try to get Dietl involved in the project. According to Sergio, Dietl thought it was a great idea.

We got through about 50 pages of it, with the centerpiece—and Sergio's self-proclaimed claim to fame—his takeover of a strip club. Scores, on 60th Street between 1st and 2nd Avenue, has since become the most famous strip joint in the world. It has franchises all over the country and is often featured on the Howard Stern show. According to

Sergio, on Halloween night in 1990, shortly after it opened, he walked into Scores.

Sergio boasted that he took the place over with what he called a "tough-guy bluff." In dropping the Gotti name, even though he had no association with Gotti, he told the two owners that they couldn't run a joint in that part of town without "a friend," and that he was their new "friend." He immediately tightened security by bringing in his own "pals," meaning bouncers, as well as some other muscle provided by his dad, Mikey Hop.

In exchange for his weekly "juice," Sergio increased revenues with better security and kept the drug dealers away. He also established the "President's Room," where celebrities would be shielded from the regular customers. The President's Room, Sergio wrote, "Was written up so much that the place became an icon unto itself where celebrities met and were seen. And celebrities love to be seen."

Demi Moore visited the President's Room to study the art of striptease for her 1996 movie *Striptease*. Sergio had me write synopses about her and other regulars. Of Moore, he wrote: "She is a beautiful woman even when she was smoking those horrible cigars. We always thought she was a real animal, but she never suggested she was available to anyone but the asshole, Bruce Willis. She spent many hours watching the gals do their routines, asked questions, and she obviously got it right if you saw the movie."

On Madonna: "She loved to have the girls dance only for her and she sure smiled a lot at them. She may be bisexual, but if she is a freaky and kinky lady, she never demonstrated that in this place."

On Mickey Rourke: "Not an unlikable fellow when he was straight, but the coke and booze turned him into a mean-spirited, physical, and foolish drunk. When he was on his worst coke rage, we beat the shit out of him, threw him into 60th Street, and then he went to the Plaza Hotel and trashed the room he was staying in. He continues to be an out-of-control drunk—some guys will never change."

On former pitcher David Cone: "Cone would get so drunk he would yell at the girls dancing in their birthday suits and start throwing beer glasses. How this guy could pitch as well as he did and drink as much as he did is nothing but a major miracle."

Sergio added: "Other assholes—Barry Bonds, Bobby Bonilla, Mike Tyson, Van Damme."

The Sergio names were on Gotti Jr.'s indictment because their false, big-mouth claims to work for both Gotti Jr. and Sr. were captured on FBI wiretaps at Scores. The tough guy Sergios might have been in their glory at Scores, but they were scared to death of Junior in jail. Junior told me that not only weren't the Sergios ever a part of his crew, but added, "My dad would never deal with assholes like those two. And if my dad was in this pod, they'd be dead by now for bragging about something they were never a part of."

◆   ◆   ◆

In July 1998 Porco and I approached the judge because there weren't any more hearings in the case planned until late fall. We requested that I be returned to McKean.

The judge asked me, "Do you mind if we have a hearing and only your lawyer can attend?" I told him, in so many words, "I couldn't care less." A week later they put the cuffs and irons on me and took me to Stewart Air Force Base to catch the bus to Lewisburg on my way back to McKean.

Shortly before I left, and after working hard on some wiretap research for Gotti Jr. that week, there was another $500 deposited in my commissary account. The anonymous donor was again John Gotti Jr. You gotta understand the magnitude of this for someone in my position—$500 is nothing short of Pepsi and Twinkie heaven in a county jail.

I got back to Lewisburg on my way to McKean, and it was just as I'd left it: filthy, cockroach-infested, and with inedible food. The weekly bus to McKean had left the day I arrived and doomed me to another seven days of Lewisburg hell. It was July, and it felt like it was 110 degrees in the cell all the time. You sit there in boxer shorts and no shirt and drip sweat all day. It was unbearable.

On my second day at Lewisburg, I caught a big break when a cop knocked on my door and said, "McLain—you wanna be my orderly for the next six days?"

I said, "Yes, sir, I want to be your orderly." I was a minimum-security prisoner with a limp because of my bad knees, and they knew I wasn't running anywhere. For three or four hours a night I was allowed out of the cell to sweep, mop, clean the shower, and pack clothes for guys who were leaving. It was a relief. They had fans in the hallways, and it gave me a chance to use the phone and take a shower every day. It's amazing how we take the phones for granted. Had I not been an orderly, I would have had no phones or outside contact until I got back to McKean.

It's remarkable how adaptable human beings become when thrown into situations where they have no control. Your keepers can do whatever they want to you whenever they want to do it. My experience in prison helped me understand why Hitler had so little resistance in murdering millions of innocent people.

In a captive situation, your keepers allow you whatever minimal freedom you have. You begin to think they won't hurt you if you say, "yes, sir," and "no, sir." The cops who brought me food for signed baseballs could have done anything to me when I was in isolation. They could have starved me if they wanted to or shoved me down a flight of stairs and simply reported, "He fell." They are able to play with your psyche so that you develop an assumption of trust—the sense that they will take care of you if you don't cross the line.

If the warden put us all against a wall and said, "Let's go to a new camp in Ohio today," we'd have lined up and gotten on the bus, just like the concentration camp prisoners got on the train that took them to the gas chambers.

Saying that something like the Holocaust could never happen again is naïve. I came to realize that the assumption process that comes with being a prisoner could happen at any time.

Thirty of us went back to McKean on the next bus out. I'd been in McKean nine months previous, but they still put me through the same intake evaluation all over again. They strip you, check to see if you've stashed a machine gun up your asshole, and tell you to pick your balls up to make sure there isn't a machete hiding between your legs. I wondered what these guards said to their wives at night: "Hey, honey, I looked up Denny McLain's ass today and made him lift his balls—and man, he has some big balls."

I was about to be cleared to go back into the camp and put the Lewisburg and Valhalla nightmares behind me when Bob Clark, the camp administrator, approached me. He sat me down in a nearby office and with stunning frankness told me that Carol Sipperly, the U.S. attorney in Westchester, had informed him that the Gambino family had a hit on me. Gotti Jr.'s uncle and one of Carlo Gambino's sons had arrived at McKean and were doing 30 to 40 years each as part of a huge heroin ring.

I wasn't going back to the camp after all. I was being sent to the depths and bleakness of the isolation unit—into what they call "protective custody."

Chapter 32

Segregated

Carol Sipperly had insisted to Bob Clark that they needed to confine me for my own safety. John Gotti Jr.'s uncle, Peter Gotti, as well as a son of Carlo Gambino were prisoners at the FCI in McKean, but could still hurt me even though I was in the camp. In theory, she was right. There were some violent people in the camp—dope dealers, informants, and the like who would even hurt you for $200 in commissary cash. A $20,000 hit on the outside can be bought for peanuts from guys in jail.

"You've got a live case," Clark continued, "and if we put you in the camp you might flee."

I said, "Flee? That's bullshit, Bob. I'll show up to sign autographs at the first card show, and that'll be it for fleeing."

Sipperly was still trying to get me to cooperate against Gotti Jr. despite the fact that she knew I had no information about him. Prosecutors just want convictions, remember? It was the same reason they sent me to the Big A back in the '80s. I didn't know the guys Gotti Jr. worked with any more than I knew Sy Sher's inner circle back then.

I told Clark that the concept of me cooperating against Gotti Jr. was preposterous and that Sipperly ought to just give it up. I told him I had breakfast, lunch, and dinner with Gotti Jr. in New York, and we had long

343

ago determined we had no connection to each other. I explained that Sipperly had to know that by now.

Clark had no choice. I was headed to segregation, and he at least gave me a nice 10 foot by 14 foot cell that even had a shower in it. But I was still alone with no chance to move around. They were treating me not so much like an inmate, but as a cooperating witness. Since the government was still expecting me to provide them information about Gotti Jr. and the prepaid card business, I got consideration as one of the good guys.

The cops knew I wasn't in isolation because I was being punished, and they took care of me. I showed them all the respect I could because without them, I'd get nothing. We're locked down and have to be taken care of individually. They've got to feed you, get you reading material, bring you mail—and they're servicing 110 guys.

You can't have ballpoints in isolation because they think you'll use one to kill yourself. They gave me those little half pencils about three inches long that I could barely feel in my hands. When I complained enough, a cop gave me pens after a day or two, but I had to hide them each time a counselor or someone walked by my cell. So I'm in jail conspiring with a cop to hold a couple of pens.

By the fourth or fifth day, I was about to go out of my mind from boredom and inactivity. A counselor checks on you every day to see if you're going to kill yourself as a result of the stress of isolation, and I got a break when one of them asked me if I'd sign some baseballs for his brother who needed them for a charity auction.

"Bring 'em on," was the easy answer. He brought me four dozen balls. I later found out the guy took a dozen for himself and sold them for $25 each.

I signed another 100 or so over the next three months for various cops, and it's very much against the rules for inmates to do any favors for cops. That's because there will always come a time when the inmate needs a favor in return, be it cigarettes or commissary money. In my case, it was batteries for my radio.

The problem was, they only let you have two batteries at a time, and those need to be in the radio. You can't keep extra batteries in segregation—presumably so you don't figure out a way to shock yourself to death. I would have gone berserk without my radio, and the cops supplied me with all the batteries I needed.

The cops also took care of me when it came to the phone. They have to bring you the phone and dial the number for you, and they gave me access on a daily basis.

Kissing ass is a fact of life for inmates, and it's possible that my friendliness and cooperation paid off. After about two months in segregation, a guy from administration stopped by my cell with the good news: "The warden says you can be an orderly at night."

It was great news. I wanted to get out of the isolation unit so badly that the thought of doing laundry and getting the showers ready out on the pods was comforting. My first night as an orderly happened to be laundry day, and I went to the 80 cells in segregation to ask guys what size jumpsuit I'd be delivering the next night.

Gotti Jr.'s uncle Peter and the Gambino grandson were in a cell together in the segregation unit below me for threatening to kill somebody behind the wall in the FCI.

Their names were on the cell door because guys get moved in and out and the guards need to know who's who. I knocked on the cell door. I was tempted to say, "Hey, I was just with your nephew," but I thought better of it.

"Gentlemen, I'm the orderly. What size suit you want tomorrow?"

Gambino got out of the lower bunk, puts his face to the slot in the door, and said, "I gotta tell you my size every other day? What are you, a f*ckin' idiot?"

"Look asshole," I said. "You don't have to tell me. I'll bring you a four-X or a small, I don't care. This is the first night I've done this. So, let's start over and I'll take your order."

They'd been in the hole for six months with no hope of coming out and didn't give a shit about anything. You just can't believe what happens to people. Peter Gotti said from the bed, "He's having bad day," and told me their sizes.

Every guy in isolation had a different story. One guy's wife visited him in the camp and then stashed four pounds of lobster out in the woods for him to retrieve. As soon as he picked it up, half a dozen cops nabbed him.

There was a guy on my isolation tier they called Fat Fred. Everybody has to have a job, but Fat Fred refused to work. He was an obese white guy with an Afro-like hairdo doing 25 years for drugs. He had been in seven prisons in six years and had refused to work everywhere he went. All he'd do was eat his three meals and stuff his face with commissary food. After about three weeks in isolation, they decided to cut off his commissary.

Fred's way of fighting back was to plug up his sink and flood the place. When water started coming into the other cells, guys hit their panic buttons. Since we're alone most of the day, each cell has a panic button. You don't like to use it unless you have to, and they were all going off. One of the newer cops ran into the unit and, when he turned the corner, it was like he was playing on the water slide and skidded about 25 feet in his brand new uniform.

For several days afterward, I'd hear Fat Fred moaning. Pissing off the cops is not taken lightly, and getting disciplined can be extremely ugly.

I must've read close to 100 books in the hole at McKean, and even wrote one about an airline pilot who traveled the world and killed people just for the fun of it. I went through a few sets of batteries a day, trying to keep my mind occupied in a seven foot by nine foot cell with no air-conditioning in the middle of summer.

Segregated

I'd asked the cops on a regular basis to keep pumping Bob Clark about when I'd be getting out of isolation and put back in the camp. I'd been in the hole for three months when he sent word that I'd be out in a few weeks, perhaps by Thanksgiving.

It was great news, and the next day they came by and said, "Pack up your shit." I'm thinking, Wow, two weeks early, no less!

A half hour later two cops unlocked my door to say, "Turn around."

I was confused. "Why the handcuffs?" I could just walk over to the camp. I didn't get it.

They said matter of factly, "You're going back to New York."

Chapter 33

Valhalla Redux

Going back to Valhalla, the pigsty of the world, was still better than spending 16 hours a day in lockup. You can't come close to comprehending the mind-numbing boredom of segregation. So I found myself looking forward to getting back in the law library, watching TV, maybe writing a book and listening to good New York radio.

What was bizarre about going back to Valhalla was that we had heard that John Gotti Jr. had already made bail and was about to complete a deal with the government. While in the hole at McKean, I'd read in the paper that Gotti Jr. had put up his $4 million estate on Long Island and was on a tether, allowed to leave only to see his attorney, get a haircut, or go to a medical appointment.

Gotti Jr. had apparently been reporting an income of about $60,000 a year while living in a $4 million mansion. Must be a great money manager, huh? After they arrested him on the indictment, the Feds found $300,000 cash in a safe in his basement. Gotti Jr. told them it was money he'd gotten from wedding gifts. Some wedding, huh?

Gotti Jr. may've have settled his mess, but I still had to play out my hand in the whole nonsensical matter.

The guy who ran Receiving and Discharge at McKean said, "Strip, I have other clothes for your trip to New York."

I hadn't taken a shower, and if he had gotten too close I might have been hit with a new charge. It was the same strip-search drill again, looking everywhere, even in my armpits. He had me run my fingers through my hair, which was about an inch and a half long. And needless to say, he had me try to grab my ankles to look for the M-16 I might've hidden in my asshole.

He also gave me size 48 pants, at least four sizes too big. No candy bars and Pepsi for four months of segregation will do that. I was about 50 pounds lighter than when I first arrived at McKean. We drove to Erie, Pennsylvania, where a plane was to take me to Valhalla.

As we passed rest stops on the highway, I thought how I would die for the chance to stop at a McDonald's, even though they have the worst fries of all the fast food joints. It felt great to breathe fresh air and sit on something soft after four months on a steel bed and iron stool. I could have sat there for days and just enjoyed the ride.

I was flown to Stewart Air Force Base in a gorgeous Cessna Citation jet that, according to the marshal, had been confiscated in a drug bust. I sat in my ankle chains and handcuffs and enjoyed that ride, too. It doesn't take much beyond the humdrum and monotony to excite you in jail, and plane rides have always been my passion. Just think about the money that the Feds wasted on this trip by flying me on a chartered jet.

When we landed in New York, I was told to pick up my box of legal materials and carry it the 15 feet from the plane to the van. But I couldn't do it with handcuffs on, and the marshal gave me a dirty look before putting it in the back of the van for me.

We got to Valhalla an hour later, and I waited another five hours in a holding cell. I finally got booked at 9:00 PM, and for the fourth time in the last day, I picked up my balls and endured the search routine. I had a roaring headache because I needed my blood pressure pills, and when the nurse checked me as part of the entry process, my blood pressure was 160 over 110, and she allowed me to take two of my pills.

Valhalla Redux

By about 11:00, I was finally led to my cell, and I'll be damned if it wasn't the same one I had during my previous seven-month stay. They gave me a blanket and two sheets but no pillow. By midnight, my 19-hour day was over—most of it spent in cuffs and shackles that cut and scraped my ankles and wrists.

Before I went to the courthouse for an 8:00 AM hearing, I ran into Greg DePalma out on the pod. DePalma was a made member of the Gambino family and was also on the Gotti Jr. indictment.

The Feds had dozens of hours of DePalma on tape bragging about his criminal exploits. He did have a few things to brag about—he was a partner of Frank Sinatra's decades ago when the Westchester Theatre was in its hey day. He told me he had lung cancer and was scheduled to start chemotherapy that day. The problem for the government was that his testimony was vital, the trial might not start for a few months, and he might not last that long.

If it hadn't been for DePalma's bragging on taped conversations with the old man Sergio, the two of them would have never been in this indictment. It was a perfect example of why you should keep your mouth shut, especially if you're a bad guy.

The judge held a 20-minute hearing that had nothing to do with me and announced that the next hearing wouldn't be until December 14, 1998, almost a full month away. I couldn't believe I was flown on a private jet for this.

I waited in the holding cell for the trip back to jail, and a guard brought baloney sandwiches. Typically, there was no mustard or mayo on the sandwich, and I asked why. He grunted the usual, "I forgot." These assholes rarely bothered to put any condiments on anything. Compared to what I'd been eating lately, it would have been a major league sandwich if it had a layer of mayo on it.

I met with Dominic Porco, my attorney who I hadn't seen in four months, and he complimented me on how much weight I'd lost. I explained to him why the isolation diet works better than Jenny Craig and also hit him up for $60 to buy soap, shampoo, Ho Hos, and Diet Pepsi.

My goal for the evening was to let Sharon know I was in Valhalla, and rather than make her pay $3.99 for the first minute and 40 cents for every minute after, I played the collect-call game. Prisoners will learn how to cheat or compromise just about anything. Here's how the payphone scam works: they give you five seconds to say your name on a collect call, and the prisoner would use those five seconds to quickly say, "Only accept if you need to talk to me." If the party doesn't accept, the prisoner keeps calling back and cramming five seconds of information into as many calls as their dialing finger can handle. There were times that I saw guys make 20 or 30 calls to get the message across.

Think of charging $3.99 a minute in a day and age when you can call direct anywhere in the country for pennies. The fact didn't escape me that I was falsely indicted for phone fraud while those whores charged $3.99 a minute. I ask you, who was stealing from whom?

◆　　　◆　　　◆

There's always a need for ingenuity in jail, and "hot coffee" is another trick. The prisoner tightly wraps toilet paper into the shape of a round cylinder and hangs the coffee in a glass or tin cup above the cylinder. He lights the toilet paper, and after 30 seconds, the coffee was flaming.

If you were caught with a weapon, you could spend months or more in the hole, so guys filled socks with bars of soap, and you'd rather be hit by a truck. I saw a sock full of soap crush a guy's nose one night after he was accused of hogging the phone.

I happened to be watching when a guy walked up behind the victim and said, "Hey, pal, look at this." When he turned to look, the sock hit him with the speed of a Randy Johnson fastball. As the guy fought to stay on his feet, he dropped the phone. The sock slugger casually picked it up and made his call. Minutes later the Darth Vaders arrived on the scene and had their fun, turning our cells upside-down again.

Getting out of isolation and reacquainting with Valhalla soon wore thin, and I felt myself sinking into another depression. I hadn't seen my family in 17 months because Michelle was reluctant to have her kids visit a jail. Sharon had divorced me and had been on her own without me going on a year and a half. Although we still talked, I was finding it harder to sustain the faith that I'd eventually win her back.

Part of the Peet conviction was garnishment of my baseball pension, and I desperately needed it. Sharon missed the house payment this month, and we were in danger of going into default on it. Thank God Lou Boudreau stepped up and paid the rent.

I clung to any hope I could find, and my Detroit attorney, Chris Andreoff, was appealing my case in Cincinnati that week. His wife Nancy accepted my collect call and told me that Chris thought we had a chance. I went to sleep that night thinking that if we lost the appeal and I faced four more years in jail, I'd never get Sharon back. I thought I might have to consider going to see Kristin in the afterlife sooner than later.

Things had changed dramatically at Valhalla in the four months I'd been away. The noise level was noticeably louder, and the population had almost completely turned over. People go in and out so quickly at a county jail, and except for the Sergios, I didn't know anybody.

I'd talk to Stephen Sergio from time to time and continued helping him on his autobiography. I'd listen in on his meetings with his crooked-nose guys and be amused by their war stories. "Hey, remember when I got that guy in the 7-Eleven?" Or, "Remember when I robbed that candy store?" It was all so infantile. And they'd always brag about the strip club Scores. Meanwhile, the two guys who owned Scores are doing 20 to 30 years each for defrauding an insurance company for $60 million.

I'd gotten pretty good at writing letters for the prisoners who were about to get sentenced. The judge will allow an inmate to talk before the sentence is handed down. The inmate says how sorry he is and how he'll never do anything to put him in this position again. I wrote at least a dozen of these to the various judges and may have helped a few get less time than expected. Not bad for two cases of Diet Pepsi per letter.

No system is perfect. One of my "clients" appeared before the same judge another client had seen the week before. The judge remarked that while his letter and his plea were passionate, he was sure he had heard something similar just a week or so ago. Oops.

With Gotti Jr. gone, a Mr. T look-alike named Willie ran the pod. Willie was huge, muscular, and had a reputation to match. He was accused of two murders, and since I had been made law librarian again, I won quick favor with Willie by doing some legal research for him. No self-respecting pod boss would ever allow his typist and legal assistant to get hurt.

Like I had in snuggling up to Gotti Jr., I ate with this guy, did his research, and even tried giving him legal advice. I convinced him to cop a plea and move on with his sentence. He wound up cooperating with the government in other criminal matters and got about 15 years.

Things were much more chaotic under Willie than they had been when Gotti Jr. was running the pod. Fights were breaking out all the time over nothing, and the Darth Vaders were in the pod almost every week to break something up. The weak were also being taken advantage of more often. Things were being stolen from their cells, and their trays would be strong-armed in the food line.

Prostitution seemed to have picked up. One whore was so busy, he had two pimps getting him business. It was later found out that he had AIDS and never told anyone.

There were so many things that drove me crazy at Valhalla—like waiting behind guys to use the phone. They'd stand there in baggy pants halfway down their asses with a hand inside playing with their balls. Then they use the same hand to talk on the phone before I had to put it up to my ear and mouth. I witnessed guys masturbating while on the phone, not even caring that others were watching while they talked to their girls.

◆   ◆   ◆

At Valhalla, the parade of new inmates is never ending. Here's a look at a few who arrived within a few days:

> • A pair of brothers ripped off a gas station and whacked the owner with a hammer, seriously injuring him. Both looked about 15, but one was 21 and the other was 18. The 18-year-old had a clean record before following his brother's lead.
> • A 40-year-old guy named Pop tried robbing a drug dealer in the guy's apartment. The dealer made a move for Pop's gun, and Pop shot him. To make sure the dealer wouldn't cause any more problems, Pop shot him four more times. He was to be sentenced in a month.
> • A guy named Rick was nabbed by the Guiliani crime team for masturbating in the bushes in Central Park. He was waiting to be bailed out. In the meantime, he sat in Valhalla with robbers, murders, and rapists. For that?
> • Another guy awaiting bail was a purse-snatcher named Mo who'd been arrested 51 times, by his count, and bragged that he'd never had to seriously hurt a woman whose purse he stole. What a humanitarian.

In early 1999 Gotti Jr. plead guilty to racketeering and cut a deal with the government that included a fine and a five-year jail term. Of course, it still didn't mean that they were done with me. Porco came to me at one point and said, "They're willing to put the case away if you'll plead guilty and take an 18-month continuous sentence."

In other words, if I admitted to something, they'd put the 18 months alongside what I was already serving, and it wouldn't cost me any more jail time.

In a perfect world, when someone makes a mistake, they admit it and you move on. But the government doesn't work that way when they know they're wrong. After spending hundreds of thousands on the Gotti Jr. charges, they were still determined not to admit any mistakes. Sipperly had screwed up this part of the indictment badly and wanted me to help her out by admitting to the charges.

She had gotten some mileage out of linking me with Gotti Jr., helping to inspire a *New York Daily News* headline back when the indictment came down that read, Link—The 30-Game Winner and the Don.

I still might have given her what she wanted—that's how badly I wanted to get out of Valhalla—but Porco started to fashion an endgame that would avoid having us admit anything.

The U.S. Attorney's office had called in a supervisor to attempt to untangle the Gotti Jr. mess. Porco arranged a meeting and presented him with a 100-page file that showed document after document, deposit after deposit, which detailed the history of our phone business. He accumulated documents in the MCI case that proved that monies we had sent MCI had then been sent to the Cayman Islands as part of MCI's fraud and had nothing to do with Gotti Jr.

When the MCI guys were questioned in a deposition in Atlanta, they were asked whether Denny McLain was in on it. The answer according to the deposition was, "No, we scammed his company, too."

My case was dismissed in April 1999. It came as no surprise to me that the same media outlets that made screaming headlines when I was indicted with Gotti Jr. barely recognized the fact that the indictment was dropped.

Valhalla Redux

Two months later the proper paperwork was filed, and I was on my way back to McKean to finish out my time.

Chapter 34

Happy Camper

When Judge Parker, a fair and really good guy, dismissed my case at the courthouse in White Plains, he asked me if I had anything to say.

I looked at him and said, "Yes. Your Honor, can I go home now?"

He, the spectators, and attorneys in the courtroom had a laugh. Judge Parker chuckled, smiled, and said, "Home—I'm not so sure. But probably to a better place than Valhalla."

That was an understatement. After my paperwork was processed, I parted via the old routine: the van to Stewart Air Force Base, the flight to stinking hot Lewisburg, and finally the van to McKean.

Lewisburg—take three—was as awful as ever. Mid-July, no air-conditioning, and my cell was right next to the hot water pipe that fed the whole cellblock. And, of course, all of the little critters and cock-roaches were still happily at play.

I only had to stay for a day this time before returning to McKean. When I got to Receiving and Discharge at McKean, the cop recognized me and said, "Sorry I have to do this." I ran my fingers through my hair, showed him my pits, picked up my balls and, before I grabbed my ankles and turned around, I said, "Be careful, I got a Twinkie up my ass and it might hit you in the face."

"Then we'll split it," he said with a laugh. I filled out the requisite eight to 10 pages of health information, next-of-kin documents, and the rest of the garbage still in the computer system from the five other times I'd been through this drill. I was escorted to a small office to reacquaint with Camp Administrator Bob Clark and a few of his minions.

Clark asked, "Any reason why you shouldn't be in the camp? Anybody after you?"

"No, sir. No reason. I just want to be able to breathe again." This was exciting. I hadn't been in the camp since November 1997, and now it was July of 1999.

My first job was to work in the welding shop. I couldn't hammer a nail, much less weld, which is a skilled job. They needed some reorganization, and my job was clerical, to keep track of all the tools in the machine shop and update the chit system for the borrowing of tools. If a tool was ever missing or not returned, there was hell to pay. Everybody got locked down to make sure it wasn't being used as a weapon. If a tool was tossed over the fence into the big prison, it could be used to bust locks, bust heads, or whatever else.

After a few months I told the cop in charge, "I've got nothing else to do. I reorganized the place, so let me weld." Whether it's a screwdriver or a saw, I'll eventually hurt myself. But I was bored.

I'd seen enough to understand basic welding, and a few days later they gave me a simple task of welding a pipe to a cross bar with no fancy seams involved. I was told to make it firm and not to worry about it looking pretty. I put on the fireproof gloves, the face shield, and the leather apron so I didn't set myself on fire, and I was alone in the barn, welding away. Since it was late summer and hot as hell, I had the two large, noisy fans that looked like propellers on a DC-3 blowing on me. As I was welding, I didn't see that my sparks were being blown behind me. I'm feeling like Willie the Welder, sweat pouring out of every part of my body, all my protection in place, thinking, *How hard is this?*

All of a sudden, an inmate who worked with me came running into the room, screaming over the din of the fans, "McLain what the hell are you doing? This place is on fire!"

Sparks had been flying into a 50-pound drum filled with paper a few feet behind me, and the damn barrel had caught on fire. The cop asked me why I was trying to burn the building down, thanked me for my reorganization efforts, told me I needed a job better suited to me, and sent me to administration for reassignment.

As luck would have it, I got a break and landed another job as a driver. I'd pick up the night shift at the power plant at 4:30 AM and run prisoners and personnel around the camp all day.

One afternoon in the fall, I was picking up workers at the maintenance building. There were about 25 guys in maintenance, cutting grass, trimming bushes, and goofing off. The geese would come by the hundreds in the fall, and their shit was everywhere. They're a pain in the ass, but it's a protected species and if you touch them it's a federal crime.

One of the maintenance guys was a kid from Tennessee they called Spanky, who was dumb as a rock and had a dumb name to match. Spanky was a driver for the maintenance crew and had succeeded in purposely running over one of the geese because he and his guys wanted to eat it.

They hadn't had fresh fowl in years, and they put the goose in the back of the truck as they pulled in after their shift. It was my job to drive them back to the units.

The maintenance boss saw the goose in the back of truck and asked Spanky, "What's with the goose?"

"We're gonna cook it."

"Are all you guys from Tennessee this stupid?" the boss railed. "We can get five years for killing a f*ckin' goose. Get rid of it now."

Spanky told him he'd bury the goose, and he and a few jerkoffs on his crew picked up a few nearby shovels. But when Spanky went to pick up the goose, it sprang back to life and started limping around the yard on one good leg. The yard was fenced in, and Spanky and the morons chased it around the yard for what seemed like 10 minutes until one of them finally whacked it with his shovel and put an end to the pursuit.

They started digging a hole to bury it as they'd promised to do. But when the boss left, instead of burying it, Spanky put the goose in his gunnysack and got into my van. "Don't talk," he said, "and we'll let you eat some of it."

"Sure, Spanky, that'd be great." I shook my head and drove them home. If I got caught with this goose in my van by the wrong cop, we'd all go to the hole.

I saw one of Spanky's crew that evening, and he told me that Spanky hid the goose under his bed and was going to take it to the Indian smokehouse area to feather it, gut it, and cut it up before the 9:00 PM body count.

There was a special area for Native Americans behind the kitchen. There were probably about two inmates with Indian blood, but since the Indians enjoyed some special privileges, about 70 guys claimed to have Indian ancestry. There was a teepee, a prayer room, and an area where rocks were arranged in a circle for a symbolic ritual.

There were two microwaves for the four floors of our housing unit, and Spanky and his pals got up at 2:00 AM to start cooking the goose. I didn't happen to wake up, but another guy told me that the aroma was fabulous and powerful enough to smell it in Pittsburgh. Spanky and his gang got their goose and ate it, too. Hey, this is prison, and anything to interrupt the monotony can't be a bad thing.

◆　　　　◆　　　　◆

Body counts were done several times a day, with the main ones at 4:00 PM after work, and at 9:00 PM before bed. You had to be by your bunk and standing up. The cops took the body counts very seriously, and if you messed with their count by saying, "Hey, you missed number 14," they could lock everyone down for as long as they wanted.

There were also body counts when we were asleep, with the last one at about 5:00 in the morning before guys got up to go to work.

The first week I was back at McKean, an escape took place. An Iranian, who should have been in the FCI as a level three or four inmate, was incorrectly placed in the camp. On a Monday morning, two days after he arrived, he passed the 5:00 AM body count. He then took a camp bus to the back of the FCI, where all the workshops were, walked through woods, and met a pal who drove him away. With a 10-hour head start, he made it to Canada by the time he failed to clear the 4:00 PM count.

The count took about 20 minutes, and when it was over, you'd hear, "Count clear—count clear." It wasn't clearing after 20 minutes, and we were all standing there with our fingers up our noses. Dinner was at 5:00, but by 5:00 we were still standing by our bunks when the captain of security started bringing around the mug books.

All 210 of us had a mug shot and an ID number. They came by me and I said, "McLain 04000-018." It matched, and they moved on. They knew right away who'd escaped, but they have to follow policy. They're always following policy, whether it's having you hold your ankles to check your asshole for rifles or going through the body-count routine.

While the captain was checking each of us, there was a patrol scouring every inch of the camp. They didn't know if the missing inmate had been beaten up or was killed and was lying face down in a field somewhere.

By 6:00 PM they were still doing the mug shots even though everybody knew that the f*cking Iranian was the so-called "walkaway." Part of the routine is to check under the beds, in the lockers, and behind the desks. The guy was 6' and 200 pounds—how can he be behind a desk that's up against the wall? One guy said, "Look in the left-hand drawer, maybe he's there."

◆   ◆   ◆

After a few years of driving, a job in the safety office opened up, and I was hired. We would make sure that the fire extinguishers were properly filled and installed, and we disbursed cleaning materials to the orderlies and to the units for use in the cells. It's Lysol, soap, mops, mop heads, waste cans, lights, and the most popular product of all, wax.

Guys loved to shine their cubes until you could see your reflection in the floor. Neat freaks who couldn't control the common areas tried to make up for it in their own little space. They'd kill hours waxing their cubes.

Like cigarettes and food, wax was money and was in limited supply. We would water it down and barter it as contraband for commissary items. A gallon of wax would bring at least $10 of commissary cash, and the stolen wax required no investment. We were required to write everything down, and if the boss ever bothered to do an audit, we would have all wound up in the hole forever.

Around the time I was put in charge of the safety office, I was also asked to become the camp's softball commissioner. Softball is taken very seriously in leagues all around America, but not like it is in prison. League winners at McKean were awarded commissary credits. The commissioner's job paid $30 a month, good money in a system that paid 11¢ an hour.

Inmates were always bitching about playing time and the other usual baseball bullshit, and the administration figured that I'd know how to handle that stuff.

I put together four teams of 20 men each and scheduled a 60-game season. I figured I could partially solve the playing-time issue by making

Happy Camper

a rule that each lineup would have 12 players. Ten would play the field and 12 would bat, with two players serving as designated hitters.

You would have thought I'd committed murder. Guys blasted me, saying things like, "You can't change the rules of the game, you fat f*ck."

I had water tossed on my bed and shit tossed on my floor. A lousy new rule designed to get more guys in the lineup created this much hell. But I needed the $30 a month and needed to stick to my decisions. I was the Bowie Kuhn of McKean and I held my ground.

The baseball season was the best time of the year because guys got outside and exercised. But you've never seen full-contact softball like it's played in prison. Tempers were combustible, and there were hard tags and brutal collisions on the base paths. The umpires were constantly under attack, and some were also on the take. I wish I had video of some of these games and incidents. They'd outsell *When Animals Attack* and maybe even *Girls Gone Wild*.

For some reason, the basketball games didn't arouse the same passion. Guys would have beefs and argue and shove, but I only witnessed one really ugly incident.

A new inmate named Hammer arrived around the middle of the season. He looked about 6'5" and was a rock-solid 250-plus pounds. He was immediately put on one of the four teams and used his bulk to move people around à la Shaquille O'Neal.

The best athlete in camp was Kiki, who was in his mid-thirties, built like a Sherman tank, and finishing up the last few years of a 15-year sentence for drug dealing. He was quiet, respectful, and well liked—the sort of guy who would loan commissary to the poorer guys. He was also the best basketball player, and at about 6'4", he could dunk.

The Hammer and Kiki went head to head all game long. With about a minute to go and with almost all 210 of us on hand, Kiki went to lay the ball in on a fast break when Hammer pushed him in the back and sent him stumbling into the unpadded steel pole that held the basket up. You could hear his head clang off it, and he went down in a heap.

Kiki appeared to be unconscious for a second or two, and when he remembered he'd been shoved intentionally, he put his hand on his bleeding head, walked over to Hammer, and without raising his voice or pointing his finger said, "I'll see you in the unit. Be there motherf*cker."

The game ended with Kiki on the bench, a blood-stained towel on his bleeding head and a golf ball–sized knot on his forehead. I went over to Kiki. "Forget it," I said. "It's not worth it. He's a scumbag. If you hurt him, you could do more time."

"He disrespected me," Kiki answered. "If I don't get him, the whole compound will think I'm a pussy."

"Nobody in here thinks you're a pussy," I argued, "and you're going home in 20 months. If you hurt him you might do 20 more years."

I walked with Kiki back to the pod where the asshole Hammer was waiting for him. I'd done all the peacemaking I could do, so I got out of the way. Hammer took one step toward him, and Kiki nailed him in the jaw with a glorious hook from right field. Hammer slumped to the floor, and the fight was over in a second.

It was thrilling. I started yelling, "Down goes Hammer! Down goes Hammer!" like Howard Cosell's, "Down goes Frazier! Down goes Frazier!" when George Foreman knocked him out in 1973. I started counting to 10, but I could have counted for 10 minutes before someone threw a bucket of water on him and he started to come around.

Hammer wound up with a concussion and a broken jaw. Some of us were called into the administration office for an investigation, but the code of silence was enforced. I eventually told one of the counselors on the promise he wouldn't report it. He asked, "Do you think anyone's in danger?"

"Hell no," I said. "The Hammer's claws have been removed."

No one went to the hole, and Kiki went home on time.

Chapter 35

Bryant

In the fall of 1999, Bryant Gumbel came to McKean to do a piece on me for his HBO show, *Real Sports*. With his experience in shaping interviews, his freedom to add disparaging remarks with no rebuttal, his producer's ability to create drama, his scriptwriter's skill at crafting a perception, and my failure to understand accountability, he ate me alive.

Me, the former media pro, wound up falling into the same trap I often set for the guests on my shows: get them frustrated and lead them to an emotional explosion.

I gave Gumbel every word and emotion he needed to make me look exactly like a self-centered jerk, and it was a blowout. I had always been guilty of grandiosity and embellishment—always craving attention and the good sound byte—and I really bit myself in the ass in this one.

The HBO piece aired in October 1999 and started with a full-screen close-up of an angry Denny, sounding like a man who had been dealt a terrible injustice.

> **Denny:** I didn't do this. I had nothing to do with this. Not one damn thing. And I'm here for no reason. No reason at all!
> **Bryant (Looking at Denny both puzzled and bemused):** So Denny had nothing to do with this?

367

Denny: Not a goddamn thing!
Bryant: Then you're here for no reason all?
Denny: You heard me. No reason at all!

The interview wasn't 15 seconds old, and I was already a loser, instantly exposed. And done in by no less than "Mr. Integrity" himself, Bryant Gumbel, a guy who cheated on his wife for years with many women before finally suffering public exposure for it.

What a beautiful pair of bedfellows we made.

I wasn't able to see the segment when it aired live, but the warden later gave me a tape to watch in the church chapel. A handful of inmates came in to see it with me.

From those first fateful seconds until it faded to black, all I did was scream at Gumbel for making me look so bad. I still couldn't grasp that my pathetic performance might actually be my fault.

As I watched, I could envision the millions of viewers shaking their heads. I could all but hear them thinking, *What's wrong with this guy? How can he look Bryant Gumbel in the eye and tell him he had nothing to do with landing himself in jail—again?*

It was the 1970 Poor, Dumb Denny *Sports Illustrated* headline all over again. I was reconstructing events in a way that made me appear to be the only victim, rather than accepting my culpability in perpetrating the events at Peet Packing.

It was true that Roger Smigiel and Jeff Egan were the financial experts who had masterminded and pulled off the pension scam, but I could have brought it to light on a timely basis and survived it.

Unfortunately, when I talked to Gumbel in 1999, I was still unable to see that the pension fund had been the tip of the iceberg in the larger disaster of sending 200 people at Peet Packing to the unemployment line. Somebody had to pay the price for that. Somebody had to be the face that was responsible for it. It was my face and it was my grand delusion of success that had been the driving force behind it. It had been another ugly result of my absurdly unjustified optimism: that no matter what the odds were, I would find a way to win.

I didn't know how to objectively take a big-picture view of my thoughts and actions to see how illogical they had been—how I had led myself to believe that I could buy a financially destitute 100-year old company with a losing culture in place and magically turn it around.

No one could ever talk any sense to the old Denny. No one! Not even Sharon, the woman I had both tortured and worshipped since we were 19 years old.

Just like Bowie Kuhn had said back in 1970, I'd allowed myself to be duped by a list of bad actors—from the Peet brothers to Egan and Smigiel. I'd always wound up with these Damon Runyon characters, like Sy Sher, Barry Nelson…the list goes on. Where did they come from and how did I find them? Why did I do what I did with them?

I shouldn't have gotten emotional with Bryant, but I couldn't help myself. Obviously, I was in jail for a reason, yet there I was, shouting, "I didn't do this and I'm here for no reason!" As if the world was going to believe that I just fell out of the sky into McKean correctional in an awful case of mistaken identity.

After my opening rave, an eloquent Gumbel continued his voice-over with shots of me in prison and in my baseball glory days:

> Dennis Dale McLain sounds like a man who's been wronged, yet his whole life suggests a sad lack of total innocence. His is a tale of an athlete who once seemed headed for Cooperstown and wound up in Bradford, Pennsylvania, instead.
>
> In the white-hot summer of 1968, a year otherwise dominated by war, protest, and assassination, a 24-year-old

right-hander from Chicago could do no wrong. It was the Year of the Pitcher, and Denny McLain had as great a season as a pitcher ever has.

It was a hell of a story for HBO: baseball player marries his sweetheart, the daughter of a Hall-of-Fame player; enjoys a meteoric rise to stardom; burns out his arm; and turns everything good in his life to ruin. He then goes to jail, rises to stardom again in a different field, and then turns it all to shit again, even more spectacularly than the first time.

Then, with a wonderful opportunity to explain his side on national television, he affirms his delusion by ranting and raving, "I'm here for no reason."

Fiction can't come close to the story Bryant was telling.

Bryant talked about my first trip to jail in the '80s:

> After 29 months in jail for racketeering and other offenses, McLain then moved his family back to Detroit and embarked on a remarkable comeback. Embraced by his former fans, he was soon making over $400,000 a year hosting a popular morning radio program and successful TV show with local sportscaster Eli Zaret.
>
> **Bryant (to Sharon):** He came out a free man. A changed man?
>
> **Sharon:** So we thought.
>
> **Eli:** He was making big money. Denny was a great entertainer who understood how to engage an audience. You couldn't have landed better on your feet. He would talk about the misery of jail, how awful it was, the vermin, the maggots, the inhumanity, how he would never go back, how thankful he was to get back on his feet.

Gumbel then went into Kristin's death and, as if he cued me to do it, got me to cry like a baby on camera.

At least he let me show I had a heart.

> **Sharon:** It [Kristin's death] just destroyed him. He wasn't happy with anything anymore. Nothing was the same. He wasn't happy on the radio. He was just searching for something that wasn't there.
>
> **Eli:** Everything has been hell in his life since then, but let's face it, Denny creates his own hell in many ways. He certainly didn't create his daughter's death, but the decisions he made after that were all too typical of what happened in his life. He was always looking for the thrill of the big score. Denny was always saying, "This'll be the big one."

Bryant used Eli's line to segue to this:

> McLain thought he found his biggest score in 1993, when he and a partner, Roger Smigiel, purchased a 100-year-old financially troubled meat-packing plant in the small town of Chesaning, Michigan. So enamored was Denny that he eventually quit his radio and TV jobs to run Peet Packing full time.
>
> **Sharon:** I didn't understand it. What does he know about running a meat-packing company?
>
> **Eli:** I asked him, "Why would you do this?" And he said, "Because it was a sleeping giant" and because he, the great Denny McLain, would be able to turn it around.
>
> Bryant voice-over: Within 15 months of McLain purchasing the company, Peet Packing was bankrupt and over

200 people were out of work. Shortly thereafter, McLain, Smigiel, and their accountant, Jeffrey Egan, were indicted for concocting a scheme to steal over $2.5 million from the company's pension fund. McLain denied any knowledge of the scheme.

No sane man with a high-paying, glamorous job would buy a company that was on life support and in foreclosure. In fact, the whole Peet episode so blatantly didn't make sense that it eventually became the perfect example that helped me recognize my faulty reasoning.

Whatever forces had previously driven me to act in a self-destructive manner became all the more dangerous and costly when Kristin died. I'd wanted to die because of what I'd had done to her. I was incapable of dealing productively with my grief, so I frantically started running everywhere, helter-skelter. I had been like a bull in the china shop, and I'd knocked over some very costly stuff.

If I could sit over my shoulder 13 years ago and advise myself on how to cope better and prevent all the tragedies from piling up, the first thing I'd do differently was just let my guard down, cry it out, and hold my wife. I did everything you're not supposed to do to properly grieve. I felt my job was to protect Sharon the way her parents protected her from so many of life's realities. You have to realize that you're a family and you have to do it together. We all lost a part of our life and we needed to share that together.

As incredible as it sounds, Sharon's parents, sister, and brothers never talked to her about Krissie's death either. Their thinking was, "Don't say anything because it'll just upset her." Sharon's mother had told her at other times in her life, "You don't get help. You handle it yourself." That was another example of all of us doing the exact opposite of what was healthy. We were acting like, "We're strong—we can handle this." And that's just not how it was. Nobody wants to be that strong, nor should they be. Then you've lost all feeling, which we did—killing the love between us because we couldn't stand to look at each other. What we thought was normal—being strong and not breaking down—was really abnormal. Neither of us would let our guard down—we wanted to be strong for the children. Sharon didn't want them to see their mother go to pieces and think she was crazy. We didn't know how to deal with each other or the kids.

I started drinking in excess for the first time in my life. Everything in my life was gone and I was searching desperately for something I couldn't define.

But those revelations came later. At McKean, I thought it was terribly cruel that my family wouldn't visit me in jail. Again, I allowed myself to play the role of victim. All I could think was, *Why don't they come? Why not just one holiday, one birthday, one day, one moment in six years. Why not? Did they hate me that much?*

I surely thought so. In my low moments, I started praying to be gravely ill. I prayed that I could be on my deathbed to see if they would come to see me then.

If I'd been capable of putting myself in their shoes, I would have at least been able to understand that visiting me caused them great pain and they needed to deal with things their way. Instead, I felt terribly wronged and was incredibly angry about it.

Gumbel's haunting voice-over continued:

> McLain's troubles have been compounded since he went to prison. The house he shared with Sharon is nearing foreclosure, and his lucrative baseball pension, which she was awarded in the divorce, has been garnished by the government to defray the restitution order. As a result, she, too, is broke.
>
> **Bryant:** How much, Denny, do you flog yourself for the financial bind your difficulties have left her?
>
> **Denny:** Every day…

Sharon: He has no clue how hard it is for me. All I get is, "I'm in jail, and you have no idea what it's like." And no, I don't have any idea.

Bryant: In other words, he's saying, "Don't complain to me, I'm in jail." (Sharon nods in agreement)

That SOB Bryant is good. He was spinning Sharon in any direction he chose. By that point he could have gotten her to admit that I'd kidnapped the Lindberg baby. Gumbel poured it on with more voice-over:

McLain spends his days cleaning the prison cafeteria and driving the prison car. In the afternoon he reads case law in the prison's law library. He longs for a visit from the family he dishonored and seemingly tired of his ways.

Bryant: How long has it been since you've seen your grandkids?

Denny: October '97.

Bryant (Pausing for effect, as if he's adding up the months): Wow. Long time…

Denny: Sure is. (Camera stays as Denny wipes away tears)

Sharon and Michelle both expressed fear about talking to me, so that I wouldn't warp their thinking as they attempted to move on with their lives.

Sharon: I wasn't strong enough to make a difference with Denny. It breaks my heart, but he single-handedly destroyed our family. He needs to let us get our lives back together and let it be our choice if we let him back in.

Bryant: Did you ever threaten to leave him?

Bryant

Sharon: Oh, my gosh. I left him three times and he'd come after me and say, "I'm sorry; you and the kids are the most important things to me." And I took him back.

Michelle: As much as I love him, and I do miss him, I'm emotionally not ready to handle it yet. I don't want to take my kids to a correctional facility; it's not normal behavior for your grandchildren to come see you in jail.

Bryant: Which do you think is keeping you away most, anger or fear?

Michelle (glancing to Sharon): Fear, for me. It's hard to believe we were that naïve, but whatever he said, [we] believed. You didn't have a choice, it was his way and that was what it was going to be.

Sharon: A little of both for me.

Bryant: Face to face with him....

Sharon: It would be a mismatch.

Bryant: He'd win?

Michelle: He always does.

Bryant then introduced Mark Steckloff, a lawyer who's job it was to oversee restitution of the pension fund.

Bryant (to Denny): Where I think there was outrage was the report of where some of the pension money went.

Denny: Where did it go?

Steckloff: A large sum was used to pay back a personal debt which he and his partner incurred in purchasing the company. In addition, monies were used to purchase a condominium in their personal names, a Harley-Davidson motorcycle, landscaping for a residence, and a country club membership.

Despite knowing all the facts, Steckloff sat there and distorted the entire truth of the matter. His law firm made piles of money representing the pension.

That's what was so frustrating. I didn't buy the company to rip it off. I didn't buy the company to get a country club membership. Hell, I had no time to play golf, and it was Smigiel's membership anyway. It was also Smigiel's Harley. C'mon, a motorcycle? He'd given himself a $10,000 bonus and bought it. He also bought himself a $10,000 tree. I dreamt about hanging him from that goddamn tree! That stuff was insignificant in the big picture, but when you illegally come into money and then buy toys, people get inflamed.

I bought the company for an entirely different reason. I bought the company because I needed to be a hero again. I bought the company so I could be back on the mound and strike out the side and hear the roar of the crowd again. I was a modern day Don Quixote, substituting ham bones for batters, substituting truckloads of meat for victories.

I bought the company to escape my pain and try to feel good again—to be a knight in shining armor, riding to the rescue and being loved by the Peet employees. It would have been easy to steal trucks, equipment, and any number of company assets. It wasn't about stealing and looting. It was about the action, the adrenalin, the excitement of the deal. It was about liking myself and getting recognition. It was about winning.

The only thing I was right about is that I am a great salesman. I thought if I increased sales in a major way, that all the company's problems would go away. I did increase sales in a major way, but the company's problems ran much deeper. I'd been so naïve in understanding the real problems, that our inability to fill orders on increased sales actually fed the disaster.

What good is selling more meat when the machinery and the people running it are incapable of producing the meat you're selling? Business

101—hello? That was one of many valid and deep-seated reasons why Peet Packing was in foreclosure before we came along, and my ability to sell ice to Eskimos provided no real benefit at all.

Gumbel was wrapping it up now, thank God, with this voice-over:

> The jury thought Denny did [steal from the pension fund]. In return for a lighter sentence, McLain's accountant, Jeffrey Egan, testified against him, and after a three-week trial, jurors took only a few hours to convict McLain and Smigiel on all counts.
>
> In May of '97, Denny was sentenced to eight years and ordered to pay $2.5 million in restitution.
>
> Sharon started divorce proceedings the day after he left for prison.
>
> **Sharon:** I knew I had to do something because he was in jail…in jail for a long time.
>
> **Bryant:** Justifiably?
>
> **Sharon:** I think so, yes.
>
> **Bryant:** I guess at this point, Denny, you look back at your life. To what, if anything, are you willing to admit, "Hey I'm guilty."
>
> **Denny:** Look. I've made some mistakes, I've dealt with them, I've paid for them, and you move on from there. I mean, what should we do? Dwell upon what happened in 1968 or '69? You can't, Bryant. You just have to move on…you pay the penalty and you move on.

That answer was me in a nutshell. I'd finished the interview by failing to address the many people I'd hurt and left strewn in my path, selfishly focusing only on me and how I felt.

The interview was beyond excruciating at this point. Although I hadn't seen what he'd done with Sharon and Michelle until it aired, I told Bryant when he left the building that day, "You've really been unfair. Had I known that you weren't even going to give me an opportunity to explain my side, we'd have never talked."

Bryant, his brother, and I were all from Chicago. I was thinking, *So much for homies, huh?*

Meanwhile, the last of the inmates to leave the room after watching the episode was a big, bearded biker guy named John who was in jail for guns and drugs. As he left the chapel, he looked at me and said, "You owe someone an apology don't you? And she lives in Michigan."

He'd spoken more truth in that one line than anything I'd said in the interview.

God, it was lonely. Two hundred twenty men at McKean surrounded me, and at times like that, I couldn't even hear a thing. It was as if I was in a vacuum. That's how deep my depression must have been.

When this sad episode took place in October 1999 I was a broken man, divorced and unable to see my family in over two years.

I needed something or someone to finally wake me up so I could stop praying to die in my sleep. I had to find the will to survive McKean, regain my freedom, and win my family and my life back.

Chapter 36

Ed Miller

Anytime someone goes to therapy in this country and writes a book, people see the profit motive and say, "He's full of shit."

But unless we somehow see the light, we go through life repeating the same losing behavior over and over. It can last generations. For example, my father controlled and intimidated his family like his father did, and I wound up doing the same. Only when it finally clicks and you can stand apart and lay your life bare will you begin to understand why you keep on making the same mistakes and misjudgments.

My first mentors, Tom McLain and Charlie Dressen, taught me how to play baseball. But it was Ed Miller in 2002 who finally explained to me why I kept on screwing up all the good things in my life. I learned from Ed that when there's a broken part—a gap in our thinking process—we keep setting the same traps for ourselves, over and over.

I'd been in McKean Correctional for almost five years when they announced a rehab program that was available to anybody with a substance problem. Alcohol provided my escape and had come to rule my life after my daughter's death, and I used that as my ticket for entry in the program.

If you completed the program, you could get up to a year off your sentence. You'd chop down trees for 24 hours a day to get out one day earlier, much less one year earlier. That was the main reason I got into it. I'd never been capable of admitting that I was wrong, much less conceding that I might actually need help.

Ed Miller was a cop who ran the program. But he wasn't a cop in the regular sense. He didn't dress like a cop, didn't have 58 keys on his belt, carry a radio or a panic button, and he didn't use profanity like most cops. He was a devout Christian who had a soft yet commanding way.

Ed was probably making $40,000 a year. He had four children and worked his ass off every day, believing in what he did. All he ever said was, "If I can only help three or four people out of this class of 25, I've accomplished what I set out to do."

We were encouraged to ask each other pointed questions, and it made the classes confrontational in nature. For example, there was a black guy, about 25, who told the group that he had seven children with five different women and never supported any of them.

I had seen the whole sickening scene play out in prison: women visiting on the weekends and sending money to these fraudulent fathers—money that should have been used for their neglected babies. If it wasn't awful enough to abandon the children they brought into the world, they continued to abuse these women financially and spiritually.

Why would men act this way, and why would these women accept it? Can their self-esteem be that nonexistent?

I certainly had my shameful transgressions. I brought terrible pain upon my wife and kids, and I was always able to conveniently put them aside and moralize about others. I verbally attacked this particular degenerate for his selfishness and lack of manhood, and the debate carried over into the hallway after the class. Had a cop not intervened, I would have gotten the shit kicked out of me.

Ed Miller listened to these shocking disclosures every day—the stories of abusers abusing their families with no ability to comprehend their degree of despicability. A rapist justified his violence one day by saying,

Ed Miller

"If she didn't expect it, then why did she invite me to her house?" How the hell do you get through to a guy like that?

The common thread with 90 percent of these men, and I was among them, is that they were abused in one form or another as children, and I identified with the physical and psychological abuse that dominated my childhood.

Some light started to creep in. My sole reason for living was to get out of prison and love my family, and I was starting to finally understand the role I played in the bad things that kept on "happening" to me and then impacted my innocent loved ones.

I became in awe of Ed Miller and told him one day, "You need to be in private practice. You're too good at this. You need to make a real living. I don't care what city they put you in, you'll do well."

"That's not my mission in life," Ed said. "These classes are what God meant for me."

Ed was my polar opposite. My way was to always look for more action—always pursue the home-run deal and to hell with the consequences. Smelling the flowers didn't drive me. I always wanted more of something—whatever it was. Thanks to the manner and wisdom of Ed, I started learning how to slow things down. Without Ed's class, prison would have been a six-year warehouse for me. I began feeling very fortunate that I met Ed and asked him to help me with my anger.

Sharon had pounded into me that if I didn't rid myself of the anger she would abandon me altogether. She'd hit the wall with my bitching about the system and my frustration over Michelle's refusal to visit me with the grandkids.

All my life, I never heeded advice. I always had to be right. My mother had ruled my father, my father ruled me, and I ruled my family. I promised Sharon I'd learn from Ed how to be more civil to her over the phone.

At some point in the first four or five weeks of the program, it struck me that I was writing feelings down that I had never shared with anyone. And knowing that Ed was the only one reading them, a tremendous trust started to develop.

Ed explained that if I was to get better, God had to play a part. Not that I had to get down on my hands and knees, but only by accepting God's role can you be brought back to the center. And if you're in the center, you can see all around you.

I had never talked to anybody about my crushing guilt over Kristin's death. Nobody. Not even Sharon. We never talked about it. Everybody has to grieve in his or her own way, and I believe that if the two of us had gone to therapy, things might have been much, much different.

I spent nine months of four and a half days a week with Ed and the group. Monday through Thursday we'd go three to four hours in a small group and then on Friday the 100 or so in the program would combine for a big class. The tough part was getting up in front of everyone to admit your wrongdoing and thank everyone for the opportunity to be a part of the program. I'd also get one-on-one sessions with Ed that were incredibly helpful.

If you go to therapy four days a week and care about some wellness in your life, you will sooner or later address yourself. I couldn't have done it when I was 25, 35, or even 45. But I had to decide: do I want to continue to be this guy who is mad at the world and bullshits everybody, or do I want to come to some level of sobriety? My definition of sobriety didn't have to do with alcohol. It was about reducing the anger so I could stand back from myself and understand if I was dealing with reality or just lying to myself again.

I surprised myself with the things I said to Eddie Miller because all of a sudden I knew that these were my honest impressions of myself. I wouldn't allow myself to lie or embellish around him, and I said things that I would never have even said to my priest.

Ed Miller

On more than one occasion I broke down and cried like baby with Ed, and I'd never even done that in front of my wife or children. Ed identified my menagerie of demons—greed, lack of patience, lack of tolerance, selfishness, egoism, delusions of grandeur, and a degree of narcissism that blocked me off from correctly seeing how my actions fit in with the world around me.

My attitude had always been that the world had to fit in with me, not me fit in with the world. Ed got me to see myself as a mere speck of dust in God's grand plan, and that He gave us free will. He allows horrible events to take place, like a sweet 26-year-old girl, who never hurt anyone in her entire life, to die in a horrible accident. "Free will," Ed said, "allows us to conduct our lives in irrational ways if we so choose." He was right, and God knows how irrational I have been in my life.

Ed's skill was being the facilitator, utilizing his calm demeanor to help me come to realizations about my life.

Ed quickly recognized that I was still pretty mad at my father 40 years after he was gone. He explained my narcissism—so-called self-love—as a means of self-protection, to fill the void of low self-esteem. All I ever cared about was how *I* felt. It was all about how things affected *me*, and I ignored the feelings of others. I found so little trust and comfort in my house, where I could get whipped at a second's notice, that the only way I could medicate my confusion, pain, and anger was pitching, playing the piano, and being the center of attention.

My whole life, I'd protected myself from all my mistakes and transgressions with the narcissist's standard answer: "Who, me? I didn't do anything wrong." In Catholic school and at home, I was always getting blamed for doing bad things. No matter what the event, the mentality was that someone had to be at blame. As a defense, I'd grown up taking the attitude that nothing was my fault and I was always the one falsely accused.

But with Kristin, it was different.

Ed made me realize that I wasn't responsible for Kristin's death. He said, "Let's see how many ways we can blame you for killing her. Did you put her out there at 2:00 in the morning? Did you park the semi improperly?"

I don't know exactly when it began, but I started to feel better about myself. I don't know if I'll ever totally forgive myself for Kristin's death, and Ed told me that would be the case. But he also said, "You can realize that there are things that occur in our lives that we have no control over. Because of your upbringing, the way the church and family controlled you, your desire is to be a controller, and you even think you're in control of things you can't possibly control.

"There are certain things you can't control. One of them is life and one of them is death." No one had ever been able to make that point before with me. I had just pounded myself for over 10 years, believing Kristin's death was entirely my fault.

If I hadn't met Eddie Miller, I'd still be angry and blaming other people for the things that went wrong. I own a telecom company now, and instead of pointing the finger of blame like the old Denny, I'll think, "Maybe I shouldn't have done it that way." If one of the techs messes up, it doesn't necessarily mean it was the tech's problem. Maybe I didn't give him the directions in detail. That's how I look at it now. I'll say, "Let's go over the proper procedure and see if we can do it better this time."

Ed's big line to me was, "You gotta let go. Just because you provide a worker with a paycheck or pay your kid's rent, it doesn't give you the right to control their lives seven days a week."

It made perfect sense. So why did it take me so long to figure these things out?

Chapter 37

Comeback

My time was up in April 2003, and although there was great expectation and anticipation to walk out that door, I was overwhelmed with apprehension. As you fall in line with the regimentation of jail, you begin to lose your sense of free choice. That's why they require inmates to spend up to the last six months of their sentence in a halfway house, and I was headed to one in Detroit.

I was due to leave at 8:00 AM on the morning of April 23, 2003, and I made arrangements with Receiving and Delivery to be the first out the door. Sharon and I were divorced, but we had talked hundreds of times and cooperated on issues that affect people after 40 years of being together. Since she was essentially all I had, she agreed to pick me up.

But I hadn't seen her in six years.

I walked out the door at 7:30 with a cart of boxes of personal belongings and legal work and saw her sitting there. I didn't get the warmest reception, but I didn't deserve one either. We talked about the kids for a while, but there was a chill between us, and I asked if we could take off and go to a Cracker Barrel Restaurant. For the first time in six years I used real silverware, napkins, and clean dishes. Even more remarkably, someone asked me what I wanted rather than just serving me whatever had been cooked.

The eggs and sausage tasted like filet mignon. You ate fast in the slammer, and I was having a tough time adjusting. "Hey, slow down. No one's going to take it away from you," Sharon remarked. We got back in the car, and I jumped on her cell phone. For six years I'd stood in line to use a pay phone for 15 minutes. But I was smilin' and dialin' on Sharon's phone for three hours of the seven-hour trip.

She dropped me off at the halfway house in Detroit, and I sensed that I'd gotten through to her a little bit. I didn't push anything because she was still of the mind-set that she was happy to be done with me. But she was nice enough to give me some money for food and toiletries and off she went. I asked if I could come and see her when they gave me visitation privileges, and she said, "Sure."

There were 50 guys in my halfway house in Detroit and more than 40 of them were black. They handed you serious, published, no-if-ands-or-buts rules, and you didn't want to violate them. The owners of the house had the power to get you sent back to the slammer with one phone call.

The first three days they only allow you to leave for a few hours to buy personal items. Knowing how desperate prisoners are for real food, they let you order in. My first meal was Kentucky Fried Chicken, and my second meal was Kentucky Fried Chicken. I got Chinese on day three and felt like I was living high on the hog.

The first serious order of business was to get a job because you can only leave the house to go to a job. And even then, you have to submit your schedule for the upcoming week so they can keep track of you. They give you a window of time to get to work and back, and you don't want to be late in either direction. If you violate the window, it can be another case of, "Here come the marshals."

The halfway house concept is a good thing for people who need help gracefully reentering society and reengaging with their families. For guys who have no family or work, it gives them up to six months to get it together. I met some nice people there, but I didn't think I needed the halfway house to help me get started. And sure enough, I ran into a road-block almost as soon as I arrived.

I had autograph signings set up at two card shows in Detroit and told my case officer about them. My plan was to get a day job and do card shows on the weekends. The extra money would really help me get back on my feet. But the caseworker surprised me by saying, "Geez, Denny, I don't know if they'll let you make public appearances."

"You gotta be kidding!" I whined. "This is what I do. I make public appearances. I do Denny McLain, and that means being in public. As it is, you guys get 25 percent of everything that we make. You should be jumping up and down about the money I can make with a few card shows."

It was true. I was required to give the halfway house 25 percent of my income up to $10,000 a month. It's because the Bureau of Prisons doesn't own the halfway houses, and the owners need the salaries of their residents as a key revenue source. I'd been making 11¢ an hour in prison, and now the halfway house wanted 25 percent of my money.

The caseworker told me she'd have to get permission from her people at the Justice Department. I called my attorney, Chris Andreoff. "Shit, Denny," Andreoff said, "that's what you do for a living. Al Taubman went right back to work running malls when he got out after the Sotheby's thing." And in 2005 Martha Stewart came out, lived at home with a tether, and was doing TV shows and making personal appearances. I wanted to know why it was different for me.

The caseworker called me back and said, "Sorry. They told me, 'no way.' They said you may have no profile and attract no crowds while in the halfway house."

"But that's what I do—I attract crowds!" They wouldn't budge.

Do you see why the government can be so totally incompetent? It's more about control than it is money or taxpayer consideration. They would rather have me lose income and keep me on a tether than pay my own way.

I called an old friend who worked as a real estate broker, but he wouldn't give me a job. I told him, "Look, pay me $200 a week so I have a place to go. I'll pay you back when I'm out." Still the answer was, "No."

I had to accept that it was like I had the plague, and people just wanted to steer clear of me. Fortunately, an old friend, Glenn Miller, owned a 7-Eleven store, and the minute I called him he said, "You're hired."

The first day at the 7-Eleven, somebody called a radio and a television station, and within hours the TV trucks were rolling up looking for a story. I tried to stop them from coming into the store because I was forbidden from doing interviews. The caseworker had told me, "One interview, and you'll be back at McKean."

I called Glenn to tell him what was happening and my very real concerns about publicity. But Glenn wanted to be a TV star. He said, "Let 'em in. Let's get the store a little exposure. I'll do all the interviews. As word spread that "McLain was out and he's making Slurpees," we started selling so many that the machine started breaking down every day. Meanwhile, I'm in hog heaven, eating all the hot dogs and Twinkies I wanted.

Here's how *The Detroit News* reported it:

Denny McLain Pitches Slurpees
As embezzlement sentence nears end, ex-Tiger lives in halfway house and works at 7-Eleven
By Angelique S. Chengelis / *The Detroit News*
STERLING HEIGHTS—May 15, 2003
Former Tigers pitching great Denny McLain is back—not on the mound, but behind the counter at 7-Eleven.
McLain, who fell from grace and ended up in prison twice after leading the Tigers to the 1968 World Series

championship, serves hot dogs and Slurpees instead of serving up fastballs.

It's all part of a work-release program. McLain, baseball's last 30-game winner, must live in a halfway house and hold a job as he nears the end of an eight-year federal prison sentence for embezzling.

McLain, who according to his attorney is not permitted to talk to the media, is still a fan favorite despite his troubled past.

"It's an honor to meet him," said Michael Smith, 30, of Shelby Township as McLain mingled with customers Wednesday. "I'm still shaking. It's not every day you meet a two-time Cy Young winner. He's one of the greatest pitchers ever. I can't wait to tell my dad."

The 59-year-old McLain is working at the 7-Eleven/Citgo gas station at Metropolitan Parkway (16 Mile) and Mound owned by family friend Glenn Miller. McLain could be released from prison in mid-October if he satisfies all the federal requirements.

"He needed a job, and he will be here until his term is up," said Miller, who added that he and his wife didn't think twice about hiring McLain. "He needed some help, and I'm helping him. When he asked, we did it."

McLain, known for his charm and gift of gab, captivated Detroit and the country in 1968 as he pitched his way to 30 victories—the first time that was done since Dizzy Dean did it in 1934.

But in 1970, then-Baseball Commissioner Bowie Kuhn suspended McLain for his involvement in gambling. McLain was later suspended twice more by the Tigers—once for dumping water on two sports writers.

McLain, who played the organ at clubs when not throwing a fastball, later took to the airwaves as a local morning talk show host.

On Wednesday, McLain's uniform of choice went from Tigers home whites to a short-sleeved shirt, khakis, and white sneakers.

Still, customers who stopped into the store for hot dogs and sodas felt that it was right that McLain was working his way back to freedom.

"Today, nobody's accountable anymore for anything that they do," said Carmello DiMaggio of Roseville. "He should be allowed to work as a payback." Reprinted with permission from *The Detroit News.*

Three weeks later, a local cellular guy named Duane Rao offered me a job helping him launch a prepaid phone card business. It took me from $8 an hour to $1,000 a week. Sharon bought me a used car because as long as I was still in the system, I wasn't allowed to buy anything in my name.

It was a thrill to be able to send and receive email on a computer at Duane's place and use high-speed internet. With the exception of the Valhalla Jail, I hadn't been online in years.

After I got my first check and made my first payment to the halfway house, they let me spend a Saturday with Sharon. A week after that, I got to spend the weekend with Sharon. With two and a half months to go, they allowed me to start spending weekends with Sharon. But I still had to drive back to the halfway house each Sunday and pay the juice on my income.

In your mind's eye, you expect things to appear as they were when you left. The most remarkable thing about coming home was seeing the stunning physical effects six years has on people. And with kids, like my grandkids, it was really shocking. Markey was a little man, Courtney was a girl all of a sudden, and Kristin was a rascal and a half.

My wish was to live with Sharon, and any time I was allowed to be away from the halfway house, I spent it at her condo.

In August, about four months after leaving McKean, I got down on my hands and knees and said, "Sharon, I've got a question to ask you."

She gave me an "Oh, what have you got in mind" look, and said, "Denny, don't do this."

"But," I said playfully, "we're both Catholic, and you don't want to live in sin now, do you? I want you to marry me."

"There's something wrong with me," she said smiling, "but okay, let's do it."

We planned the wedding and had it in October.

Ira Berkow covered the story in *The New York Times*.

In a Lifetime Full of Second Chances, Denny McLain Receives His Biggest

By Ira Berkow

DETROIT—Given the context, it was an extraordinary event—a small wedding attended by a handful of family members and friends. It took place October 18, at the home of Michelle and Mark Lauzon in a Detroit suburb, and was the remarriage of Michelle's parents, Sharon and Denny McLain.

It came six months after the bridegroom's release from prison. He had spent more than six years in the McKean Federal Penitentiary in Bradford, Pennsylvania, after a jury convicted him on charges including embezzlement, mail fraud, and conspiracy in connection with the theft of $2.5 million from the pension fund of a meat-packing company in which he was part owner.

At the wedding, the bride wore an elegant dress made of beige chiffon. Her once-and-future husband was decked out in a black tuxedo. A disc jockey played love songs that had been requested by the couple.

The way McLain proposed to her this second time around, he recalled at dinner recently, was "on my hands and knees. I begged her to forgive me, and told her I'd never put her through anything like that again," he said. "I had caused her so much grief. She suffered a heart attack, developed migraine headaches, got high blood pressure. I did it all to her." In a toast to his bride at the wedding, McLain said he would do everything possible "to be worthy of her affections in the future."

"One month after I hit McKean, Sharon filed divorce papers," McLain, seated in a restaurant in Detroit, said recently. "I couldn't believe it. I was livid. I called her. She said: 'I've had enough. I can't take any more.' It shook me up so bad I wanted to run out of prison and run to Detroit to see her."

McLain won 31 games in 1968 against only six losses, winning the MVP and Cy Young Awards. The next season, he shared the Cy Young Award, going 24–9. He appeared headed to the Hall of Fame. More than that, his life seemed like a fairy tale. He was a kid from a working-class family with an abusive father who grew up on the South Side of Chicago, signed out of high school at 18, and pitched a no-hitter in his first game in the minor leagues, at Harlan, Kentucky, in the Class D Appalachian League. He was in the major leagues a year later and became a 20-game winner at 22.

♦   ♦   ♦

In retrospect I can say I made a lot of mistakes, but I wasn't going to listen to anybody. I was going to do whatever I wanted, whenever I wanted to do it, and whatever happened, happened.

Sharon always would say, "Look out for Bertucci, look out for Barry Nelson, Roger Smigiel." She didn't trust any of them. She'd say, "Watch those guys, they're trying to get in your pocket." She's got some kind of intuition, and 99 out of 100 times she can she can spot the users and see 'em comin'. I've always been too primed to jump into the excitement of the next deal.

If I'd listened to Sharon, I would have never done the Farmer Peet thing. The first time she met Jeff Egan she remarked in the car coming home, "Boy, I do not like him—there's grease all over him." I said, "What the hell are you talking about?" She said, "That's a bad guy. You watch him." I said, "How can you tell? You just met him for an hour and half at dinner." She said, "I just don't like the way he talks." She was right about him, and she never cared for Smigiel either. I have been defined by any number of people—especially Ed Miller—that I can be an overwhelming depressive or an eternal optimist, and ignore all of the fires burning around me as I walk through the middle of the room.

As for the rest of my crew:

Denny Jr. owns a carpeting business in Augusta, Georgia, and is also a church elder. I've always been a Catholic. While I don't believe in everything the church stands for, I believe in its doctrine. I've always had my private moments every day when I pray and ask for forgiveness.

Dennis married Tanya, a former model. They have two beautiful little girls, real heart-grabbers.

Tim is an engineer and went to New Zealand shortly after I went to prison in 1997. I don't blame him. It was tough dealing with everything here. I suspect that some of it had to do with me, but I don't know how much. He got degrees in engineering and computer science, and he's started his own company. He travels all over Southeast Asia. He's done real well. I do know that he found a lot more peace over there than he was having here. It was a great move for him. But it's upsetting every day that goes by and I don't see his little girls, fire-engine red-headed twins Abby and Maddy, born in 2005. Tim has turned out to be a helluva father and a great husband for Janet, a former career woman with Air New Zealand.

Michelle is everything a father would want in a daughter. She got pregnant in high school, and I didn't think that relationship would last two hours. Now here they are 15 years later. Young Markey is a pillar of what a teenager should be at this point. We helped raise Markey the first few years, so we have a very special relationship with him. Mark was in the military when he was born, and they were having serious problems as a couple. I think, much like Sharon with me, Michelle laid down the law to Mark one day. The new sheriff's in town, and I think Mark doesn't want to get on the wrong side of that sheriff.

Markey is our superstar goalie, who was on the state championship Brighton High School hockey team as a freshman. He is a pistol, and his two sisters are angels. Kourtney Kristin is a gymnast, and Kristin Michelle wants to be a veterinarian.

To be a free man again and enjoy my seven gorgeous grandchildren is the light in my heart and soul.

Lastly, as long as Sharon Alice McLain is in my life, getting old is not such a bad thing. Sharon, I love you, and I know that you love me more than I deserve.

I still work in the Telecom business with Michnet Carrier Services. We do a different part of long distance called VoIP (Voice over Internet Protocol). We sell long distance, 800 numbers, phone cards. The people I deal with—the people who backed me—know me and they know what happened at Peet.

Comeback

You get up every day and you try to do the right thing. You work hard, and you have to try to help people. I've got investors in our company and you have to support them, maintain certain levels of production. And you want to make sure that they're happy, like you do with everybody you deal with.

I want to work until the day I die. I can't sit around. I can't just go get my Social Security and go to the beach. It's not me. I can't imagine not having something to do. My father taught me that good things happen to those who work long and those who work smart. It's always been true.

I try every day to apply the lessons I learned in prison. I've talked with Ed Miller a number of times to stay on track. I actually call Tim Roche more. Tim was my administration counselor. He said he had been a hard-nosed cop in the Illinois State penitentiary who learned at some point that even inmates are human beings and you have to give them consideration unless they lie to you. If your mother died or you had an illness in the family, he'd let you make a phone call in his private office rather than the dorms, where you'd have to wait to get in line and everyone would hear your call. He recognized what a human being was. Relationships like these don't often happen in jail because cops and inmates don't trust each other.

My comeback is still under construction. I'm doing the best I can, but I'm still not as good as I need to get. I believe I learned how to apply a quiet, calm wisdom in prison, and I try to use it every day. I've still got a long way to go. But when I get lost, I think I now have the roadmap to always find my way back.

No one is sorrier than I am for all the pain I have caused in this world. Sometimes I wish I had a magic wand to show people I've hurt how sorry I really am. I will continue to try to do better. At 62, I don't know how much time I have left. But one thing that I lean on is that I know I have a much better appreciation for life, family, grandkids, and other people's feelings and pain. Everyone has a story, and all of us have experienced some kind of hell in our lives.

I know now that having empathy and compassion for others gives life its meaning.

Postscript *by Michelle McLain Lauzon*

My father asked me to read this book, and the main reason I fought against doing it was because I didn't want to relive my sister's death all over again. Don't get me wrong—I think about Krissie every day. But I don't think of her as being gone. I can still see her. I see her on a beach in Florida. I see her in me, and I see her in my children's eyes. For me, Krissie's not defined by how she died.

Krissie was six years and four months older than me. And as long as I remember, I always had two moms. There was my real mom—and there was also Krissie. I was the annoying little sister, but despite our age difference, we got along great. Whenever someone would ask who my best friend was, I would say without hesitation, "My sister."

The day Krissie left us, my family changed forever. No family would be left unchanged. The horror of that day still plays in my mind if I let it. I was in Florida in 1992 attending my husband's graduation from boot camp. We all grew up in Florida, so everything around me felt very nostalgic—the smells, the sounds, the places where my family went. I can still remember hearing my dad's voice on the other line that morning. I remember saying, "Not Krissie."

Everything else from that moment on for about a month is a complete blur. I remember bits and pieces like a jigsaw puzzle. I know my brothers and I felt lost. Krissie was the glue in our family. She would pick up the pieces and put us back together. She held us strong. And for the first time in our lives she wasn't there to do that.

397

I can see my brothers and I sitting in the funeral home just staring into nothing. My mom wasn't functioning well and my dad wasn't either. We all just kind of gave up. There's not a book out there telling you what to do in a situation like that.

But there was music. Believe it or not we all found comfort in music. I know at first some people at Krissie's funeral thought we had lost it. We didn't want the traditional funeral music played. So we all sat down and put a list together of all the songs that Krissie loved and the songs that reminded us of her, and that's what was played at her funeral. I remember walking in the funeral home and hearing "My Girl" being played in the background. Strange as it sounds, I smiled. Krissie was smiling, too. I know she was.

My family has come a long way since then. We've been through some terrible things. But we are still a family. We still support each other no matter what.

My dad especially has come a long way. He has let go of some of the control he felt he had to have over us kids after Krissie's death. I know he loves my family and me. He would give up his life for any one of us. Isn't that the kind of love we all want? He just has to figure out how to give it without pushing us out. And he is.

Index

Index

Index